UTAH TRAILS
M O A B   R E G I O N

Warning: While every effort has been made to make the 4WD trail descriptions in this book as accurate as possible, some discrepancies may exist between the text and the actual trail. Hazards may have changed since the research and publication of this edition. Adler Publishing Company, Inc., and the authors accept no responsibility for the safety of users of this guide. Individuals are liable for all costs incurred if rescue is necessary.

Printed in the United States of America

Cover photos
Clockwise from bottom left: Yellow Cat Road, Eightmile Road, Bobby's Hole and Ruin Park Trail

Rear cover photos
From left: White Rim Trail, Eightmile Road

UTAH TRAILS
MOAB REGION

PETER MASSEY
AND JEANNE WILSON

ADLER
PUBLISHING

Acknowledgements

Many people and organizations have made major contributions to the research and production of this book. We owe them all special thanks for their assistance.

First, we would like to thank the following people who have played major roles in the production of this book and have been key to completing it in a timely fashion.

Cover Design Concept: **Rudy Ramos**
Editing and Proofreading: **Jeff Campbell, Alice Levine**
Graphic Design and Maps: **Deborah Rust**

We would also like to thank the many people at the Bureau of Land Management offices throughout Utah, who spent countless hours assisting us. In particular, we would like to thank Jeanie Linn at the Hanksville Field Office.

Staff at many offices of the National Forest Service also provided us with valuable assistance, particularly the offices in Price, Ferron, Teasdale, and Richfield.

We received a great deal of assistance from many other people and organizations. We would like to thank the Utah State Historical Society, the Denver Public Library Western History Department, Kari Murphy at the Moab to Monument Valley Film Commission, and the Moab Historical Society.

The book includes many photos, and we are most thankful to Alan Barnett and Tara Thompson at the Utah State Historical Society.

With a project of this size countless hours are spent researching and recording the trail information, and we would like to thank Carol and Gary Martin of the Virginian Motel in Moab for providing a base camp for our researchers and for their helpful trail suggestions.

Publisher's Note: Every effort has been taken to ensure that the information in this book is accurate at press time. Please visit our website to advise us of any changes or corrections you find. We also welcome recommendations for new 4WD trails or other suggestions to improve the information in this book.

Adler Publishing Company, Inc.
1601 Pacific Coast Highway, Suite 290
Hermosa Beach, CA 90254
Phone: 800-660-5107
Fax: 310-698-0709
4WDbooks.com

ADLER
PUBLISHING

Contents

Before You Go   **7**

Moab Region Map   **24**

Trail #1:   Shafer Trail   28

Trail #2:   White Rim Trail   31

Trail #3:   Lathrop Canyon Trail   37

Trail #4:   Taylor Canyon Trail   39

Trail #5:   Taylor Canyon Rim Trail   41

Trail #6:   Long Canyon Trail   43

Trail #7:   Mineral Point Trail   46

Trail #8:   Hell Roaring Canyon Rim Trail   48

Trail #9:   Bartlett Wash Trail   50

Trail #10: Hidden Canyon Wash Trail   53

Trail #11: Hidden Canyon Rim Trail   55

Trail #12: Hidden Canyon Rim Escape Trail   58

Trail #13: Bartlett Rim Trail   60

Trail #14: Monitor and Merrimac Trail   63

Trail #15: Klondike Bluffs Trail   68

Trail #16: Spring Canyon Point Trail   70

Trail #17: Rainbow Rocks Trail   72

Trail #18: Levi Well Trail   75

Trail #19: Crystal Geyser Trail   78

Trail #20: Yellow Cat Trail   83

Trail #21: Yellow Cat Road   90

Trail #22: Salt Valley Road   93

Trail #23: Salt Wash Overlook Trail   96

Trail #24: Dome Plateau Trail   98

Trail #25: Eye of the Whale Trail   101

Trail #26: Willow Flats Road   103

Trail #27: Winter Camp Ridge Trail   105

Trail #28: Squaw Park Trail   107

Trail #29: Wood Road   110

Trail #30: Cache Valley Trail   113

Trail #31: Anticline Overlook Trail   115

Trail #32: Eightmile Road   117

Trail #33: Elephant Hill Loop   121

Trail #34: Bobby's Hole and Ruin Park Trail   124

Trail #35: Cottonwood Canyon Trail   129

Trail #36: Beef Basin Trail   132

Trail #37: North Long Point Trail   136

Trail #38: North and South Elk Ridge Trail   138

Trail #39: Blue Mountains Road   142

Trail #40: Cottonwood Wash Trail   148

Trail #41: Johns Canyon Overlook Trail   152

Trail #42: Johns Canyon Trail   154

Trail #43: Valley of the Gods Trail   156

Trail #44: Butler Wash Road   160

Trail #45: Snow Flat Road   163

Trail #46: Comb Wash Trail   167

Trail #47: Decker Road   170

Trail #48: Montezuma Canyon Trail   173

Trail #49: Hurrah Pass Trail   179

Trail #50: Chicken Corners Trail   182

Trail #51: Gemini Bridges Trail   184

Trail #52: Bull Canyon Trail   187

Trail #53: Castleton-Gateway Road   189

Trail #54: Polar Mesa Trail   193

Trail #55: Onion Creek and Thompson Canyon Trail   196

Trail #56: Sand Flats Road   199

Trail #57: Miners Basin Trail   203

Selected Further Reading   **206**

Before You Go

Why a 4WD Does It Better

The design and engineering of 4WD vehicles provide them with many advantages over normal cars when you head off the paved road:

- improved distribution of power to all four wheels;
- a transmission transfer case, which provides low-range gear selection for greater pulling power and for crawling over difficult terrain;
- high ground clearance;
- less overhang of the vehicle's body past the wheels, which provides better front- and rear-clearance when crossing gullies and ridges;
- large-lug, wide-tread tires;
- rugged construction (including underbody skid plates on many models).

If you plan to do off-highway touring, all of these considerations are important whether you are evaluating the capabilities of your current 4WD or are looking to buy one; each is considered in detail in this chapter.

To explore the most difficult trails described in this book, you will need a 4WD vehicle that is well rated in each of the above features. If you own a 2WD sport utility vehicle, a lighter car-type SUV, or a pickup truck, your ability to explore the more difficult trails will depend on conditions and your level of experience.

A word of caution: Whatever type of 4WD vehicle you drive, understand that it is not invincible or indestructible. Nor can it go everywhere. A 4WD has a much higher center of gravity and weighs more than a car, and so has its own consequent limitations.

Experience is the only way to learn what your vehicle can and cannot do. Therefore, if you are inexperienced, we strongly recommend that you start with trails that have lower difficulty ratings. As you develop an understanding of your vehicle and of your own

taste for adventure, you can safely tackle the more challenging trails.

One way to beef up your knowledge quickly, while avoiding the costly and sometimes dangerous lessons learned from on-the-road mistakes, is to undertake a 4WD course taught by a professional. Look in the Yellow Pages for courses in your area.

Using This Book

Route Planning

The regional map on pages xx and xx provide a convenient overview of the trails in the Moab Region of Utah. Each 4WD trail is shown, as are major highways and towns, to help you plan various routes by connecting a series of 4WD trails and paved roads.

As you plan your overall route, you will probably want to utilize as many 4WD trails as possible. However, check the difficulty rating and time required for each trail before finalizing your plans. You don't want to be stuck 50 miles from the highway—at sunset and without camping gear, since your trip was supposed to be over hours ago—when you discover that your vehicle can't handle a certain difficult passage.

Difficulty Ratings

We use a point system to rate the difficulty of each trail. Any such system is subjective, and your experience of the trails will vary depending on your skill and the road conditions at the time. Indeed, any amount of rain may make the trails much more difficult, if not completely impassable.

We have rated the 4WD trails on a scale of 1 to 10—1 being passable for a normal passenger vehicle in good conditions and 10 requiring a heavily modified vehicle and an experienced driver who expects to encounter vehicle damage. Because this book is designed for owners of unmodified 4WD vehicles—who we assume do not want to damage their vehicles—most of the trails are rated 5 or lower. A few trails are included that rate as high as 7, while those rated 8 to 10 are beyond the scope of this book.

This is not to say that the moderate-rated trails are easy. We strongly recommend that inexperienced drivers not tackle trails rated at 4 or higher until they have undertaken a number of the lower-rated ones, so that they can gauge their skill level and prepare for the difficulty of the higher-rated trails.

In assessing the trails, we have always assumed good road conditions (dry road surface, good visibility, and so on). The factors influencing our ratings are as follows:

■ obstacles such as rocks, mud, ruts, sand, slickrock, and stream crossings;
■ the stability of the road surface;
■ the width of the road and the vehicle clearance between trees or rocks;
■ the steepness of the road;
■ the margin for driver error (for example, a very high, open shelf road would be rated more difficult even if it was not very steep and had a stable surface).

The following is a guide to the ratings.

Rating 1: The trail is graded dirt but suitable for a normal passenger vehicle. It usually has gentle grades, is fairly wide, and has very shallow water crossings (if any).

Rating 2: High-clearance vehicles are preferred but not necessary. These trails are dirt roads, but they may have rocks, grades, water crossings, or ruts that make clearance a concern in a normal passenger vehicle. The trails are fairly wide, making passing possible at almost any point along the trail. Mud is not a concern under normal weather conditions.

Rating 3: High-clearance 4WDs are preferred, but any high-clearance vehicle is acceptable. Expect a rough road surface; mud and sand are possible but will be easily passable. You may encounter rocks up to 6 inches in diameter, a loose road surface, and shelf roads, though these will be wide enough for passing or will have adequate pull-offs.

Rating 4: High-clearance 4WDs are recommended, though most stock SUVs are acceptable. Expect a rough road surface with rocks larger than 6 inches, but there

will be a reasonable driving line available. Patches of mud are possible but can be readily negotiated; sand may be deep and require lower tire pressures. There may be stream crossings up to 12 inches deep, substantial sections of single-lane shelf road, moderate grades, and sections of moderately loose road surface.

Rating 5: High-clearance 4WDs are required. These trails have either a rough, rutted surface, rocks up to 9 inches, mud and deep sand that may be impassable for inexperienced drivers, or stream crossings up to 18 inches deep. Certain sections may be steep enough to cause traction problems, and you may encounter very narrow shelf roads with steep drop-offs and tight clearance between rocks or trees.

Rating 6: These trails are for experienced four-wheel drivers only. They are potentially dangerous, with large rocks, ruts, or terraces that may need to be negotiated. They may also have stream crossings at least 18 inches deep, involve rapid currents, unstable stream bottoms, or difficult access; steep slopes, loose surfaces, and narrow clearances; or very narrow sections of shelf road with steep drop-offs and possibly challenging road surfaces.

Rating 7: Skilled, experienced four-wheel drivers only. These trails include very challenging sections with extremely steep grades, loose surfaces, large rocks, deep ruts, and/or tight clearances. Mud or sand may necessitate winching.

Rating 8 and above: Stock vehicles are likely to be damaged, and drivers may find the trail impassable. Highly skilled, experienced four-wheel drivers only.

Scenic Ratings

If rating the degree of difficulty is subjective, rating scenic beauty is guaranteed to lead to arguments. Utah contains a spectacular variety of scenery—from its grand canyons and towering mountains and buttes to its seemingly endless desert country. Despite the subjectivity of attempting a comparative rating of diverse scenery, we have tried to provide a guide to the relative scenic quality of the various trails. The ratings are based on a scale of 1 to 10, with 10 being the most attractive.

Remoteness Ratings

Many trails in this region are in remote mountain or desert country; sometimes the trails are seldom traveled, and the likelihood is low that another vehicle will appear within a reasonable time to assist you if you get stuck or break down. We have included a ranking for remoteness of +0 through +2. Extreme summer temperatures can make a breakdown in the more remote areas a life-threatening experience. Prepare carefully before tackling the higher-rated, more remote trails (see Special Preparations for Remote Travel, page 11). For trails with a high remoteness rating, consider traveling with a second vehicle.

Estimated Driving Times

In calculating driving times, we have not allowed for stops. Your actual driving time may be considerably longer depending on the number and duration of the stops you make. Add more time if you prefer to drive more slowly than good conditions allow.

Current Road Information

All the 4WD trails described in this book may become impassable in poor weather conditions. Storms can alter roads, remove tracks, and create impassable washes. Most of the trails described, even easy 2WD trails, can quickly become impassable even to 4WD vehicles after only a small amount of rain. For each trail, we have provided a phone number for obtaining current information about conditions.

Abbreviations

The route directions for the 4WD trails use a series of abbreviations as follows:

SO	CONTINUE STRAIGHT ON
TL	TURN LEFT
TR	TURN RIGHT
BL	BEAR LEFT
BR	BEAR RIGHT
UT	U-TURN

Using Route Directions

For every trail, we describe and pinpoint (by odometer reading) nearly every significant feature along the route—such as intersections, streams, washes, gates, cattle guards, and so on—and provide directions from these landmarks. Odometer readings will vary from vehicle to vehicle, so you should allow for slight variations. Be aware that trails can quickly change in the desert. A new trail may be cut around a washout, a faint trail can be graded by the county, or a well-used trail may fall into disuse. All these factors will affect the accuracy of the given directions.

If you diverge from the route, zero your trip meter upon your return and continue along the route, making the necessary adjustment to the point-to-point odometer readings. In the directions, we regularly reset the odometer readings—at significant landmarks or popular lookouts and spur trails—so that you won't have to recalculate for too long.

Most of the trails can be started from either end, and the route directions include both directions of travel; reverse directions are printed in blue below the main directions. When traveling in reverse, read from the bottom of the table and work up.

Route directions include cross-references whenever two 4WD trails included in this book connect; these cross-references allow for an easy change of route or destination.

Each trail includes periodic latitude and longitude readings to facilitate using a global positioning system (GPS) receiver. These readings may also assist you in finding your location on the maps. The GPS coordinates are given in the format dd°mm.mm'. To save time when loading coordinates into your GPS receiver, you may wish to include only one decimal place, since in Utah, the first decimal place equals about 165 yards and the second only about 16 yards.

Map References

We recommend that you supplement the information in this book with more-detailed maps. For each trail, we list the sheet maps and road atlases that provide the best detail for the area. Typically, the following references are given:

- Bureau of Land Management Maps
- U.S. Forest Service Maps
- Utah Travel Council Maps, Department of Geography, University of Utah—regions 1 through 5,
- *Utah Atlas & Gazetteer,* 4th ed. (Freeport, Maine: DeLorme Mapping, 2000)—Scale 1:250,000,
- Maptech-Terrain Navigator Topo Maps—Scale 1:100,000 and 1:24,000,
- *Trails Illustrated* Topo Maps; National Geographic Maps—Various scales, but all contain good detail.

We recommend the *Trails Illustrated* series of maps as the best for navigating these trails. They are reliable, easy to read, and printed on nearly indestructible plastic paper. However, this series covers only a few of the 4WD trails described in this book.

The DeLorme Atlas has the advantage of providing you with maps of the state at a reasonable price. Although its 4WD trail information doesn't go beyond what we provide, it is useful if you wish to explore the hundreds of side roads.

U.S. Forest Service maps lack the topographic detail of the other sheet maps and, in our experience, are occasionally out of date. They have the advantage of covering a broad area and are useful in identifying land use and travel restrictions. These maps are most useful for the longer trails.

Utah Travel Council maps cover Utah in five regions. They provide good overviews with a handful of 4WD trails, although with little specific detail. Four of Utah's five regions are currently available: Southwestern #4, Southeastern #5, Northern #1, and Northeastern #3. Central map #2 has been out of print for several years and it is yet undetermined when it will be available.

In our opinion, the best single option by far is the Terrain Navigator series of maps published on CD-ROM by Maptech. These CD-ROMs contain an amazing level of detail because they include the entire set of 1,941 U.S. Geological Survey topographical maps of Utah at the 1:24,000 scale and all 71 maps at the 1:100,000

scale. These maps offer many advantages over normal maps:

- GPS coordinates for any location can be found and loaded into your GPS receiver. Conversely, if you have your GPS coordinates, your location on the map can be pinpointed instantly.
- Towns, rivers, passes, mountains, and many other sites are indexed by name so that they can be located quickly.
- 4WD trails can be marked and profiled for elevation changes and distances from point to point.
- Customized maps can be printed out.

Maptech uses seven CD-ROMs to cover the entire state of Utah; they can be purchased individually or as part of a two-state package at a heavily discounted price. The CD-ROMs can be used with a laptop computer and a GPS receiver in your vehicle to monitor your location on the map and navigate directly from the display.

All these maps should be available through good map stores. The Maptech CD-ROMs are available directly from the company (800-627-7236, or on the internet at www.maptech.com).

Backcountry Driving Rules and Permits

Four-wheel driving involves special driving techniques and road rules. This section is an introduction for 4WD beginners.

4WD Road Rules

To help ensure that these trails remain open and available for all four-wheel drivers to enjoy, it is important to minimize your impact on the environment and not be a safety risk to yourself or anyone else. Remember that the 4WD clubs in Utah fight a constant battle with the government and various lobby groups to retain the access that currently exists.

The fundamental rule when traversing the 4WD trails described in this book is to use common sense. In addition, special road rules for 4WD trails apply:

- Vehicles traveling uphill have the right of way.
- If you are moving more slowly than the vehicle behind you, pull over to let the other vehicle by.
- Park out of the way in a safe place. Blocking a track may restrict access for emergency vehicles as well as for other recreationalists. Set the parking brake—don't rely on leaving the transmission in park. Manual transmissions should be left in the lowest gear.

Tread Lightly!

Remember the rules of the Tread Lightly!® program:
- Be informed. Obtain maps, regulations, and other information from the forest service or from other public land agencies. Learn the rules and follow them.
- Resist the urge to pioneer a new road or trail or to cut across a switchback. Stay on constructed tracks and avoid running over young trees, shrubs, and grasses, damaging or killing them. Don't drive across alpine tundra; this fragile environment can take years to recover.
- Stay off soft, wet roads and 4WD trails readily torn up by vehicles. Repairing the damage is expensive, and quite often authorities find it easier to close the road rather than repair it.
- Travel around meadows, steep hillsides, stream banks, and lake shores that are easily scarred by churning wheels.
- Stay away from wild animals that are rearing young or suffering from a food shortage. Do not camp close to the water sources of domestic or wild animals.
- Obey gate closures and regulatory signs.
- Preserve America's heritage by not disturbing old mining camps, ghost towns, or other historical features. Leave historic sites, Native American rock art, ruins, and artifacts in place and untouched.
- Carry out all your trash, and even that of others.
- Stay out of designated wilderness areas. They are closed to all vehicles. It is your responsibility to know where the boundaries are.
- Get permission to cross private land. Leave livestock alone. Respect landowners' rights.

Report violations of these rules to help keep these 4WD trails open and to ensure that others will have the opportunity to visit these backcountry sites. Many groups are actively seeking to close these public lands to vehicles, thereby denying access to those who are unable, or perhaps merely unwilling, to hike long distances. This magnificent countryside is owned by, and should be available to, all Americans.

Special Preparations for Remote Travel

Due to the remoteness of some areas in Utah and the very high summer temperatures, you should take some special precautions to ensure that you don't end up in a life-threatening situation:
- When planning a trip into the desert, always inform someone as to where you are going, your route, and when you expect to return. Stick to your plan.
- Carry and drink at least one gallon of water per person per day of your trip. (Plastic gallon jugs are handy and portable.)
- Be sure your vehicle is in good condition with a sound battery, good hoses, spare tire, spare fan belts, necessary tools, and reserve gasoline and oil. Other spare parts and extra radiator water are also valuable. If traveling in pairs, share the common spares and carry a greater variety.
- Keep an eye on the sky. Flash floods can occur in a wash any time you see thunderheads—even when it's not raining a drop where you are.
- If you are caught in a dust storm while driving, get off the road and turn off your lights. Turn on the emergency flashers and back into the wind to reduce windshield pitting by sand particles.
- Test trails on foot before driving through washes and sandy areas. One minute of walking may save hours of hard work getting your vehicle unstuck.

- If your vehicle breaks down, stay near it. Your emergency supplies are there. Your car has many other items useful in an emergency. Raise your hood and trunk lid to denote "help needed." Remember, a vehicle can be seen for miles, but a person on foot is very difficult to spot from a distance.

- When you're not moving, use available shade or erect shade from tarps, blankets, or seat covers—anything to reduce the direct rays of the sun.

- Do not sit or lie directly on the ground. It may be 30 degrees hotter than the air.

- Leave a disabled vehicle only if you are positive of the route and the distance to help. Leave a note for rescuers that gives the time you left and the direction you are taking.

- If you must walk, rest for at least 10 minutes out of each hour. If you are not normally physically active, rest up to 30 minutes out of each hour. Find shade, sit down, and prop up your feet. Adjust your shoes and socks, but do not remove your shoes—you may not be able to get them back on swollen feet.

- If you have water, drink it. Do not ration it.

- If water is limited, keep your mouth closed. Do not talk, eat, smoke, drink alcohol, or take salt.

- Keep your clothing on despite the heat. It helps to keep your body temperature down and reduces your body's dehydration rate. Cover your head. If you don't have a hat, improvise a head covering.

- If you are stalled or lost, set signal fires. Set smoky fires in the daytime and bright ones at night. Three fires in a triangle denote "help needed."

- A roadway is a sign of civilization. If you find a road, stay on it.

- When hiking in the desert, equip each person, especially children, with a police-type whistle. It makes a distinctive noise with little effort. Three blasts denote "help needed."

- To avoid poisonous creatures, put your hands or feet only where your eyes can see. One insect to be aware of in Southen Utah is the Africanized honeybee. Though indistinguishable from its European counterpart, these bees are far more aggressive and can be a threat. They have been known to give chase of up to a mile and even wait for people who have escaped into the water to come up for air. The best thing to do if attacked is to cover your face and head with clothing and run to the nearest enclosed shelter. Keep an eye on your pet if you notice a number of bees in the area, as many have been killed by Africanized honeybees.

- Avoid unnecessary contact with wildlife. Some mice in Utah carry the deadly hantavirus, a pulmonary syndrome fatal in 60 to 70 percent of human cases. Fortunately the disease is very rare—by May 2006, only 24 cases had been reported in Utah and 438 nationwide—but caution is still advised. Other rodents may transmit bubonic plague, the same epidemic that killed one-third of Europe's population in the 1300s. Be especially wary near sick animals and keep pets, especially cats, away from wildlife and their fleas. Another creature to watch for is the western black-legged tick, the carrier of Lyme disease. Wearing clothing that covers legs and arms, tucking pants into boots, and using insect repellent are good ways to avoid fleas and ticks.

Obtaining Permits

Backcountry permits, which usually cost a fee, are required for certain activities on public lands in Utah, whether the area is a national park, state park, national monument, Indian reservation, or BLM land.

Restrictions may require a permit for all overnight stays, which can include backpacking and 4WD or bicycle camping. Permits may also be required for day use by vehicles, horses, hikers, or bikes in some areas.

When possible, we include information about fees and permit requirements and where permits may be obtained, but these regulations change constantly. If in doubt, check with the most likely governing agency.

Assessing Your Vehicle's Off-Road Ability

Many issues come into play when evaluating your 4WD vehicle, although most of the 4WDs on the market are suitable for even the roughest trails described in this book. Engine power will be adequate in even the least-powerful modern vehicle. However, some vehicles are less suited to off-highway driving than others, and some of the newest, carlike sport utility vehicles simply are not designed for off-highway touring. The following information should enable you to identify the good, the bad, and the ugly.

Differing 4WD Systems

All 4WD systems have one thing in common: The engine provides power to all four wheels rather than to only two, as is typical in most standard cars. However, there are a number of differences in the way power is applied to the wheels.

The other feature that distinguishes nearly all 4WDs from normal passenger vehicles is that the gearboxes have high and low ratios that effectively double the number of gears. The high range is comparable to the range on a passenger car. The low range provides lower speed and more power, which is useful when towing heavy loads, driving up steep hills, or crawling over rocks. When driving downhill, the 4WD's low range increases engine braking.

Various makes and models of SUVs offer different drive systems, but these differences center on two issues: the way power is applied to the other wheels if one or more wheels slip, and the ability to select between 2WD and 4WD.

Normal driving requires that all four wheels be able to turn at different speeds; this allows the vehicle to turn without scrubbing its tires. In a 2WD vehicle, the front wheels (or rear wheels in a front-wheel-drive vehicle) are not powered by the engine and thus are free to turn individually at any speed. The rear wheels, powered by the engine, are only able to turn at different speeds because of the differential, which applies power to the faster-turning wheel.

This standard method of applying traction has certain weaknesses. First, when power is applied to only one set of wheels, the other set cannot help the vehicle gain traction. Second, when one powered wheel loses traction, it spins, but the other powered wheel doesn't turn. This happens because the differential applies all the engine power to the faster-turning wheel and no power to the other wheels, which still have traction. All 4WD systems are designed to overcome these two weaknesses. However, different 4WDs address this common objective in different ways.

Full-Time 4WD. For a vehicle to remain in 4WD all the time without scrubbing the tires, all the wheels must be able to rotate at different speeds. A full-time 4WD system allows this to happen by using three differentials. One is located between the rear wheels, as in a normal passenger car, to allow the rear wheels to rotate at different speeds. The second is located between the front wheels in exactly the same way. The third differential is located between the front and rear wheels to allow different rotational speeds between the front and rear sets of wheels. In nearly all vehicles with full-time 4WD, the center differential operates only in high range. In low range, it is completely locked. This is not a disadvantage because when using low range the additional traction is normally desired and the deterioration of steering response will be less noticeable due to the vehicle traveling at a slower speed.

Part-Time 4WD. A part-time 4WD system does not have the center differential located between the front and rear wheels. Consequently, the front and rear drive shafts are both driven at the same speed and with the same power at all times when in 4WD.

This system provides improved traction because when one or both of the front or rear wheels slips, the engine continues to provide power to the other set. However, because such a system doesn't allow a difference in speed between the front and rear sets of wheels, the tires scrub when turning, placing additional strain on the whole drive system.

Therefore, such a system can be used only in slippery conditions; otherwise, the ability to steer the vehicle will deteriorate and the tires will quickly wear out.

Some vehicles, such as Jeeps with Selectrac and Mitsubishi Monteros with Active Trac 4WD, offer both full-time and part-time 4WD in high range.

Manual Systems to Switch Between 2WD and 4WD. There are three manual systems for switching between 2WD and 4WD. The most basic requires stopping and getting out of the vehicle to lock the front hubs manually before selecting 4WD. The second requires you to stop, but you change to 4WD by merely throwing a lever inside the vehicle (the hubs lock automatically). The third allows shifting between 2WD and 4WD high range while the vehicle is moving. Any 4WD that does not offer the option of driving in 2WD must have a full-time 4WD system.

AutomatedSwitching Between 2WD and 4WD. Advances in technology are leading to greater automation in the selection of two- or four-wheel drive. When operating in high range, these high-tech systems use sensors to monitor the rotation of each wheel. When any slippage is detected, the vehicle switches the proportion of power from the wheel(s) that is slipping to the wheels that retain grip. The proportion of power supplied to each wheel is therefore infinitely variable as opposed to the original systems where the vehicle was either in two-wheel drive or four-wheel drive.

In recent years, this process has been spurred on by many of the manufacturers of luxury vehicles entering the SUV market—Mercedes, BMW, Cadillac, Lincoln, and Lexus have joined Range Rover in this segment.

Manufacturers of these higher-priced vehicles have led the way in introducing sophisticated computer-controlled 4WD systems. Although each of the manufacturers has its own approach to this issue, all the systems automatically vary the allocation of power between the wheels within milliseconds of the sensors' detecting wheel slippage.

Limiting Wheel Slippage

All 4WDs employ various systems to limit wheel slippage and transfer power to the wheels that still have traction. These systems may completely lock the differentials or they may allow limited slippage before transferring power back to the wheels that retain traction.

Lockers completely eliminate the operation of one or more differentials. A locker on the center differential switches between full-time and part-time 4WD. Lockers on the front or rear differentials ensure that power remains equally applied to each set of wheels regardless of whether both have traction. Lockers may be controlled manually, by a switch or a lever in the vehicle, or they may be automatic.

The Toyota Land Cruiser offers the option of having manual lockers on all three differentials, while other brands such as the Mitsubishi Montero offer manual lockers on the center and rear differential. Manual lockers are the most controllable and effective devices for ensuring that power is provided to the wheels with traction. However, because they allow absolutely no slippage, they must be used only on slippery surfaces.

An alternative method for getting power to the wheels that have traction is to allow limited wheel slippage. Systems that work this way may be called limited-slip differentials, posi-traction systems, or in the center differential, viscous couplings. The advantage of these systems is that the limited difference they allow in rotational speed between wheels enables such systems to be used when driving on a dry surface. All full-time 4WD systems allow limited slippage in the center differential.

For off-highway use, a manually locking differential is the best of the above systems, but it is the most expensive. Limited-slip differentials are the cheapest but also the least satisfactory, as they require one wheel to be slipping at 2 to 3 mph before power is transferred to the other wheel. For the center differential, the best system combines a locking differential and, to enable full-time use, a viscous coupling.

Tires

The tires that came with your 4WD vehicle may be satisfactory, but many 4WDs are fitted with passenger-car tires. These are unlikely to be the best choice because they are less rugged and more likely to puncture on rocky trails. They are particularly prone to sidewall damage as well. Passenger vehicle tires also have a less aggressive tread pattern than specialized 4WD tires, and provide less traction in mud.

For information on purchasing tires better suited to off-highway conditions, see Special 4WD Equipment, page 20.

Clearance

Road clearances vary considerably among different 4WD vehicles—from less than 7 inches to more than 10 inches. Special vehicles may have far greater clearance. For instance, the Hummer has a 16-inch ground clearance. High ground clearance is particularly advantageous on the rockier or more rutted 4WD trails in this book.

When evaluating the ground clearance of your vehicle, you need to take into account the clearance of the bodywork between the wheels on each side of the vehicle. This is particularly relevant for crawling over larger rocks. Vehicles with sidesteps have significantly lower clearance than those without.

Another factor affecting clearance is the approach and departure angles of your vehicle—that is, the maximum angle the ground can slope without the front of the vehicle hitting the ridge on approach or the rear of the vehicle hitting on departure. Mounting a winch or tow hitch to your vehicle is likely to reduce your angle of approach or departure.

If you do a lot of driving on rocky trails, you will inevitably hit the bottom of the vehicle sooner or later. When this happens, you will be far less likely to damage vulnerable areas such as the oil pan and gas tank if your vehicle is fitted with skid plates. Most manufacturers offer skid plates as an option. They are worth every penny.

Maneuverability

When you tackle tight switchbacks, you will quickly appreciate that maneuverability is an important criterion when assessing 4WD vehicles. Where a full-size vehicle may be forced to go back and forth a number of times to get around a sharp turn, a small 4WD might go straight around. This is not only easier, it's safer.

If you have a full-size vehicle, all is not lost. We have traveled many of the trails in this book in a Suburban. That is not to say that some of these trails wouldn't have been easier to negotiate in a smaller vehicle! We have noted in the route descriptions if a trail is not suitable for larger vehicles.

In Summary

Using the criteria above, you can evaluate how well your 4WD will handle off-road touring, and if you haven't yet purchased your vehicle, you can use these criteria to help select one. Choosing the best 4WD system is, at least partly, subjective. It is also a matter of your budget. However, for the type of off-highway driving covered in this book, we make the following recommendations:

■ Select a 4WD system that offers low range and, at a minimum, has some form of limited slip differential on the rear axle.

■ Use light truck, all-terrain tires as the standard tires on your vehicle. For sand and slickrock, these will be the ideal choice. If conditions are likely to be muddy, or if traction will be improved by a tread pattern that will give more bite, consider an additional set of mud tires.

■ For maximum clearance, select a vehicle with 16-inch wheels or at least choose the tallest tires that your vehicle can accommodate. Note that if you install tires with a diameter greater than standard, the odometer will under calculate the distance you have traveled. Your engine braking and gear ratios will also be affected.

■ If you are going to try the rockier 4WD trails, don't install a sidestep or low-hanging front bar. If you have the option, have underbody skid plates mounted.

■ Remember that many of the obstacles

you encounter on backcountry trails are more difficult to navigate in a full-size vehicle than in a compact 4WD.

Four-Wheel
Driving Techniques

Safe four-wheel driving requires that you observe certain golden rules:

- Size up the situation in advance.
- Be careful and take your time.
- Maintain smooth, steady power and momentum.
- Engage 4WD and low-range gears before you get into a tight situation.
- Steer toward high spots, trying to put the wheel over large rocks.
- Straddle ruts.
- Use gears and not just the brakes to hold the vehicle when driving downhill. On very steep slopes, chock the wheels if you park your vehicle.
- Watch for logging and mining trucks and smaller recreational vehicles, such as all-terrain vehicles (ATVs).
- Wear your seat belt and secure all luggage, especially heavy items such as tool boxes or coolers. Heavy items should be secured by ratchet tie-down straps rather than elastic-type straps, which are not strong enough to hold heavy items if the vehicle rolls.

Utah's 4WD trails have a number of common obstacles, and the following provides an introduction to the techniques required to surmount them.

Rocks. Tire selection is important in negotiating rocks. Select a multiple-ply, tough sidewall, light-truck tire with a large-lug tread.

As you approach a rocky stretch, get into 4WD low range to give yourself maximum slow-speed control. Speed is rarely necessary, since traction on a rocky surface is usually good. Plan ahead and select the line you wish to take. If a rock appears to be larger than the clearance of your vehicle, don't try to straddle it. Check to see that it is not higher than the frame of your vehicle once you get a wheel over it. Put a wheel up on the rock and slowly climb it, then gently drop over the other

side using the brake to ensure a smooth landing. Bouncing the car over rocks increases the likelihood of damage, because the body's clearance is reduced by the suspension compressing. Running boards also significantly reduce your clearance in this respect. It is often helpful to use a "spotter" outside the vehicle to assist you with the best wheel placement.

Steep Uphill Grades. Consider walking the trail to ensure that the steep hill before you is passable, especially if it is clear that backtracking is going to be a problem.

Select 4WD low range to ensure that you have adequate power to pull up the hill. If the wheels begin to lose traction, turn the steering wheel gently from side to side to give the wheels a chance to regain traction.

If you lose momentum, but the car is not in danger of sliding, use the foot brake, switch off the ignition, leave the vehicle in gear (if manual transmission) or park (if automatic), engage the parking brake, and get out to examine the situation. See if you can remove any obstacles, and figure out the line you need to take. Reversing a couple of yards and starting again may allow you to get better traction and momentum.

If halfway up, you decide a stretch of road is impassably steep, back down the trail. Trying to turn the vehicle around on a steep hill is extremely dangerous; you will very likely cause it to roll over.

Steep Downhill Grades. Again, consider walking the trail to ensure that a steep downhill is passable, especially if it is clear that backtracking uphill is going to be a problem.

Select 4WD low range and use first gear to maximize braking assistance from the engine. If the surface is loose and you are losing traction, change up to second or third gear. Do not use the brakes if you can avoid it, but don't let the vehicle's speed get out of control. Feather (lightly pump) the brakes if you slip while braking. For vehicles fitted with an antilock breaking system, apply even pressure if you start to slip; the ABS helps keep vehicles on line.

Travel very slowly over rock ledges or ruts. Attempt to tackle these diagonally, letting one wheel down at a time.

If the back of the vehicle begins to slide

around, gently apply the throttle and correct the steering. If the rear of the vehicle starts to slide sideways, do not apply the brakes.

Sand. As with most off-highway situations, your tires are the key to your ability to cross sand. It is difficult to tell how well a particular tire will handle in sand just by looking at it, so be guided by the manufacturer and your dealer.

The key to driving in soft sand is floatation, which is achieved by a combination of low tire pressure and momentum. Before crossing a stretch of sand, reduce your tire pressure to between 15 and 20 pounds. If necessary, you can safely go to as low as 12 pounds. As you cross, maintain momentum so that your vehicle rides on the top of the soft sand without digging in or stalling. This may require plenty of engine power. Avoid using the brakes if possible; removing your foot from the accelerator alone is normally enough to slow or stop. Using the brakes digs the vehicle deep in the sand.

Pump the tires back up as soon as you are out of the sand to avoid damaging the tires and the rims. Pumping the tires back up requires a high-quality air compressor. Even then, it is a slow process.

In the backcountry of Utah, sandy conditions are commonplace. You will therefore find a good compressor most useful.

Slickrock. When you encounter slickrock, first assess the correct direction of the trail. It is easy to lose sight of the trail on slickrock, because there are seldom any developed edges. Often the way is marked with small rock cairns, which are simply rocks stacked high enough to make a landmark.

All-terrain tires with tighter tread are more suited to slickrock than the more open, luggier type tires. As with rocks, a multiple-ply sidewall is important. In dry conditions, slickrock offers pavement-type grip. In rain or snow, you will soon learn how it got its name. Even the best tires may not get an adequate grip. Walk steep sections first; if you are slipping on foot, chances are your vehicle will slip, too.

Slickrock is characterized by ledges and long sections of "pavement." Follow the guidelines for travel over rocks. Refrain from speeding over flat-looking sections, because you may hit an unexpected crevice or water pocket, and vehicles bend easier than slickrock! Turns and ledges can be tight, and vehicles with smaller overhangs and better maneuverability are at a distinct advantage—hence the popularity of the compacts in the slickrock mecca of Moab, Utah.

On the steepest sections, engage low range and pick a straight line up or down the slope. Do not attempt to traverse a steep slope sideways.

Mud. Muddy trails are easily damaged, so they should be avoided if possible. But if you must traverse a section of mud, your success will depend heavily on whether you have open-lugged mud tires or chains. Thick mud fills the tighter tread on normal tires, leaving the tire with no more grip than if it were bald. If the muddy stretch is only a few yards long, the momentum of your vehicle may allow you to get through regardless.

If the muddy track is very steep, uphill or downhill, or off camber, do not attempt it. Your vehicle is likely to skid in such conditions, and you may roll or slip off the edge of the road. Also, check to see that the mud has a reasonably firm base. Tackling deep mud is definitely not recommended unless you have a vehicle-mounted winch—and even then—be cautious, because the winch may not get you out. Finally, check to see that no ruts are too deep for the ground clearance of your vehicle.

When you decide you can get through and have selected the best route, use the following techniques to cross through the mud:

■ Avoid making detours off existing tracks to minimize environmental damage.

■ Select 4WD low range and a suitable gear; momentum is the key to success, so use a high enough gear to build up sufficient speed.

■ Avoid accelerating heavily, so as to minimize wheel spinning and to provide maximum traction.

■ Follow existing wheel ruts, unless they are too deep for the clearance of your vehicle.

■ To correct slides, turn the steering wheel in the direction that the rear wheels are skidding, but don't be too aggressive or you'll overcorrect and lose control again.

- If the vehicle comes to a stop, don't continue to accelerate, as you will only spin your wheels and dig yourself into a rut. Try backing out and having another go.
- Be prepared to turn back before reaching the point of no return.

Stream Crossings. By crossing a stream that is too deep, drivers risk far more than water flowing in and ruining the interior of their vehicles. Water sucked into the engine's air intake will seriously damage the engine. Likewise, water that seeps into the air vent on the transmission or differential will mix with the lubricant and may lead to serious problems in due course.

Even worse, if the water is deep or fast flowing, it could easily carry your vehicle downstream, endangering the lives of everyone in the vehicle.

Some 4WD manuals tell you what fording depth the vehicle can negotiate safely. If your vehicle's owner's manual does not include this information, your local dealer may be able to assist. If you don't know, then avoid crossing through water that is more than a foot or so deep.

The first rule for crossing a stream is to know what you are getting into. You need to ascertain how deep the water is, whether there are any large rocks or holes, if the bottom is solid enough to avoid bogging down the vehicle, and whether the entry and exit points are negotiable. This may take some time and involve getting wet, but you take a great risk by crossing a stream without first properly assessing the situation.

The secret to water crossings is to keep moving, but not too fast. If you go too fast, you may drown the electrics, causing the vehicle to stall midstream. In shallow water (where the surface of the water is below the bumper), your primary concern is to safely negotiate the bottom of the stream, to avoid any rock damage, and to maintain momentum if there is a danger of getting stuck or of slipping on the exit.

In deeper water (between 18 and 30 inches), the objective is to create a small bow wave in front of the moving vehicle. This requires a speed that is approximately walking pace. The bow wave reduces the depth of the water around the engine compartment. If the water's surface reaches your tailpipe, select a gear that will maintain moderate engine revs to avoid water backing up into the exhaust; and do not change gears midstream.

Crossing water deeper than 25 to 30 inches requires more extensive preparation of the vehicle and should be attempted only by experienced drivers.

Snow. The trails in this book that receive heavy snowfall are closed in winter. Therefore, the snow conditions that you are most likely to encounter are an occasional snowdrift that has not yet melted or fresh snow from an unexpected storm. Getting through such conditions depends on the depth of the snow, its consistency, the stability of the underlying surface, and your vehicle.

If the snow is no deeper than about 9 inches and there is solid ground beneath it, crossing the snow should not be a problem. In deeper snow that seems solid enough to support your vehicle, be extremely cautious: If you break through a drift, you are likely to be stuck, and if conditions are bad, you may have a long wait.

The tires you use for off-highway driving, with a wide tread pattern, are probably suitable for these snow conditions. Nonetheless, it is wise to carry chains (preferably for all four wheels), and if you have a vehicle-mounted winch, even better.

Vehicle Recovery Methods

If you do enough four-wheel driving, you are sure to get stuck sooner or later. The following techniques will help you get back on the go. The most suitable method will depend on the equipment available and the situation you are in—whether you are stuck in sand, mud, or snow, or are high-centered or unable to negotiate a hill.

Towing. Use a nylon yank strap of the type discussed in the Special 4WD Equipment section below. This type of strap will stretch 15 to 25 percent, and the elasticity will assist in extracting the vehicle.

Attach the strap only to a frame-mounted tow point. Ensure that the driver of the stuck vehicle is ready, take up all but about 6 feet of slack, then move the towing vehicle away at a moderate speed (in most circumstances this means using 4WD low range in second gear) so that the elasticity of the strap is employed in the way it is meant to be. Don't take off like a bat out of hell or you risk breaking the strap or damaging a vehicle.

Never join two yank straps together with a shackle. If one strap breaks, the shackle will become a lethal missile aimed at one of the vehicles (and anyone inside). For the same reason, never attach a yank strap to the tow ball on either vehicle.

Jacking. Jacking the vehicle allows you to pack rocks, dirt, or logs under the wheel or to use your shovel to remove an obstacle. However, the standard vehicle jack is unlikely to be of as much assistance as a high-lift jack. We highly recommend purchasing a good high-lift jack as a basic accessory if you decide that you are going to do a lot of serious, off-highway four-wheel driving. Remember a high-lift jack is of limited use if your vehicle does not have an appropriate jacking point. Some brush bars have two built-in forward jacking points.

Tire Chains. Tire chains can be of assistance in both mud and snow. Cable-type chains provide much less grip than link-type chains. There are also dedicated mud chains with larger, heavier links than on normal snow chains. It is best to have chains fitted to all four wheels.

Once you are bogged down is not the best time to try to fit the chains; if at all possible, try to predict their need and have them on the tires before trouble arises. An easy way to affix chains is to place two small cubes of wood under the center of the stretched-out chain. When you drive your tires up on the blocks of wood, it is easier to stretch the chains over the tires because the pressure is off of them.

Winching. Most recreational four-wheel drivers do not have a winch. But if you get serious about four-wheel driving, this is probably the first major accessory you should consider buying.

Under normal circumstances, a winch would be warranted only for the more diffi-cult 4WD trails in this book. Having a winch is certainly comforting when you see a difficult section of road ahead and have to decide whether to risk it or turn back. Also, major obstacles can appear when you least expect them, even on trails that are otherwise easy.

Owning a winch is not a panacea to all your recovery problems. Winching depends on the availability of a good anchor point, and electric winches may not work if they are submerged in a stream. Despite these constraints, no accessory is more useful than a high-quality, powerful winch when you get into a difficult situation.

If you acquire a winch, learn to use it properly; take the time to study your owner's manual. Incorrect operation can be extremely dangerous and may cause damage to the winch or to your anchor points, which are usually trees.

Navigation by the Global Positioning System (GPS)

Although this book is designed so that each trail can be navigated simply by following the detailed directions provided, nothing makes navigation easier than a GPS receiver.

The global positioning system (GPS) consists of a network of 24 satellites, nearly 13,000 miles in space, in six different orbital paths. The satellites are constantly moving at about 8,500 miles per hour and make two complete orbits around the earth every 24 hours.

Each satellite is constantly transmitting data, including its identification number, its operational health, and the date and time. It also transmits its location and the location of every other satellite in the network.

By comparing the time the signal was transmitted to the time it is received, a GPS receiver calculates how far away each satellite is. With a sufficient number of signals, the receiver can then triangulate its location. With three or more satellites, the receiver can determine latitude and longitude coordinates. With four or more, it can calculate elevation. By constantly making these calculations, it can determine speed and direction. To facilitate these calculations, the time data broadcast by GPS is accurate to within 40 billionths of a second.

The U.S. military uses the system to provide positions accurate to within half an inch. When the system was first established, civilian receivers were deliberately fed slightly erroneous information in order to effectively deny military applications to hostile countries or terrorists—a practice called selective availability (SA). However on May 1, 2000, in response to the growing importance of the system for civilian applications, the U.S. government stopped intentionally downgrading GPS data. The military gave its support to this change once new technology made it possible to selectively degrade the system within any defined geographical area on demand. This new feature of the system has made it safe to have higher-quality signals available for civilian use. Now, instead of the civilian-use signal having a margin of error between 20 and 70 yards, it is only about one-tenth of that.

A GPS receiver offers the four-wheeler numerous benefits:

■ You can track to any point for which you know the longitude and latitude coordinates with no chance of heading in the wrong direction or getting lost. Most receivers provide an extremely easy-to-understand graphic display to keep you on track.

■ It works in all weather conditions.

■ It automatically records your route for easy backtracking.

■ You can record and name any location, so that you can relocate it with ease. This may include your campsite, a fishing spot, or even a silver mine you discover!

■ It displays your position, enabling you to pinpoint your location on a map.

■ By interfacing the GPS receiver directly to a portable computer, you can monitor and record your location as you travel (using the appropriate map software) or print the route you took.

However, remember that GPS units can fail, batteries can go flat, and tree cover and tight canyons can block the signals. Never rely entirely on GPS for navigation. Always carry a compass for backup.

Special 4WD Equipment

Tires

When 4WD touring, you will likely encounter a variety of terrain: rocks, mud, talus, slickrock, sand, gravel, dirt, and bitumen. The immense array of tires on the market includes many specifically targeted at one or another of these types of terrain, as well as tires designed to adequately handle a range of terrain.

Every four-wheel driver seems to have a preference when it comes to tire selection, but most people undertaking the 4WD trails in this book will need tires that can handle all of the above types of terrain adequately.

The first requirement is to select rugged, light-truck tires rather than passenger-vehicle tires. Check the size data on the sidewall: it should have "LT" rather than "P" before the number. Among light-truck tires, you must choose between tires that are designated "all-terrain" and more-aggressive, wider-tread mud tires. Either type will be adequate, especially on rocks, gravel, talus, or dirt. Although mud tires have an advantage in muddy conditions and soft snow, all-terrain tires perform better on slickrock, in sand, and particularly on ice and paved roads.

When selecting tires, remember that they affect not just traction but also cornering ability, braking distances, fuel consumption, and noise levels. It pays to get good advice before making your decision.

Global Positioning System Receivers

GPS receivers have come down in price considerably in the past few years and are rapidly becoming indispensable navigational tools. Many higher-priced cars now offer integrated GPS receivers, and within the next few years, receivers will become available on most models.

Battery-powered, hand-held units that meet the needs of off-highway driving currently range from less than $100 to a little over $300 and continue to come down in price. Some high-end units feature maps that are incorporated in the display, either from a built-in database or from interchangeable memory cards. Currently, only a few of these maps include 4WD trails.

If you are considering purchasing a GPS unit, keep the following in mind:

- Price. The very cheapest units are likely outdated and very limited in their display features. Expect to pay from $125 to $300.
- The display. Compare the graphic display of one unit with another. Some are much easier to decipher or offer more alternative displays.
- The controls. GPS receivers have many functions, and they need to have good, simple controls.
- Vehicle mounting. To be useful, the unit needs to be placed where it can be read easily by both the driver and the navigator. Check that the unit can be conveniently located in your vehicle. Different units have different shapes and different mounting systems.
- Map data. More and more units have map data built in. Some have the ability to download maps from a computer. Such maps are normally sold on a CD-ROM. GPS units have a finite storage capacity and having the ability to download maps covering a narrower geographical region means that the amount of data relating to that specific region can be greater.
- The number of routes and the number of sites (or "waypoints") per route that can be stored in memory. For off-highway use, it is important to be able to store plenty of waypoints so that you do not have to load coordinates into the machine as frequently. Having plenty of memory also ensures that you can automatically store your present location without fear that the memory is full.
- Waypoint storage. The better units store up to 500 waypoints and 20 reversible routes of up to 30 waypoints each. Also consider the number of characters a GPS receiver allows you to use to name waypoints. When you try to recall a waypoint, you may have difficulty recognizing names restricted to only a few characters.
- Automatic route storing. Most units automatically store your route as you go along and enable you to display it in reverse to make backtracking easy.

After you have selected a unit, a number of optional extras are also worth considering:

- A cigarette lighter electrical adapter.

Despite GPS units becoming more power efficient, protracted in-vehicle use still makes this accessory a necessity.

- A vehicle-mounted antenna, which will improve reception under difficult conditions. (The GPS unit can only "see" through the windows of your vehicle; it cannot monitor satellites through a metal roof.) Having a vehicle-mounted antenna also means that you do not have to consider reception when locating the receiver in your vehicle.
- An in-car mounting system. If you are going to do a lot of touring using the GPS, consider attaching a bracket on the dash rather than relying on a Velcro mount.
- A computer-link cable and digital maps. Data from your GPS receiver can be downloaded to your PC; maps and waypoints can be downloaded from your PC; or if you have a laptop computer, you can monitor your route as you go along, using one of a number of inexpensive map software products on the market.

Yank Straps

Yank straps are industrial-strength versions of the flimsy tow straps carried by the local discount store. They are 20 to 30 feet long and 2 to 3 inches wide, made of heavy nylon, rated to at least 20,000 pounds, and have looped ends.

Do not use tow straps with metal hooks in the ends (the hooks can become missiles in the event the strap breaks free). Likewise, never join two yank straps together using a shackle.

CB Radios

If you are stuck, injured, or just want to know the conditions up ahead, a citizen's band (CB) radio can be invaluable. CB radios are relatively inexpensive and do not require an Federal Communications Comission license. Their range is limited, especially in very hilly country, as their transmission patterns basically follow lines of sight. Range can be improved using single sideband (SSB) transmission, an option on more expensive units. Range is even better on vehicle-mounted units that have been professionally fitted to ensure that the antenna and cabling are matched appropriately.

Winches

There are three main options when it comes to winches: manual winches, removable electric winches, and vehicle-mounted electric winches.

If you have a full-size 4WD vehicle—which can weigh in excess of 7,000 pounds when loaded—a manual winch is of limited use without a lot of effort and considerable time. However, a manual winch is a very handy and inexpensive accessory if you have a small 4WD. Typically, manual winches are rated to pull about 5,500 pounds.

An electric winch can be mounted to your vehicle's trailer hitch to enable it to be removed, relocated to the front of your vehicle (if you have a hitch installed), or moved to another vehicle. Although this is a very useful feature, a winch is heavy, so relocating one can be a two-person job. Consider that 5,000-pound-rated winches weigh only about 55 pounds, while 12,000-pound-rated models weigh around 140 pounds. Therefore, the larger models are best permanently front-mounted. Unfortunately, this position limits their ability to winch the vehicle backward.

When choosing among electric winches, be aware that they are rated for their maximum capacity on the first wind of the cable around the drum. As layers of cable wind onto the drum, they increase its diameter and thus decrease the maximum load the winch can handle. This decrease is significant: A winch rated to pull 8,000 pounds on a bare drum may only handle 6,500 pounds on the second layer, 5,750 pounds on the third layer, and 5,000 pounds on the fourth. Electric winches also draw a high level of current and may necessitate upgrading the battery in your 4WD or adding a second battery.

There is a wide range of mounting options—from a simple, body-mounted frame that holds the winch to heavy-duty winch bars that replace the original bumper and incorporate brush bars and mounts for auxiliary lights.

If you buy a winch, either electric or manual, you will also need quite a range of additional equipment so that you can operate it correctly:

- at least one choker chain with hooks on each end,
- winch extension straps or cables,
- shackles,
- a receiver shackle,
- a snatch block,
- a tree protector,
- gloves.

Grill/Brush Bars and Winch Bars

Brush bars protect the front of the vehicle from scratches and minor bumps; they also provide a solid mount for auxiliary lights and often high-lift jacking points. The level of protection they provide depends on how solid they are and whether they are securely mounted onto the frame of the vehicle. Lighter models attach in front of the standard bumper, but the more substantial units replace the bumper. Prices range from about $150 to $450.

Winch bars replace the bumper and usually integrate a solid brush bar with a heavy-duty winch mount. Some have the brush bar as an optional extra to the winch bar component. Manufacturers such as Warn, ARB, and TJM offer a wide range of integrated winch bars. These are significantly more expensive, starting at about $650.

Remember that installing heavy equipment on the front of the vehicle may necessitate increasing the front suspension rating to cope with the additional weight.

Portable Air Compressors

Most portable air compressors on the market are flimsy models that plug into the cigarette lighter and are sold at the local discount store. These are of very limited use for four-wheel driving. They are very slow to inflate the large tires of a 4WD vehicle; for instance, to reinflate from 15 to 35 pounds typically takes about 10 minutes for each tire. They are also unlikely to be rated for continuous use, which means that they will overheat and cut off before completing the job. If you're lucky, they will start up again when they have cooled down, but this means that you are unlikely to reinflate your tires in less than an hour.

The easiest way to identify a useful air compressor is by the price—good ones cost $200 or more. Many of the quality units feature a Thomas-brand pump and are built to last. Another good unit is sold by ARB. All these pumps draw between 15 and 20 amps and thus should not be plugged into the cigarette lighter socket but attached to the vehicle's battery with clips. The ARB unit can be permanently mounted under the hood. Quick-Air makes a range of units including a 10-amp compressor that can be plugged into the cigarette lighter socket and performs well.

Auxiliary Driving Lights

There is a vast array of auxiliary lights on the market today and selecting the best lights for your purpose can be a confusing process.

Auxiliary lights greatly improve visibility in adverse weather conditions. Driving lights provide a strong, moderately wide beam to supplement headlamp high beams, giving improved lighting in the distance and to the sides of the main beam. Fog lamps throw a wide-dispersion, flat beam; and spots provide a high-power, narrow beam to improve lighting range directly in front of the vehicle. Rear-mounted auxiliary lights provide greatly improved visibility for backing up.

For off-highway use, you will need quality lights with strong mounting brackets. Some high-powered off-highway lights are not approved by the Department of Transportation for use on public roads.

Roof Racks

Roof racks can be excellent for storing gear, as well as providing easy access for certain weatherproof items. However, they raise the center of gravity on the vehicle, which can substantially alter the rollover angle. A roof rack is best used for lightweight objects that are well-strapped down. Heavy recovery gear and other bulky items should be packed low in the vehicle's interior to lower the center of gravity and stabilize the vehicle.

A roof rack should allow for safe and secure packing of items and be sturdy enough to withstand knocks.

Packing Checklist

Before embarking on any 4WD adventure, whether a lazy Sunday drive on an easy trail or a challenging climb over rugged terrain, be prepared. The following checklist will help you gather the items you need.

Essential

❑ Rain gear
❑ Small shovel or multipurpose ax, pick, shovel, and sledgehammer
❑ Heavy-duty yank strap
❑ Spare tire that matches the other tires on the vehicle
❑ Working jack and base plate for soft ground
❑ Maps
❑ Emergency medical kit, including sun protection and insect repellent
❑ Bottled water
❑ Blankets or space blankets
❑ Parka, gloves, and boots
❑ Spare vehicle key
❑ Jumper leads
❑ Heavy-duty flashlight
❑ Multipurpose tool, such as a Leatherma
❑ Emergency food—high-energy bars or similar

Worth Considering

❑ Global Positioning System (GPS) receiver
❑ Cell phone
❑ A set of light-truck, off-highway tires and matching spare
❑ High-lift jack
❑ Additional tool kit
❑ CB radio
❑ Portable air compressor
❑ Tire gauge
❑ Tire-sealing kit
❑ Tire chains
❑ Handsaw and ax
❑ Binoculars
❑ Firearms
❑ Whistle
❑ Flares
❑ Vehicle fire extinguisher
❑ Gasoline, engine oil, and other vehicle fluids
❑ Portable hand winch
❑ Electric cooler

If Your Credit Cards Aren't Maxed Out

❑ Electric, vehicle-mounted winch and associated recovery straps, shackles, and snatch blocks
❑ Auxiliary lights
❑ Locking differential(s)

Trails in the Moab Region

- ■ #01   Shafer Trail *(page 28)*
- ■ #02   White Rim Trail *(page 31)*
- ■ #03   Lathrop Canyon Trail *(page 37)*
- ■ #04   Taylor Canyon Trail *(page 39)*
- ■ #05   Taylor Canyon Rim Trail *(page 41)*
- ■ #06   Long Canyon Trail *(page 43)*
- ■ #07   Mineral Point Trail *(page 46)*
- ■ #08   Hell Roaring Canyon Rim Trail *(page 48)*
- ■ #09   Bartlett Wash Trail *(page 50)*
- ■ #10   Hidden Canyon Wash Trail *(page 53)*
- ■ #11   Hidden Canyon Rim Trail *(page 55)*
- ■ #12   Hidden Canyon Rim Escape Trail *(page 58)*
- ■ #13   Bartlett Rim Trail *(page 60)*
- ■ #14   Monitor & Merrimac Trail *(page 63)*
- ■ #15   Klondike Bluffs Trail *(page 68)*
- ■ #16   Spring Canyon Point Trail *(page 70)*
- ■ #17   Rainbow Rocks Trail *(page 72)*
- ■ #18   Levi Well Trail *(page 75)*
- ■ #19   Crystal Geyser Trail *(page 78)*
- ■ #20   Yellow Cat Trail *(page 83)*
- ■ #21   Yellow Cat Road *(page 90)*
- ■ #22   Salt Valley Road *(page 93)*
- ■ #23   Salt Wash Overlook Trail *(page 96)*
- ■ #24   Dome Plateau Trail *(page 98)*
- ■ #25   Eye of the Whale Trail *(page 101)*
- ■ #26   Willow Flats Road *(page 103)*
- ■ #27   Winter Camp Ridge Trail *(page 105)*
- ■ #28   Squaw Park Trail *(page 107)*
- ■ #29   Wood Road *(page 110)*
- ■ #30   Cache Valley Trail *(page 113)*
- ■ #31   Anticline Overlook Trail *(page 115)*
- ■ #32   Eightmile Road *(page 117)*
- ■ #33   Elephant Hill Loop *(page 121)*
- ■ #34   Bobby's Hole & Ruin Park Trail *(page 124)*
- ■ #49   Hurrah Pass Trail *(page 179)*
- ■ #50   Chicken Corners Trail *(page 182)*
- ■ #51   Gemini Bridges Trail *(page 184)*
- ■ #52   Bull Canyon Trail *(page 187)*
- ■ #53   Castleton-Gateway Road *(page 189)*
- ■ #54   Polar Mesa Trail *(page 193)*
- ■ #55   Onion Creek & Thompson Canyon Trail *(page 196)*
- ■ #56   Sand Flats Road *(page 199)*
- ■ #57   Miners Basin Trail *(page 203)*

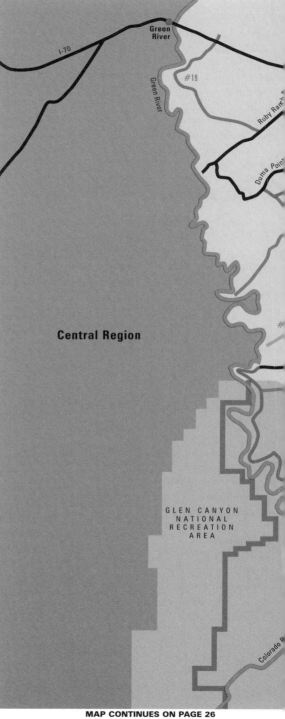

Central Region

MAP CONTINUES ON PAGE 26

escent Junction

I-70

#21

Utah 128

#22

#20

#29

US 191

#23

#24

Blue Hills Road

18

ARCHES
NATIONAL PARK

#28

#11

#15

#27

#12

#14

#10

#26

#25

#30

#55

#54

#13

#9

Dubinky Well Road

Utah 128

#7

Utah 313

#51

Utah 279

Moab

#53

TRAIL TO
GATEWAY,
COLORADO

#52

#56

#57

COLORADO BORDER

#5

#49

US 191

#1

#2

La Sal Mt. Road
(FR 062)

MANTI
LA SAL
NATIONAL
FOREST

Utah 313

#50

#3

Utah 46

La Sal Junction

La Sal

#31

#32

US 191

N

#33

CANYONLANDS
NATIONAL
PARK

Trails in the Moab Region

- #34 Bobby's Hole & Ruin Park Trail *(page 124)*
- #35 Cottonwood Canyon Trail *(page 129)*
- #36 Beef Basin Trail *(page 132)*
- #37 North Long Point Trail *(page 136)*
- #38 North and South Elk Ridge Trail *(page 138)*
- #39 Blue Mountains Road *(page 142)*
- #40 Cottonwood Wash Trail *(page 148)*
- #41 Johns Canyon Overlook Trail *(page 152)*
- #42 Johns Canyon Trail *(page 154)*
- #43 Valley of the Gods Trail *(page 156)*
- #44 Butler Wash Road *(page 160)*
- #45 Snow Flat Road *(page 163)*
- #46 Comb Wash Trail *(page 167)*
- #47 Decker Road *(page 170)*
- #48 Montezuma Canyon Trail *(page 173)*

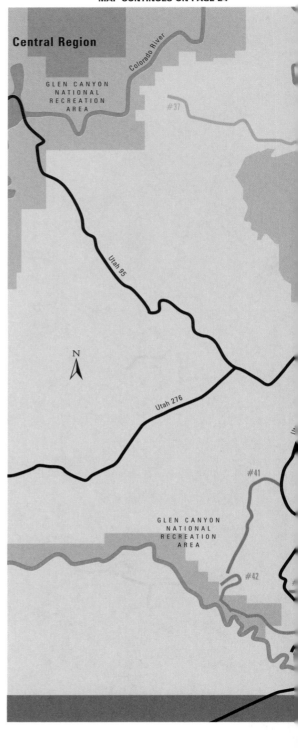

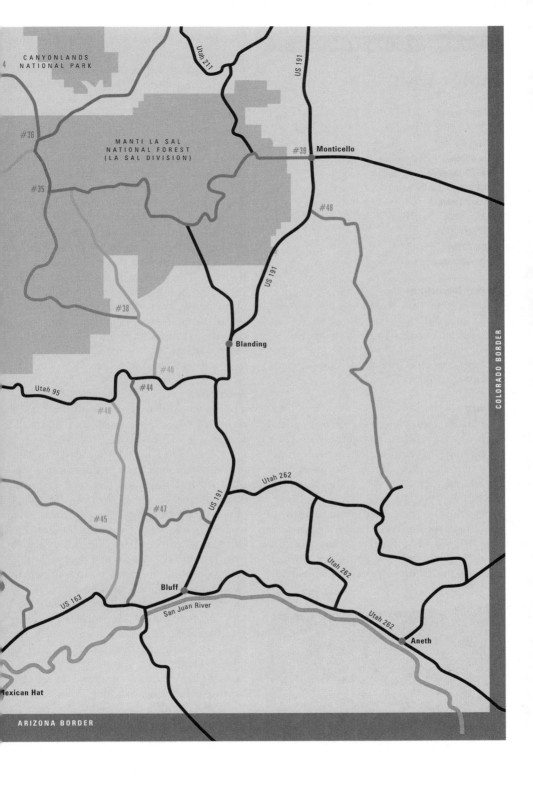

CANYONLANDS
NATIONAL PARK

Utah 211

US 191

#36

MANTI LA SAL
NATIONAL FOREST
(LA SAL DIVISION)

#39 Monticello

#35

#48

US 191

#38

Blanding

#40

#44

Utah 95

#46

Utah 262

#47

US 191

#45

Utah 262

Bluff

US 163

San Juan River

Utah 262

Aneth

COLORADO BORDER

Mexican Hat

ARIZONA BORDER

Shafer Trail

STARTING POINT Island in the Sky Road (Utah 313) in Canyonlands National Park
FINISHING POINT Potash, at Utah 279
TOTAL MILEAGE 19 miles
UNPAVED MILEAGE 17 miles
DRIVING TIME 2 hours
ELEVATION RANGE 3,900–5,900 feet
USUALLY OPEN Year-round
DIFFICULTY RATING 3
SCENIC RATING 10
REMOTENESS RATING +0

Special Attractions

- Island in the Sky region of Canyonlands National Park.
- Steep descent down tight switchbacks from rim.
- Views over the Colorado River and canyon country.

History

The Shafer Trail was named after Frank and John Shafer, ranchers in the area in 1914. Along with their family, they cut a steep stock trail into the cliffs of the canyon so they could drive their cattle down from the top of the mesa to graze by the river in winter. In summer, cattle grazed on the mesa tops. In the 1950s during the uranium boom, the trail was widened to allow the ore trucks to drive to Moab, carrying ore from the uranium mines in Lathrop and Taylor Canyons.

Canyonlands NP sign as you enter Island in the Sky District

Today, the Shafer Canyon area is often used by the movie industry. Many car commercials are filmed in the area, and the heroines in the movie *Thelma and Louise* took their famous final leap into Shafer Canyon from Fossil Point, now renamed Thelma and Louise Point.

At the base of the trail, there is an active potash mining operation. Utah is the nation's leading producer of phosphates, 95 percent of which are used in fertilizer. Solution mining replaced the more dangerous underground mining in 1972. The potash layer is leeched out in a salt solution and the resultant sludge is pumped to the surface into settling ponds, which can be seen beside the trail. The combined surface area of the ponds is over 400 acres. The vivid blue color of the ponds is actually a dye that is added to speed evaporation. As the water evaporates, the salt and potash remain. The by-product salt is not wasted; it is used for highway de-icing and industrial purposes.

Description

The ore trucks may be gone, but there is still plenty of traffic moving up and down the Shafer Trail. This incredible drive takes you from the Island in the Sky down to the potash works at the base of the trail in a very short time. The graded dirt road gradually descends as it leaves the canyon rim, wrapping back to the north, where it can be seen from the viewpoint opposite the visitor center. Almost immediately it turns into a shelf road, cut into the cliff on one side, with staggering drops on the other. It starts to switchback, and the grade increases, but it is still suitable for high-clearance vehicles with good tires in dry weather. The surface is mainly graded dirt, but because of its steepness, the trail does wash out. The lower end can be rough. There are a reasonable number of passing places for most of its length; remember that uphill vehicles have right of way.

After 4.3 miles, the switchbacks come to an end, and the trail undulates down to the potash works. The turnoff for Trail #2: White Rim Trail is reached at 5.1 miles. The lower end of the trail follows the Colorado

Shafer Trail looking along Shafer Canyon

River for a short way, with views over the Goose Neck section. There are a couple of wide, sandy washes; look carefully for the trail leading out, as it is easy to miss.

From top to bottom, this trail offers magnificent views. The road may be closed at both the top and bottom in adverse weather, and the creeks may be impassable following heavy rain.

Current Road Information
Canyonlands National Park
Island in the Sky Ranger District
(435) 259-4712

Map References
BLM   La Sal, Moab
USGS 1:24,000   Musselman Arch, Shafer
        Basin, Gold Bar Canyon
        1:100,000 La Sal, Moab
Maptech CD-ROM: Moab/Canyonlands
Trails Illustrated, #501; #210

Utah Atlas & Gazetteer, p. 30
Utah Travel Council #5 (incomplete)
Other: Latitude 40—Moab West
          Canyon Country Off-Road Vehicle
          Trail Map—Island Area

Route Directions

▼ 0.0   Zero trip meter and turn south from
           Utah 313 onto the marked Shafer Trail.
5.1 ▲   Trail ends at Utah 313. Turn right for
           Moab, left for the Island in the Sky
           Visitor Center.
           GPS: N 38°28.29' W 109°48.66'

▼ 0.1 SO Park information board and trail closure
           gate. Trail descends along narrow shelf
           road with numerous switchbacks.
5.0 ▲ SO Park information board and trail closure
           gate.

▼ 4.3 SO End of switchbacks.
0.8 ▲ SO Trail rises steeply and switchbacks
           along a narrow shelf road to the
           canyon rim.

▼ 5.1 TL Trail closure gate, then sign, left for
           potash works, straight on for Trail #2:
           White Rim Trail. Zero trip meter.
0.0 ▲   Continue west on Shafer Trail.
           GPS: N 38°27.57' W 109°47.65'

▼ 0.0   Continue northeast on Shafer Trail.
7.2 ▲ TR Sign, left is Trail #2: White Rim Trail,
           right is Island in the Sky Visitor Center.
           Trail closure gate. Zero trip meter at
           turn.

▼ 0.7 SO Cross through creek.
6.5 ▲ SO Cross through creek.

▼ 1.0 SO Shafer Camp on left, permit required.
6.2 ▲ SO Shafer Camp on right, permit required.

▼ 1.2 SO Drop into creek bed.
6.0 ▲ SO Leave creek bed.

▼ 1.3 SO Leave creek bed.
5.9 ▲ SO Drop into creek bed.

Trail #1: Shafer Trail

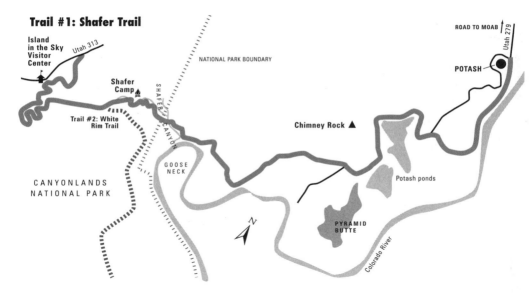

▼ 1.6   SO Leave Canyonlands National Park, enter BLM land.
5.6 ▲   SO Leave BLM land, enter Canyonlands National Park. Fee area.
        GPS: N 38°27.77' W 109°46.19'

▼ 2.2   BR View of Colorado River from rim. Do not follow creek bed; trail follows rim above the river.
5.0 ▲   BL Leaving Colorado River. Stay on graded track; do not follow creek bed.

▼ 2.4   SO Goose Neck section of Colorado River, overlook on right.
4.8 ▲   SO Goose Neck section of Colorado River, overlook on left.

▼ 2.7   SO Track on right.
4.5 ▲   SO Track on left.

▼ 4.2   SO Colorado River viewpoint on right. Directly above is Dead Horse Point State Park, the far side of the river is Chicken Corners.
3.0 ▲   SO Colorado River viewpoint on left. Directly above is Dead Horse Point State Park, the far side of the river is Chicken Corners.
        GPS: N 38°27.21' W 109°43.94'

▼ 5.7   SO Cross wash, track on right.
1.5 ▲   SO Track on left, cross wash.

▼ 5.8   SO Track on left.
1.4 ▲   SO Track on right.

▼ 6.0   SO Track on right, gate. Trail standard improves.
1.2 ▲   SO Trail becomes rougher at gate. Track on left.

▼ 6.6   SO Chimney Rock on left, Pyramid Butte on right.
0.6 ▲   SO Chimney Rock on right, Pyramid Butte on left.

▼ 7.2   SO Leave BLM lands through gate. Trail passes through private property, potash settling ponds on right. Zero trip meter.
0.0 ▲   Continue into BLM land.
        GPS: N 38°28.49' W 109°41.30'

▼ 0.0   Continue toward potash works.
6.7 ▲   SO Enter BLM lands through gate. Zero trip meter.

▼ 1.4   SO Track on left.
5.3 ▲   SO Track on right.

▼ 2.2   SO Leave potash ponds.
4.5 ▲   SO Potash settling ponds on the left.

▼ 3.1   SO Stop sign, private roads right and left.

| 3.6 ▲ | SO | Stop sign, private roads right and left. |

| ▼ 3.2 | BL | Numerous tracks on right and left. Remain on public road. |
| 3.5 ▲ | BR | Remain on public road. |

| ▼ 5.2 | SO | Boat launching area on Colorado River on right. Pavement begins. |
| 1.5 ▲ | SO | Pavement ends. Boat launching area on Colorado River on left. Numerous tracks on right and left, remain on public road. |

| ▼ 6.7 | | Trail ends at the start of Utah 279. Continue straight on to Moab. |
| 0.0 ▲ | | Trail begins at the potash works at end of Utah 279; sign reads, "Unimproved Road, next 10 miles." Zero trip meter and continue straight on. |

GPS: N 38°31.43' W 109°39.20'

Driving along the rock ledge above Buck Canyon

MOAB REGION TRAIL #2

White Rim Trail

STARTING POINT Canyonlands National Park, 5.1 miles along Trail #1: Shafer Trail
FINISHING POINT Mineral Bottom
TOTAL MILEAGE 68.4 miles
UNPAVED MILEAGE 68.4 miles
DRIVING TIME 2 days
ELEVATION RANGE 3,900–6,000 feet
USUALLY OPEN Year-round
DIFFICULTY RATING 4
SCENIC RATING 9
REMOTENESS RATING +1

Special Attractions
- Long two-day trail within Canyonlands National Park.
- Access to hiking trails.
- Wide variety of scenery and rock formations.

History
The White Rim came together as a trail using the network of uranium roads that were created during the boomtimes of the 1950s. It gained its name from the white sandstone rim that most of the trail follows.

Evidence of the region's earliest human inhabitants can be seen at Fort Bottom, accessed via a short hiking trail from the 4WD road. Moki Fort at the end of the hiking trail is an Anasazi rock structure dating back almost a millennium when the Anasazi farmed alongside the Colorado River.

Most of the later history of the trail relates to the ranchers and uranium miners, who pushed their way into the region and left their impressions of the territory in some of the names they gave to features along the trail. Hardscrabble Hill was the original rough, steep cow trail that wound its way down to Hardscrabble Bottom. The narrow shelf road is referred to as "Walker Cut," after Mark Walker who apparently blasted or cut the cow trail around the edge of the hill just after the turn of the 19th century. He also built a small cabin at Fort Bottom, often called "Outlaw Cabin," possibly because of the horse-thieving that happened in the region. (Just above Taylor Canyon is Horsethief Point.)

Musselman Arch, 3 miles into the trail,

CANYONLANDS GEOLOGY

The Canyonlands encompass the southeastern corner of Utah. This striking region displays excellent examples of layer cake geology. Layer cake geology involves the gradual layering of hard and soft sedimentary deposits. In the Canyonlands, these layers have eroded into the many mesas, buttes, and canyon walls.

The general uplift of western North America during the last 15 million years lifted Utah by as much as 5,000 feet. The increased gradient of the rivers and streams in the Canyonlands region greatly increased the rate at which they eroded the horizontal beds of layered, sedimentary rock. Despite their increased speeds, these rivers maintained the meandering courses that were established prior to the uplift, when they were flowing nearly at sea level. Along their path, the rivers cut deep, steep-sided canyons, revealing colorful layers of sedimentary rock. The results of this erosion form the striking scenery typically associated with the Canyonlands area today. Pockets of volcanic activity, such as the La Sal and the Henry Mountains, only occasionally break this even pattern.

was named after Ross A. Musselman, who operated a rock shop and tour business in Moab. He also developed the Pack Creek Ranch, now a country inn, located 5 miles south of Moab. The arch was named by National Geographical Society writer Jack Breed in recognition of Musselman, who had assisted Breed in his research on the region.

Murphy Hogback was named after Otho, Jack, and Tom Murphy, the stockmen who built a trail over the ridge in the 1910s to facilitate the movement of cattle down to the White Rim.

The Murphys also named White Crack, where the present-day national park campsite is situated. Tom Murphy spotted a narrow "white crack" in the white sandstone, and in the 1910s the Murphys blasted a rough cow trail through the gap, opening up access to grazing areas in the south. In the 1950s it was widened with a bulldozer to work uranium mines down below. This trail is now closed to vehicle use.

Description

This extremely long trail can be completed in a single day, but that leaves no time to explore the side canyons or to appreciate the varied scenery. The trail is best completed over two days with an overnight camp. Campsites must be booked in advance with the National Park Service, and a backcountry permit is required. A special permit is not needed to drive the trail in one day, just the normal park entrance fee.

The White Rim Trail officially starts at the same point as Trail #1: Shafer Trail. After descending the initial switchbacks into Shafer Basin, the White Rim Trail diverges and follows the edge of the Island in the Sky plateau to its southernmost point. You pass many points of interest along the way: overlooks for the Colorado River Goose Neck, Musselman Arch (which is so large you can walk onto it), and views of Airport Butte and Washer Woman Arch (which, when seen side on, looks like a woman in a long skirt bending over a tub). You can see the turn for Trail #3: Lathrop Canyon Trail, a spur trail leading to the Colorado River, as you proceed south around the rim. The trail then runs around the edge of Monument Basin, with its spurs, spires, and sandstone formations.

The western side of the trail is no less scenic. It passes through Soda Springs Basin and Holeman Spring Basin before dropping to travel above or alongside the Green River. The western side contains slightly more difficult sections of trail.

For the most part, the trail surface is a mix of broken rock and dirt. The trail is graded, but there are washouts and some moderately difficult sections over slickrock and loose broken rock. On the western side of the trail, there are some steep climbs and short sections of shelf road as the trail climbs around the rim and down along the Green

River. Some of the surface is loose, but the trail is well within the capabilities of a high-clearance SUV. For the most part, the trail follows the White Rim, often running very close to the steep drop from the plateau. The entire trail has views to keep you glued to the window, but it's better still to get out frequently to peer into the canyons or to hike a tantalizing rise. The trail is nearly 70 miles of 4WD road, and from the end there are still 38 miles of dirt road and paved highway back to Moab.

The national park campsites are spread fairly evenly around the trail, roughly 10 miles apart. Sites are numbered, and visitors are required to select their campsite in advance. Perhaps the most popular is White Crack, which is roughly halfway around the trail. However, most of the sites are exposed, with little shade or shelter from the winds, which can spring up from nowhere. Some of the sites along the Green River have some shade. The visitor center at the Island in the Sky has photos of many of the campsites to help you choose, but be aware that at popular times of the year, typically late spring through early fall, you must book your site at least several weeks in advance. All of the campsites have pit toilets. To us, the best campsites are Murphy Campsite A (for its great view) and Potato Bottom Campsite A (for the cottonwoods and river).

The trail is open year-round, but snow or heavy rain can temporarily close the trail. Information on trail conditions can be obtained from the Information Center in Moab or from the Island in the Sky Visitor Center. In particular, the exit from the trail up the Mineral Bottom Road switchbacks and along the dirt road out to Utah 313 can become impassable after rain. The trail is also popular with mountain bikers, who typically take three to four days to complete it.

Current Road Information

Canyonlands National Park
Island in the Sky Ranger District
(435) 259-4712

Monument Basin falls off to the side of White Rim Trail

Map References

BLM   La Sal, Hanksville, San Rafael
Desert, Moab

USGS 1:24,000   Musselman Arch,
Monument Basin, Turks Head,
Upheaval Dome, Horsethief
Canyon, Bowknot Bend, Mineral
Canyon, The Knoll
1:100,000 La Sal, Hanksville, San
Rafael Desert, Moab

Maptech CD-ROM: Moab/Canyonlands;
Central/San Rafael

Trails Illustrated, #501; #210

Utah Atlas & Gazetteer, p. 30

Utah Travel Council #5

Other: Latitude 40—Moab West
Canyon Country Off-Road Vehicle
Trail Map—Island Area

Route Directions

▼ 0.0   After descending switchbacks on Trail
#1: Shafer Trail for 5.1 miles, zero trip
meter and proceed east along White
Rim Trail.

10.8 ▲   End at intersection with Trail #1:
Shafer Trail. Right goes to potash
works. Left travels 5.1 miles up
switchbacks to Utah 313.
GPS: N 38°27.57′ W 109°47.65′

▼ 1.2   SO   Goose Neck Trail on left, 0.5-mile hike
to Colorado River viewpoint.

9.6 ▲   SO   Goose Neck Trail on right, 0.5-mile hike
to Colorado River viewpoint.
GPS: N 38°27.30′ W 109°46.41′

▼ 2.9   TR   Colorado River Overlook is straight on.

7.9 ▲   TL   Colorado River Overlook is to the right.
GPS: N 38°26.28′ W 109°45.97′

▼ 3.1   SO   Musselman Arch on left.

7.7 ▲   SO   Musselman Arch on right.
GPS: N 38°26.20′ W 109°46.16′

▼ 4.3   SO   Cross through wash. Musselman
Canyon is on the left.

6.5 ▲   SO   Musselman Canyon is on the right;
cross through wash.
GPS: N 38°25.84′ W 109°47.11′

▼ 10.7   SO   Lathrop hiking trail is on the right.

0.1 ▲   SO   Lathrop hiking trail is on the left.
GPS: N 38°24.09′ W 109°47.59′

▼ 10.8   SO   Track on left is Trail #3: Lathrop
Canyon Trail to the Colorado River.
Zero trip meter.

0.0 ▲   Continue around the White Rim.
GPS: N 38°24.02′ W 109°47.62′

▼ 0.0   Continue around the White Rim.

10.9 ▲   SO   Track on right is Trail #3: Lathrop
Canyon Trail to the Colorado River.
Zero trip meter.

▼ 0.7   SO   Airport Campsites A and B on the right.

10.2 ▲   SO   Airport Campsites A and B on the left.
GPS: N 38°23.45′ W 109°47.53′

▼ 1.2   SO   Airport Campsites C and D on the right.

9.7 ▲   SO   Airport Campsites C and D on the left.
GPS: N 38°23.23′ W 109°47.93′

▼ 1.3   SO   Washer Woman Arch can be seen to
the west.

9.6 ▲   SO   Washer Woman Arch can be seen to
the west.

▼ 4.8   SO   Cross through wash at head of Buck
Canyon.

6.1 ▲   SO   Cross through wash at head of Buck
Canyon.
GPS: N 38°22.85′ W 109°50.09′

▼ 5.4   SO   Cross through wash.

5.5 ▲   SO   Cross through wash.

▼ 6.7   SO   Cross through wash.

4.2 ▲   SO   Cross through wash.

▼ 7.7   SO   Cross through wash on rock ledge;
great views into Buck Canyon.

3.2 ▲   SO   Cross through wash on rock ledge;
great views into Buck Canyon.
GPS: N 38°21.08′ W 109°50.31′

▼ 8.3   SO   Cross through wash.

2.6 ▲   SO   Cross through wash.

Trail #2: White Rim Trail

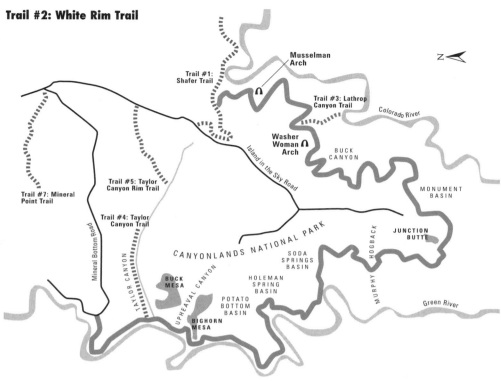

▼ 10.6 SO Gooseberry hiking trail on the right goes 3 miles to the top of the rim.

0.3 ▲ SO Gooseberry hiking trail on the left goes 3 miles to the top of the rim.

GPS: N 38°20.14′ W 109°49.66′

▼ 10.7 SO Cross through rocky wash. Care needed to avoid scraping undercarriage.

0.2 ▲ SO Cross through rocky wash. Care needed to avoid scraping undercarriage.

▼ 10.8 SO Cross through wash, followed by Gooseberry Campsite A on the left.

0.1 ▲ SO Gooseberry Campsite A on the right, then cross through wash.

▼ 10.9 SO Track on right goes to Gooseberry Campsite B. Zero trip meter.

0.0 ▲ Continue around the White Rim.

GPS: N 38°19.80′ W 109°49.59′

▼ 0.0 Continue along the White Rim.

7.7 ▲ SO Track on left goes to Gooseberry Campsite B. Zero trip meter.

▼ 0.4 SO Cross through wash.

7.3 ▲ SO Cross through wash.

▼ 3.6 SO Edge of Monument Basin.

4.1 ▲ SO Leaving Monument Basin.

▼ 4.4 SO Cross through wash.

3.3 ▲ SO Cross through wash.

▼ 4.7 SO Cross through wash.

3.0 ▲ SO Cross through wash.

▼ 5.2 SO Cross through wash.

2.5 ▲ SO Cross through wash.

▼ 5.9 SO Cross through wash.

1.8 ▲ SO Cross through wash.

▼ 7.7 BR Leaving Monument Basin. White Crack Campground on left. Zero trip meter.

0.0 ▲ Continue around the White Rim. Edge of Monument Basin.

GPS: N 38°16.46′ W 109°51.75′

▼ 0.0 Continue around the White Rim.
7.3 ▲ SO White Crack Campground on right.
       Zero trip meter.

▼ 1.1 SO Cross through wash many times in the
       next 5.1 miles.
6.2 ▲ SO Cross through wash, end of wash
       crossings.

▼ 6.2 SO Murphy hiking trail on right. End of
       wash crossings.
1.1 ▲ SO Murphy hiking trail on left. Cross
       through wash many times in the next
       5.1 miles.
       GPS: N 38°19.15′ W 109°53.61′

▼ 6.9 SO Start of narrow shelf road climbing to
       Murphy Hogback.
0.4 ▲ SO End of descent from Murphy Hogback.

▼ 7.3 SO Top of Murphy Hogback. Murphy
       Campsite A on left. Zero trip meter.
0.0 ▲ Continue around White Rim.
       GPS: N 38°19.31′ W 109°54.36′

▼ 0.0 Continue around White Rim.
9.9 ▲ SO Murphy Campsite A on right. Zero trip
       meter.

▼ 0.1 SO Murphy Campsite B on right, then
       Murphy hiking trail on right.
9.8 ▲ SO Murphy hiking trail on left, then
       Murphy Campsite B on left.
       GPS: N 38°19.40′ W 109°54.40′

▼ 0.2 SO Murphy Campsite C on left. Trail
       descends from Murphy Hogback into
       Soda Springs Basin with views to
       Candlestick Tower.
9.7 ▲ SO Murphy Campsite C on right. Top of
       Murphy Hogback.

▼ 2.7 SO Cross through wash. Many wash
       crossings in the next 10.5 miles as
       trail passes through Soda Springs
       Basin, then Holeman Spring Basin.
7.2 ▲ SO Cross through wash.

▼ 9.9 SO Boundary Campsite on right. Zero trip
       meter.

0.0 ▲ Continue around White Rim.
       GPS: N 38°22.46′ W 109°57.87′

▼ 0.0 Continue along White Rim.
9.7 ▲ SO Boundary Campsite on left. Zero trip
       meter.

▼ 3.3 SO Cross through wash.
6.4 ▲ SO Cross through wash. Many wash
       crossings in the next 10.5 miles as
       trail passes through Holeman Spring
       Basin, then Soda Springs Basin.

▼ 8.1 SO Cross through wash. Trail runs close to
       Green River.
1.6 ▲ SO Cross through wash.

▼ 9.0 SO Cross through wash.
0.7 ▲ SO Cross through wash.

▼ 9.3 SO Cross through wash.
0.4 ▲ SO Cross through wash.

▼ 9.7 SO Potato Bottom Campsite A on left
       beside river. Zero trip meter.
0.0 ▲ Continue around White Rim.
       GPS: N 38°25.30′ W 110°00.19′

▼ 0.0 Continue around White Rim.
4.1 ▲ SO Potato Bottom Campsite A on right
       beside river. Zero trip meter.

▼ 0.6 SO Potato Bottom Campsite B on left.
3.5 ▲ SO Potato Bottom Campsite B on right.

▼ 0.7 SO Potato Bottom Campsite C on left.
3.4 ▲ SO Potato Bottom Campsite C on right.
       GPS: N 38°25.84′ W 110°00.53′

▼ 0.9 SO Cross through wash.
3.2 ▲ SO Cross through wash.

▼ 1.7 SO Start of narrow shelf road.
2.4 ▲ SO Shelf road ends.

▼ 2.5 SO Hiking trail on left goes to Fort Bottom.
       Views ahead to Hardscrabble Bottom.
1.6 ▲ SO Hiking trail on right goes to Fort
       Bottom.
       GPS: N 38°26.65′ W 110°01.02′

▼ 4.1   BR   End of shelf road, then track on left
               goes to Hardscrabble Bottom
               Campsite. Zero trip meter.
0.0 ▲   Continue along White Rim Trail.
               GPS: N 38°27.20' W 110°00.45'

▼ 0.0   Continue along White Rim Trail.
1.9 ▲   BL   Track on right goes to Hardscrabble
               Bottom Campsite. Start of narrow shelf
               road. Zero trip meter.

▼ 0.7   SO   Views ahead into Upheaval Bottom.
1.2 ▲   SO   Views ahead into Hardscrabble
               Bottom.

▼ 1.3   SO   Upheaval Dome Loop hiking trail on
               right, then cross through wash.
0.6 ▲   SO   Cross through wash, then Upheaval
               Dome Loop hiking trail on left.
               GPS: N 38°28.06' W 109°59.90'

▼ 1.4   SO   Cross through wash.
0.5 ▲   SO   Cross through wash.

▼ 1.9   SO   Track on right is Trail #4: Taylor
               Canyon Trail. Zero trip meter.
0.0 ▲   Continue along White Rim Trail.
               GPS: N 38°28.52' W 109°59.87'

▼ 0.0   Continue along White Rim Trail.
2.4 ▲   SO   Track on left is Trail #4: Taylor Canyon
               Trail. Zero trip meter.

▼ 0.1   SO   Labyrinth Campsite B on left.
2.3 ▲   SO   Labyrinth Campsite B on right.

▼ 0.2   SO   Track on left goes to Labyrinth
               Campsite A.
2.2 ▲   SO   Track on right goes to Labyrinth
               Campsite A.
               GPS: N 38°28.48' W 110°00.01'

▼ 0.3   SO   Start of narrow shelf road.
2.1 ▲   SO   End of shelf road.

▼ 0.4   SO   End of shelf road.
2.0 ▲   SO   Start of narrow shelf road.

▼ 1.8   SO   Small corral in rock alcove on right.

0.6 ▲   SO   Small corral in rock alcove on left.

▼ 2.2   SO   Cross through wash.
0.2 ▲   SO   Cross through wash.

▼ 2.4   SO   Cattle guard. Leaving Canyonlands
               National Park. Zero trip meter.
0.0 ▲   Continue into national park.
               GPS: N 38°30.01' W 110°01.43'

▼ 0.0   Continue out of national park.
3.7 ▲   SO   Cattle guard. Entering Canyonlands
               National Park. Zero trip meter.

▼ 2.7   SO   Cattle guard.
1.0 ▲   SO   Cattle guard.

▼ 3.7   Trail ends at the intersection with
               Mineral Bottom Road. Turn left for spur
               trail to Mineral Bottom, turn right for
               Utah 313 and Moab.
0.0 ▲   Trail starts at the intersection with the
               Mineral Bottom Road and the White
               Rim Trail. Turn west at the sign for
               Canyonlands National Park and zero
               trip meter.
               GPS: N 38°31.03' W 110°00.25'

MOAB REGION TRAIL #3

Lathrop Canyon Trail

STARTING POINT Trail #2: White Rim Trail
FINISHING POINT Colorado River
TOTAL MILEAGE 3.5 miles
UNPAVED MILEAGE 3.5 miles
DRIVING TIME 45 minutes (one-way)
ELEVATION RANGE 3,900–4,400 feet
USUALLY OPEN Year-round
DIFFICULTY RATING 4
SCENIC RATING 8
REMOTENESS RATING +1

Special Attractions

■ Sandy spur trail off Trail #2: White Rim
   Trail.
■ Access to the Colorado River.
■ Shady riverside picnicking.

Trail #3: Lathrop Canyon Trail

History

Howard Lathrop, a sheepman from Colorado, built a trail from the canyon rim to the Colorado River in the 1940s. Today's trail was cut through in the early 1950s to gain river access in order to supply water for the uranium mine higher up in Lathrop Canyon, above the White Rim Trail. Today, the river access is used by river operators as a pickup point.

Description

This short spur trail drops 500 feet down Lathrop Canyon to finish at the Colorado River. It is the only place on the eastern side of Trail #2: White Rim Trail where it is possible to get down to the river, and if you have only a limited amount of time, driving the eastern side of the White Rim Trail, including the Shafer Trail switchbacks, as far as Lathrop Canyon makes a pleasant and popular day trip. This trek allows sufficient time to view the Goose Neck and Musselman Arch as well as have a riverside picnic in one day.

Any 4WD vehicle capable of accessing the top of the trail via the White Rim will have no trouble negotiating the Lathrop Canyon Trail. The major difficulty on the trail is the loose, deep sand at the lower end of the canyon. There are a couple of large ledges that may be difficult to climb back up, but the worst one has a detour around the

A tight fit beneath a tree along a detour of the Lathrop Canyon Trail

wash that avoids it. Tall vehicles will find the detour a problem though, as a tree limb hangs down far enough that it may catch a high roofline or roof rack.

The trail ends at a clearing in the tamarisks alongside the Colorado River. There are picnic tables in the shade and a pit toilet. You can see the river through a gap in the tamarisks. The site is for day use only; no camping is allowed.

Current Road Information
Canyonlands National Park
Island in the Sky Ranger District
(435) 259-4712

Map References
BLM   La Sal
USGS 1:24,000   Musselman Arch,
        Monument Basin
        1:100,000 La Sal
Maptech CD-ROM: Moab/Canyonlands
Trails Illustrated, #501; #210
Utah Atlas & Gazetteer, p. 30
Utah Travel Council #5
Other: Latitude 40—Moab West

Route Directions

▼ 0.0   10.8 miles along Trail #2: White Rim Trail from the junction with Trail #1: Shafer Trail, turn southeast at the sign for Lathrop Canyon and zero trip meter. Trail immediately drops steeply.
         GPS: N 38°24.02′ W 109°47.62′

▼ 0.2 SO Cross through wash. Trail follows wash and drops into tight canyon. There are many wash crossings to the end of the trail.

▼ 3.3 SO Picnic table on left underneath large cottonwoods.
         GPS: N 38°22.28′ W 109°46.44′

▼ 3.4 SO Steep, soft sand as trail drops in and out of wash. A couple of ledges to watch. The trail forks a couple of times with the fork following the wash. These are alternate routes that rejoin the trail before the end.

▼ 3.5   Trail ends at clearing beside the Colorado River with three picnic tables and river access.
         GPS: N 38°22.17′ W 109°46.37′

Taylor Canyon Trail

STARTING POINT Trail #2: White Rim Trail
FINISHING POINT Trailhead to Moses Rock and Taylor Canyon
TOTAL MILEAGE 4.8 miles
UNPAVED MILEAGE 4.8 miles
DRIVING TIME 30 minutes (one-way)
ELEVATION RANGE 4,000–4,400 feet
USUALLY OPEN Year-round
DIFFICULTY RATING 2
SCENIC RATING 9
REMOTENESS RATING +1

Special Attractions
■ Interesting spur trail to complement Trail #2: White Rim Trail.
■ Moses and Zeus rocks.
■ Access to hiking trails up Taylor Canyon.

History
Taylor Canyon is named after a prominent early cattleman in the area, Arth Taylor. Taylor arrived in Moab in the late 1800s and ran both cattle and sheep, whichever was the most profitable at the time. The Taylor family members were entrepreneurs who had several ventures over the years in and around Moab, including operating a rowboat ferry on the Colorado River, managing the first general store in Moab, and winning a contract for putting through the grade for the Denver & Rio Grande Railroad for part of the stretch between Grand Junction and Green River.

In the 1920s, Taylor Canyon was a good place to try to catch a burro. A prospector named Turner came here and then moved on, but he left his burros behind.

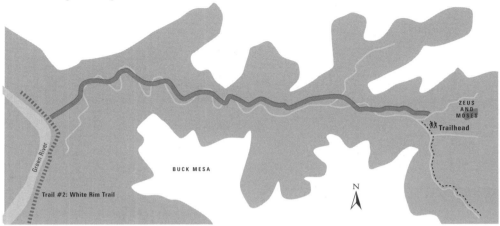

Description

This short spur trail from Trail #2: White Rim Trail gives access to the Moses hiking trail and to trails up Taylor Canyon. The Moses and Zeus rocks, large Entrada sandstone formations that are supposed to resemble stooping figures of the prophet and the god, are prominent at the end of the trail, high on the cliff to the north.

There is a single camping area at the end of the trail; reservations are required with the National Park Service.

The trail is generally easy as it follows along the wash in Taylor Canyon. It crosses the wash numerous times in the first 4 miles, at times running along the sandy wash. The trail has no real changes in gradient, and the wash bottom is firm. The trail is slightly sandy in dry weather.

Current Road Information

Canyonlands National Park
Island in the Sky Ranger District
(435) 259-4712

Map References

BLM   La Sal (incomplete)
USGS 1:24,000   Upheaval Dome
        1:100,000 La Sal (incomplete)
Maptech CD-ROM: Moab/Canyonlands
Trails Illustrated, #210
Utah Atlas & Gazetteer, p. 30
Utah Travel Council #5
Other: Latitude 40—Moab West
        Canyon Country Off-Road Vehicle
        Trail Map—Island Area

Route Directions

The trail enters a wash as the canyon rock formations tower above

▼ 0.0   From Trail #2: White Rim Trail, close to the Labyrinth Campsites, turn east on the Taylor Canyon Trail at the sign and zero trip meter.
        GPS: N 38°28.53′ W 109°59.86′

▼ 0.5	SO	Trail enters wash. Many wash crossings or sections within the wash in the next 3.5 miles.
▼ 4.0	SO	Trail leaves wash.
▼ 4.6	SO	Taylor Campsite on right.
		GPS: N 38°28.58' W 109°55.35'

| ▼ 4.8 | | Trail ends at trailhead for Moses hiking trail. Moses and Zeus rocks are ahead to the east. |
| | | **GPS: N 38°28.57' W 109°55.20'** |

MOAB REGION TRAIL #5

Taylor Canyon Rim Trail

STARTING POINT Island in the Sky Road (Utah 313)
FINISHING POINT Taylor Canyon Rim
TOTAL MILEAGE 4.8 miles
UNPAVED MILEAGE 4.8 miles
DRIVING TIME 45 minutes (one-way)
ELEVATION RANGE 5,200–6,000 feet
USUALLY OPEN Year-round
DIFFICULTY RATING 3
SCENIC RATING 8
REMOTENESS RATING +0

Special Attractions
- Beehive Butte and Whitbeck Rock.
- Short, easy hiking trail to rewarding viewpoint.
- Views over the Island in the Sky area of Canyonlands National Park.

Description
This short spur trail leads to a Taylor Canyon overlook in the Island in the Sky district of Canyonlands National Park. The trail starts at Island in the Sky Road, 2.4 miles south of Dead Horse Point Road. The trail, which is not signposted, leads to the south toward the large dome of Whitbeck Rock. To the right is prominent Beehive Butte, a large dome standing by itself on the plateau. The trail runs along a very loose, sandy plateau, on the western edge of Whitbeck Rock, and then gradually descends to run along an old seismic line toward the canyon rim. The drop down is very loose and sandy, with some deep sections of powder-fine sand. Vehicle marks show where vehicles have slid to the edge, unable to turn the corner in the sand. This section is more difficult in very dry weather. As the trail descends, you start to get views of the Island in the

A view of the Island in the Sky from an unnamed butte behind the trail

Sky district. On a clear day it is possible to see as far as the Henry Mountains to the west. The trail passes an unnamed butte and continues to the park boundary. Vehicle access stops at this point. Leave your vehicle and hike the 1.3 miles to the rim of Taylor Canyon. The viewpoint from the end is very rewarding—including Taylor, Rough, and Trail Canyons. You can see the wash and the remains of old vehicle tracks far below, the Green River Canyon to the right, and Upheaval Dome ahead. For those not wishing to hike as far, there is a nice viewpoint 0.4 miles from the end of the vehicle trail, looking east over Taylor and Rough Canyons.

This track provides access to some very quiet, little-used backcountry campsites. The best sites are after the drop-off to the point where juniper and pinyon trees provide some shade. The hardest part of the trail is the soft sand, although there are some deep washouts near the beginning. The soft sand makes this a brutal ride for mountain bikers.

Current Road Information

BLM Moab Field Office
82 East Dogwood, Suite M
Moab, UT 84532
(435) 259-2100

Map References

BLM   Moab, La Sal
USGS 1:24,000   The Knoll, Musselman
       Arch, Upheaval Dome
       1:100,000 Moab, La Sal
Maptech CD-ROM: Moab/Canyonlands
Trails Illustrated, #501; #210
Utah Atlas & Gazetteer, p. 30
Utah Travel Council #5
Other: Latitude 40—Moab West
       Canyon Country Off-Road Vehicle
       Trail Map—Island Area

Route Directions

▼ 0.0   From the Island in the Sky Road,
            2.4 miles south of Dead Horse Point
            Road, turn west on unmarked, ungraded sandy trail and zero trip meter.
            GPS: N 38°31.00' W 109°48.02'

▼ 0.4   BL Track on right.
▼ 1.0   BL Track on right goes to Beehive Butte.
            Whitbeck Rock is on the left.
            GPS: N 38°30.89' W 109°49.17'

▼ 1.1   SO Track on left.
▼ 1.6   BL Track on right.
▼ 2.0   BL Track on right.
▼ 2.1   SO Track on right rejoins. Trail descends.

Trail #5: Taylor Canyon Rim Trail

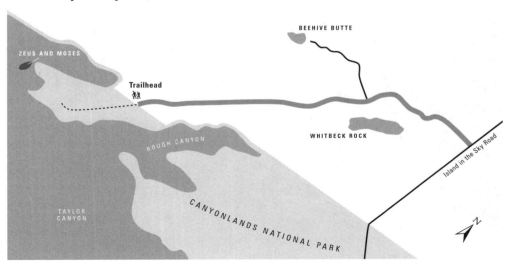

▼ 2.2 SO Two tracks on left and track on right. Second track on left goes to campsite with good views.
GPS: N 38°30.33' W 109°50.28'

▼ 2.8 SO Faint track on right opposite unnamed butte.
GPS: N 38°30.12' W 109°50.67'

▼ 3.1 SO Track on right before slickrock area and track on left. Keep going to the southwest.
▼ 3.4 SO Track on left.
▼ 3.8 SO Faint track on left.
▼ 4.8   Trail ends for vehicles at the boundary of Canyonlands National Park. Hike along the old vehicle trail 1.3 miles to Taylor Canyon Rim.
GPS: N 38°28.98' W 109°52.58'

A large fallen rock creates a natural tunnel along the trail

MOAB REGION TRAIL #6

Long Canyon Trail

STARTING POINT Dead Horse Point Road (Utah 313)
FINISHING POINT Potash Road (Utah 279) at Jug Handle Arch
TOTAL MILEAGE 7.2 miles
UNPAVED MILEAGE 7.2 miles
DRIVING TIME 45 minutes
ELEVATION RANGE 3,900–6,100 feet
USUALLY OPEN Year-round
DIFFICULTY RATING 3
SCENIC RATING 9
REMOTENESS RATING +0

Special Attractions
■ Steep, narrow trail in tight red sandstone canyon.
■ Jug Handle Arch.
■ Views east to the La Sal Mountains and down into Long Canyon.

Description
The Long Canyon Trail (or as it is more popularly called, Pucker Pass) makes an exciting alternative way back to Moab from the Island in the Sky district. It was named Pucker Pass by some imaginative Jeepers back in the days when a drive down the canyon was a lot more hair-raising than it is now. The trail leaves Dead Horse Point Road and travels in a plumb line across Big Flat until it reaches the top of Long Canyon. From here it drops steeply down into the extremely narrow, sandstone-walled canyon.

After 3.3 miles, the trail goes underneath a huge slab of sandstone that fell down from the cliff face. The huge block has remained tilted at a precarious angle over the trail, luckily allowing vehicles to pass easily underneath. From here, the canyon opens up a bit, but it still switchbacks steeply down before joining Long Canyon Creek. For the last few miles, the trail crosses Long Creek several times before finishing on Potash Road (Utah 279) in the Jug Handle Arch parking area. True to its name, this unusual arch bends out from the cliff exactly like the jug handle. The area of cliffs bordering Potash Road is popular with rock climbers, and it is not unusual to see several groups swaying precariously from the cliff face.

The surface along this trail is generally pretty smooth. There are a few lumpy sections on the switchbacks, but normally nothing to catch an unwary undercarriage.

Looking up the switchbacks of Long Canyon Trail

There is a long section of narrow shelf road running down the canyon that's wide enough for a single vehicle, and it has a sufficient number of passing places.

The trail is normally open year-round, but heavy rains or snow can make it impassable. Snow remains for a long time in the narrow canyon, which sees little sunlight in winter, and can become dangerously icy. Given the long drop if you slip, this is one trail to avoid in the snow. Camping is restricted in the upper canyon to protect the bighorn sheep habitat.

Current Road Information
BLM Moab Field Office
82 East Dogwood, Suite M
Moab, UT 84532
(435) 259-2100

Map References
BLM   Moab
USGS 1:24,000   Gold Bar Canyon,
        The Knoll
        1:100,000 Moab
Maptech CD-ROM: Moab/Canyonlands
Trails Illustrated, #501; #210
Utah Atlas & Gazetteer, p. 30
Utah Travel Council #5
Other: Latitude 40—Moab West
        Canyon Country Off-Road Vehicle
        Trail Map—Island Area

Route Directions

▼ 0.0   From Dead Horse Point Road (Utah
            313), 1.5 miles from the junction with
            the Island in the Sky Road, turn east
            on the unmarked Long Canyon Road
            and zero trip meter.
3.3 ▲   Trail finishes on Dead Horse Point
            Road, 1.5 miles from the junction with
            the Island in the Sky Road. Turn left to
            visit Dead Horse Point, turn right for
            the Island in the Sky and Moab.
            GPS: N 38°32.71′ W 109°45.82′

▼ 0.1   SO Track on left.
3.2 ▲   SO Track on right.

▼ 0.5   SO Track on right.
2.8 ▲   SO Track on left.

▼ 0.9   SO Track on left.
2.4 ▲   SO Track on right.
            GPS: N 38°32.62′ W 109°44.73′

▼ 1.8   SO Track on left.
1.5 ▲   SO Track on right.

▼ 2.0   SO Track on left.
1.3 ▲   SO Track on right.

▼ 2.4   SO Track on left.
0.9 ▲   SO Track on right.

▼ 2.5   SO Track on right.
0.8 ▲   SO Track on left.

▼ 2.8   SO Long Canyon on the right.
0.5 ▲   SO Leaving Long Canyon.

▼ 2.9   SO Track on right. Trail starts to switch-
             back down into Long Canyon.
0.4 ▲   SO Track on left. End of climb up Long
             Canyon.
             GPS: N 38°32.50′ W 109°42.41′

▼ 3.3   SO Trail passes underneath huge fallen
             boulder tilted over the trail. Zero trip
             meter.
0.0 ▲   Continue to climb up Long Canyon.
             GPS: N 38°32.62′ W 109°42.36′

▼ 0.0   Continue down Long Canyon.
3.9 ▲   SO Trail passes underneath huge fallen
             boulder tilted over the trail. Zero trip
             meter.

▼ 1.7   SO Cross through wash.
2.2 ▲   SO Cross through wash.

▼ 1.8   SO Cross through wash. End of descent.
2.1 ▲   SO Cross through wash. Start of climb.

▼ 2.1   SO Cross over wash and track on right.
1.8 ▲   SO Cross over wash and track on left.

▼ 2.4   SO Cross through Long Creek Wash.

1.5 ▲   SO Cross through Long Creek Wash.

▼ 2.7   SO Cross through Long Creek Wash.
1.2 ▲   SO Cross through Long Creek Wash.

▼ 2.8   SO Camping permitted past this point.
1.1 ▲   SO No camping past this point.
             GPS: N 38°32.73′ W 109°40.12′

▼ 3.0   SO Cross over Long Creek.
0.9 ▲   SO Cross over Long Creek.

▼ 3.1   SO Cross over Long Creek.
0.8 ▲   SO Cross over Long Creek.

▼ 3.5   SO Track on left.
0.4 ▲   SO Track on right.

▼ 3.8   SO Trail enters the Jug Handle Arch park-
             ing area. The Jug Handle Arch is on
             the left.
0.1 ▲   SO The Jug Handle Arch is on the right. Trail
             leaves out the back of the parking area.

▼ 3.9   Cross over railroad tracks, then trail
             finishes at Potash Road (Utah 279).
             Turn left to join US 191.
0.0 ▲   On Potash Road (Utah 279), 12.7 miles
             from US 191, turn into the Jug Handle
             parking area, cross railroad tracks and
             zero trip meter. There is no sign for the
             trail from Potash Road.
             GPS: N 38°32.79′ W 109°38.83′

Trail #6: Long Canyon Trail

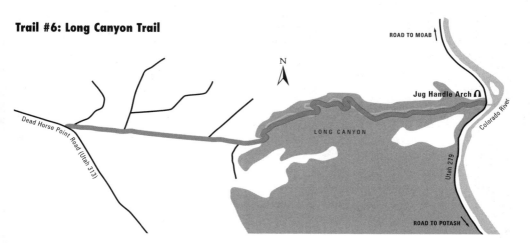

Mineral Point Trail

STARTING POINT 0.4 miles south of mile marker 11 on Utah 313
FINISHING POINT Mineral Point
TOTAL MILEAGE 11.6 miles
UNPAVED MILEAGE 11.6 miles
DRIVING TIME 45 minutes (one-way)
ELEVATION RANGE 4,700–5,800 feet
USUALLY OPEN Year-round
DIFFICULTY RATING 2
SCENIC RATING 8
REMOTENESS RATING +0

Special Attractions

■ Panoramic views from Mineral Point over the Green River.
■ Easy and scenic high-clearance road.
■ Provides access to a large network of interesting trails.

Description

This short spur trail runs out onto Mineral Point, one of the long ridges that overlooks the Green River. The trail is graded dirt along its entire length and is suitable in dry weather for high-clearance 2WDs. However, in wet weather the trail is often impassable to all vehicles because of the clinging red mud. The surface in dry weather is sandy with patches of southeast Utah's ubiquitous powder-fine sand traps. There are some minor rocky sections at the far end and a few small washes.

The main trail is easy to navigate and well defined, although there are no signs, and it connects to a maze of smaller tracks, some of which lead to other good viewpoints—Trail #8: Hell Roaring Canyon Rim Trail is a loop spur off this route.

Mineral Point is a broad, gently sloping ridge that tapers down to the viewpoint over the Green River. The original tracks were put through for mineral exploration. As you descend gradually, there are views over the broad plateau and over to the Henry Mountains. At the end, the Green River is far below and the Maze district of Canyonlands National Park is visible on the far side.

Current Road Information

Canyonlands National Park
Island in the Sky Ranger District
(435) 259-4712

Map References

BLM   Moab
USGS 1:24,000   The Knoll, Mineral
            Canyon
       1:100,000 Moab
Maptech CD-ROM: Moab/Canyonlands
Trails Illustrated, #501; #210
Utah Atlas & Gazetteer, p. 30

View of Green River from the end of Mineral Point Trail

Trail #7: Mineral Point Trail

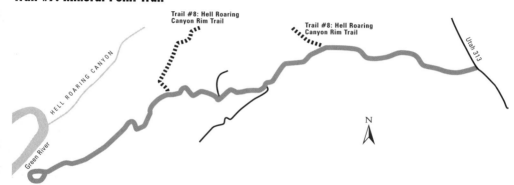

Utah Travel Council #5
Other: Latitude 40—Moab West
        Canyon Country Off-Road Vehicle
        Trail Map—Island Area

Route Directions

▼ 0.0   Trail starts 0.4 miles south of mile
           marker 11 on Utah 313. Turn west
           on unmarked road and zero trip
           meter.
           GPS: N 38°35.23' W 109°48.32'

▼ 0.3   SO   Track on left.
▼ 0.4   SO   Track on left.
▼ 0.5   SO   Track on left.
▼ 0.9   SO   Track on left.
▼ 1.1   SO   Track on left.
▼ 1.2   SO   Track on left.
▼ 1.6   SO   Two tracks on right, then track on left.
▼ 1.8   SO   Track on right.
▼ 1.9   SO   Track on right.
           GPS: N 38°35.45' W 109°50.29'

▼ 2.2   SO   Old corral on right.
▼ 2.9   SO   Track on right.
           GPS: N 38°35.51' W 109°51.30'

▼ 3.0   SO   Track on right.
▼ 3.3   SO   Track on left.
▼ 3.6   SO   Track on right toward ridge is Trail #8:
             Hell Roaring Canyon Rim Trail, and
             track on left. Zero trip meter.
           GPS: N 38°35.51' W 109°52.16'

▼ 0.0   Continue along trail.
▼ 0.1   SO   Cross through wash.
▼ 0.3   SO   Track on right.
▼ 0.8   SO   Cross through small wash.
▼ 3.0   SO   Track on right alongside butte, and
             track on left.
           GPS: N 38°34.46' W 109°54.84'

▼ 3.6   SO   Cross through wash.
▼ 3.8   SO   Track on right.
▼ 4.3   SO   Track on right is end of Trail #8:
             Hell Roaring Canyon Rim Trail. Zero trip
             meter.
           GPS: N 38°34.45' W 109°56.08'

▼ 0.0   Continue toward Mineral Point.
▼ 0.8   SO   Track on left.
▼ 0.9   SO   Track on left.
▼ 1.0   SO   Cross through wash.
▼ 1.6   SO   Track on right.
▼ 2.4   BL   Track on right to oil drilling site.
           GPS: N 38°33.21' W 109°58.06'

▼ 2.6   SO   Track on left.
▼ 2.8   SO   Tracks on right and left.
▼ 3.4   SO   Track on right.
           GPS: N 38°32.89' W 109°59.15'

▼ 3.6   BL   Start of small loop at end of trail.
▼ 3.7   Trail ends at farthest point of loop on
           Mineral Point. Walk out onto the rocks
           for the best views of Green River and
           the Maze area of Canyonlands National
           Park.
           GPS: N 38°32.83' W 109°59.44'

Hell Roaring Canyon Rim Trail

STARTING POINT Trail #7: Mineral Point Trail, 3.6 miles from Utah 313

FINISHING POINT Trail #7: Mineral Point Trail, 7.9 miles from Utah 313

TOTAL MILEAGE 5.7 miles

UNPAVED MILEAGE 5.7 miles

DRIVING TIME 1 hour

ELEVATION RANGE 5,300–5,800 feet

USUALLY OPEN Year-round

DIFFICULTY RATING 4

SCENIC RATING 8

REMOTENESS RATING +0

Special Attractions

- Challenging trail that makes a spur loop off Trail #7: Mineral Point Trail.
- Views into Hell Roaring Canyon.

Description

This short trail is picked up along Trail #7: Mineral Point Trail; it starts and finishes on Mineral Point Road and makes a pleasant side trip. It travels on smaller, ungraded sandy and rocky tracks along a ridge top on Mineral Point, offering wide-ranging views, before dropping to visit the edge of Hell Roaring Canyon.

There are many small, unmarked trails leading off from this trail, so pay close attention to the route to avoid getting lost. However, most of the side trails are dead ends or rejoin the route later, so it is hard to go too far wrong.

Within the first mile, this route climbs onto the ridge. Ahead are the Henry Mountains and the Maze district of Canyonlands National Park. The Needles, large buttes that are passed on Trail #16: Spring Canyon Point Trail, are to the right and to the left are the La Sal Mountains and the Abajo, or Blue, Mountains near Monticello.

The trail leaves the ridge and drops through a maze of small tracks to wrap around the edge of a small canyon, a tributary of the main Hell Roaring Canyon. It then descends to the bench directly above Hell Roaring Canyon. This descent is the most difficult part of the trail, with a couple of rock steps and some loose sand, but it is normally easily passable by most SUVs. You'll get the best viewpoints over Hell Roaring Canyon by walking a short distance to the edge of the rim. For those wanting to camp, this trail has better spots to pitch a tent than the main Mineral Point Trail, including some pleasant spots near the rim.

Looking down into Hell Roaring Canyon

Trail #8: Hell Roaring Canyon Rim Trail

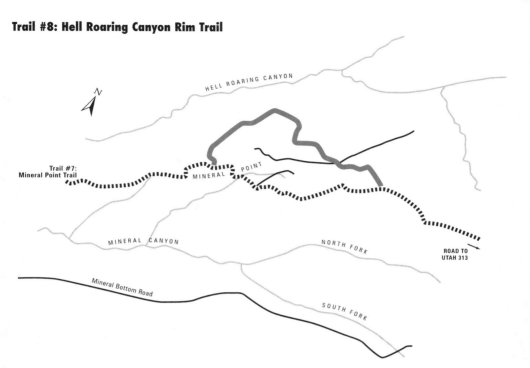

Current Road Information

BLM Moab Field Office
82 East Dogwood, Suite M
Moab, UT 84532
(435) 259-2100

Map References

BLM   Moab
USGS 1:24,000 The Knoll, Mineral
        Canyon
        1:100,000 Moab
Maptech CD-ROM: Moab/Canyonlands
Trails Illustrated, #210
Utah Atlas & Gazetteer, p. 30
Utah Travel Council #5
Other: Latitude 40—Moab West
        Canyon Country Off-Road Vehicle
        Trail Map—Island Area

Route Directions

▼ 0.0   From Trail #7: Mineral Point Trail, 3.6
          miles from the start, turn northwest on
          an unmarked sandy track and zero trip
          meter.

5.7 ▲   Trail ends at the junction with Trail #7:

Mineral Point Trail. Turn left to exit to
Utah 313, turn right to continue to
Mineral Point.
GPS: N 38°35.51' W 109°52.16'

▼ 0.5   TL   Turn onto unmarked track in front of
               rise.
5.2 ▲   TR   Turn onto unmarked track at the end of
               the rise.
          GPS: N 38°35.74' W 109°52.80'

▼ 0.6   TR   Track on left. Trail climbs onto ridge.
5.1 ▲   TL   Track on right. Trail leaves ridge.

▼ 1.1   SO   Track on left. Continue along ridge.
4.6 ▲   SO   Track on right. Continue along ridge.
          GPS: N 38°35.51' W 109°53.33'

▼ 1.3   TL   Turn left at T-intersection, track on right.
4.4 ▲   TR   Track straight ahead.
          GPS: N 38°35.58' W 109°53.46'

▼ 1.4   SO   Track on right.
4.3 ▲   SO   Track on left.

▼ 1.5   TR   Small intersection.

4.2 ▲	TL	Small intersection.

GPS: N 38°35.49′ W 109°53.67′

▼ 1.7	SO	Track on right.
4.0 ▲	SO	Track on left.

▼ 1.8	BL	Track on right.
3.9 ▲	BR	Track on left.

▼ 1.9	BL	Track on right.
3.8 ▲	BR	Track on left.

GPS: N 38°35.72′ W 109°54.05′

▼ 2.4	SO	Track on right.
3.3 ▲	SO	Track on left.

▼ 3.2	SO	Cross through wash.
2.5 ▲	SO	Cross through wash.

GPS: N 38°36.01′ W 109°54.98′

▼ 3.4	BL	Track on right goes to viewpoint over Hell Roaring Canyon.
2.3 ▲	BR	Track on left goes to viewpoint over Hell Roaring Canyon.

GPS: N 38°35.98′ W 109°55.18′

▼ 3.9	SO	Cross through slickrock wash.
1.8 ▲	SO	Cross through slickrock wash.

▼ 4.5	SO	Cross through wash.
1.2 ▲	SO	Cross through wash.

▼ 5.3	TL	Intersection. Follow more-used track to the left and pass to the south of the ridge.
0.4 ▲	TR	Pass to the south of the ridge, then intersection. Follow more-used track to the right.

GPS: N 38°34.68′ W 109°56.36′

▼ 5.7		Trail ends back on Trail #7: Mineral Point Trail. Turn right to continue to Mineral Point, turn left to exit to Utah 313.
0.0 ▲		From Trail #7: Mineral Point Trail, 7.9 miles from the start, turn northwest on an unmarked sandy track and zero trip meter.

GPS: N 38°34.45′ W 109°56.08′

Bartlett Wash Trail

STARTING POINT Blue Hills Road, 2.2 miles west of US 191
FINISHING POINT Dubinky Well Road, 1.6 miles northeast of junction with Spring Canyon Road
TOTAL MILEAGE 7.3 miles
UNPAVED MILEAGE 7.3 miles
DRIVING TIME 1 hour
ELEVATION RANGE 4,600–5,200 feet
USUALLY OPEN Year-round
DIFFICULTY RATING 3
SCENIC RATING 8
REMOTENESS RATING +0

Special Attractions

■ Easy to moderate trail along wide, sandy valley.
■ Access to the mountain bike slickrock play area.
■ Shady picnicking under large cottonwoods alongside the wash.

Description

Bartlett Wash Trail is a pleasant alternative to Trail #10: Hidden Canyon Wash Trail for those not wanting to tackle the deep sand along Hidden Canyon. The trail is graded at the start and for much of its length, but it does have some moderately sandy sections, and toward the end where it joins Dubinky Well Road, there are some rocky ledges and slickrock sections.

The trail leaves Blue Hills Road at the same point as Trail #10: Hidden Canyon Wash Trail, but it diverges within the first mile. Bartlett Wash Trail follows a smaller graded road and drops down into Bartlett Wash. The first section has some large cottonwoods in the wide part of the wash, which provide a pleasant place for a picnic, although there are no tables or facilities. People have camped here, but it is not advisable so close to the wash.

Once it enters the valley, the trail crosses the wash many times. There are several

Looking back across Bartlett Wash Trail

forks, and in a couple of places it is possible to follow along in the wash as an alternative to the trail. After 2.4 miles from the start of the trail, a mountain bike–only trail leaves the wash to the right and climbs onto the sandy ridges. This eventually gives access to the large slickrock domes between Bartlett Wash and Hidden Canyon. Mountain bikers can connect the two canyons in this way.

The valley gradually rises until it passes the far end of Trail #10: Hidden Canyon Wash Trail. From here, the trail runs across the benches, past large sandstone buttes, until it gradually climbs to finish on Dubinky Well Road, 1.6 miles northwest of junction with Spring Canyon Road.

Current Road Information
BLM Moab Field Office
82 East Dogwood, Suite M
Moab, UT 84532
(435) 259-2100

Map References
BLM   Moab
USGS 1:24,000 Jug Rock
       1:100,000 Moab
Maptech CD-ROM: Moab/Canyonlands
Trails Illustrated, #501 (incomplete)
Utah Atlas & Gazetteer, p. 40
Other: Latitude 40—Moab West
       Canyon Country Off-Road Vehicle
       Trail Map—Island Area

Route Directions

▼ 0.0   Trail commences on Blue Hills Road, 2.2 miles from the junction with US 191. Turn south onto smaller, unmarked graded road and zero trip meter.

1.4 ▲   Trail finishes at the junction with the graded dirt Blue Hills Road. Turn right to join US 191.
      GPS: N 38°44.69′ W 109°46.74′

▼ 0.7 TL Track straight on is Trail #10: Hidden Canyon Wash Trail.

0.7 ▲ TR Track on left is Trail #10: Hidden Canyon Wash Trail.
      GPS: N 38°44.01′ W 109°47.08′

▼ 0.9 SO Track on right.

0.5 ▲ SO Track on left.

▼ 1.1 SO Cross through the wide, sandy Bartlett Wash.

0.3 ▲ SO Cross through the wide, sandy Bartlett Wash.

▼ 1.4 TR Turn right onto unmarked roughly graded dirt trail and zero trip meter.

0.0 ▲   Continue along wider road.
      GPS: N 38°43.67′ W 109°46.47′

▼ 0.0   Continue to the southwest.

2.3 ▲ TL Turn left at T-intersection. Zero trip meter.

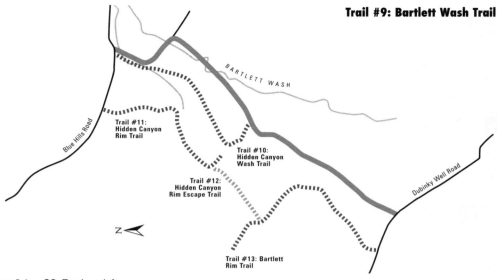

Trail #11:
Hidden Canyon
Rim Trail

Trail #10:
Hidden Canyon
Wash Trail

Trail #12:
Hidden Canyon
Rim Escape Trail

Trail #13: Bartlett
Rim Trail

▼ 0.1   SO   Track on left.
2.2 ▲   SO   Track on right.

▼ 0.3   SO   Track on left.
2.0 ▲   SO   Track on right.

▼ 0.5   SO   Trail drops down and enters the Bartlett Wash valley; Bartlett Wash is on the right.
1.8 ▲   SO   Trail leaves the Bartlett Wash valley.

▼ 0.9   SO   Cross through Bartlett Wash twice. Trail runs in or alongside the wash, crossing it many times.
1.4 ▲   SO   Cross through Bartlett Wash for final time.
    GPS: N 38°43.05' W 109°47.14'

▼ 1.0   BL   Gate in wash then bear left out of wash. Remaining in wash at this point leads to the mountain bike trail which leaves up the sand ridge to the west.
1.3 ▲   SO   Gate in wash. Turning left back up wash before the gate leads to the mountain bike trail which leaves up the sand ridge to the west.
    GPS: N 38°43.00' W 109°47.19'

▼ 1.4   BL   Fork in wash, follow graded track out of the main wash along smaller wash.
0.9 ▲   SO   Join larger wash.
    GPS: N 38°42.71' W 109°47.43'

▼ 1.5   BR   Small track on left.
0.8 ▲   BL   Small track on right.
    GPS: N 38°42.61' W 109°47.51'

▼ 1.7   SO   Track on right drops into wash.
0.6 ▲   SO   Track on left drops into wash.

▼ 1.8   SO   Cross through small wash.
0.5 ▲   SO   Cross through small wash.

▼ 2.0   SO   Old oil drilling marker on left.
0.3 ▲   SO   Old oil drilling marker on right.
    GPS: N 38°42.41' W 109°47.91'

▼ 2.3   SO   Track on right is Trail #10: Hidden Canyon Wash Trail. Zero trip meter.
0.0 ▲   Continue to the north.
    GPS: N 38°42.33' W 109°48.19'

▼ 0.0   Continue to the south.
3.6 ▲   SO   Track on left is Trail #10: Hidden Canyon Wash Trail. Zero trip meter.

▼ 0.5   SO   Track on right goes to small viewpoint.
3.1 ▲   BR   Track on left goes to a small viewpoint.

▼ 0.7   SO   Enter wash.
2.9 ▲   SO   Exit wash.

▼ 0.8   SO   Exit wash.
2.8 ▲   SO   Enter wash.

▼ 1.4	SO	Cross through wash.
2.2 ▲	SO	Cross through wash.

▼ 1.8	SO	Cross through wash.
1.8 ▲	SO	Cross through wash.

▼ 2.6	SO	Cross through wash.
1.0 ▲	SO	Cross through wash.

GPS: N 38°40.57' W 109°49.71'

▼ 3.0	SO	Cross through wash, then cross slick-rock pavement.
0.6 ▲	SO	Leave slickrock, then cross through wash.

▼ 3.2	SO	Leave slickrock.
0.4 ▲	SO	Cross slickrock pavement.

▼ 3.6		Trail ends at the junction with Dubinky Well Road. Turn left to join Spring Canyon Road or Utah 313.
0.0 ▲		Trail starts on the Dubinky Well Road, approximately 3 miles northwest of Utah 313, 1.6 miles northwest of the junction with the Spring Canyon Road. Zero trip meter and turn northeast on unmarked track.

GPS: N 38°39.80' W 109°50.30'

MOAB REGION TRAIL #10

Hidden Canyon Wash Trail

STARTING POINT Blue Hills Road, 2.2 miles west of US 191

FINISHING POINT Junction with Trail #9: Bartlett Wash Trail

TOTAL MILEAGE 4.1 miles

UNPAVED MILEAGE 4.1 miles

DRIVING TIME 45 minutes

ELEVATION RANGE 4,600–4,900 feet

USUALLY OPEN Year-round

DIFFICULTY RATING 5

SCENIC RATING 9

REMOTENESS RATING +0

Special Attractions

- Multicolored sandstone domes of Hidden Canyon.
- Fun, sandy trail to explore.
- Very pretty canyon and creek wash.

Description

This short trail leads into the extremely scenic Hidden Canyon, with its walls of colored slickrock. The canyon is not particularly deep, and it has a wide, sandy valley floor. The trail starts off as a graded track, but the road standard quickly drops to a very loose sandy track. It follows the wash into the canyon before descending to run in the wash toward Trail #9: Bartlett Wash Trail. The sand in the canyon is difficult to traverse, being very deep and loose. You will probably need to lower tire pressures to avoid bogging down.

After 3.2 miles, the trail turns left down the wash for the climb out, but you can continue ahead for a further 3.2 miles into Hidden Canyon. At that point, the trail becomes too narrow for 4WDs, but some ATVs are able to travel a little farther. Both the head of the canyon and another short spur are worth investigating on foot.

The climb up to Trail #9: Bartlett Wash Trail has the loosest and deepest sand; it's quite steep, but it's short. There are two alternative climbs, both visible when you get to the end of the canyon. At the time of writing, the left-hand climb was slightly easier, but this may not always be the case.

Current Road Information

BLM Moab Field Office
82 East Dogwood, Suite M
Moab, UT 84532
(435) 259-2100

Map References

BLM   Moab (incomplete)
USGS 1:24,000   Jug Rock (incomplete)
          1:100,000 Moab (incomplete)
Maptech CD-ROM: Moab/Canyonlands
Trails Illustrated, #501 (incomplete)
Utah Atlas & Gazetteer, p. 40
Other: Latitude 40—Moab West (doesn't show an exit from Hidden Canyon Wash)

Hidden Canyon Wash Trail runs below the viewpoint along the edge of the rim

Route Directions

▼ 0.0   Trail commences on Blue Hills Road, 2.2 miles from US 191. Turn south onto smaller, unmarked graded road and zero trip meter.

3.2 ▲   Trail finishes at the junction with the graded dirt Blue Hills Road. Turn right to join US 191.

GPS: N 38°44.69' W 109°46.74'

▼ 0.7   SO   Track on left is Trail #9: Bartlett Wash Trail.

2.5 ▲   SO   Track on right is Trail #9: Bartlett Wash Trail.

GPS: N 38°44.01' W 109°47.08'

▼ 0.9   SO   Track on right.

2.3 ▲   SO   Track on left.

▼ 1.1   SO   Corral on left, then track on left.

2.1 ▲   SO   Track on right, then corral on right.

GPS: N 38°43.75' W 109°47.21'

▼ 1.5   BL   Two tracks on right.

1.7 ▲   BR   Two tracks on left.

▼ 1.6   SO   Cross through wash.

1.6 ▲   SO   Cross through wash.

▼ 1.8   SO   Cross through fence line.

1.4 ▲   SO   Cross through fence line.

▼ 1.9   SO   Track on left.

1.3 ▲   SO   Track on right.

GPS: N 38°43.24' W 109°47.71'

▼ 2.0   SO   Cross through sandy wash.

1.2 ▲   SO   Cross through sandy wash.

▼ 2.1   SO   Join Hidden Canyon Wash, entering through the wide mouth of Hidden Canyon.

1.1 ▲   SO   Exit Hidden Canyon Wash, leaving through the wide mouth of Hidden Canyon.

▼ 2.3   SO   Exit wash.

0.9 ▲   SO   Enter wash.

▼ 2.4   BR   Track on left.

0.8 ▲   SO   Track on right.

▼ 2.5   SO   Cross through wash.

0.7 ▲   SO   Cross through wash.

▼ 2.6   SO   Faint track on right.

0.6 ▲   SO   Faint track on left.

▼ 2.8   SO   Cross through wash.

Trail #10: Hidden Canyon Wash Trail

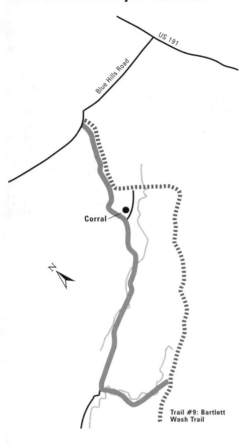

0.4 ▲   SO Cross through wash.
        GPS: N 38°42.78′ W 109°48.53′

▼ 3.0   SO Trail crests a loose and sandy rise,
            then drops down into Hidden Canyon.
0.2 ▲   SO Trail crests a loose and sandy rise.

▼ 3.2   TL Turn left and drop into wash, heading
            southeast. Trail ahead at this point
            goes another 3.2 miles into Hidden
            Canyon before becoming too narrow
            for 4WD vehicles. Zero trip meter.
0.0 ▲   Proceed to the northeast toward the
            mouth of Hidden Canyon.
        GPS: N 38°42.66′ W 109°48.85′

▼ 0.0   Proceed to the southeast and drop into
            the wash.
0.9 ▲   TR Trail exits wash. Trail to the left at this

point goes another 3.2 miles into
Hidden Canyon before becoming too
narrow for 4WD vehicles. Zero trip
meter.

▼ 0.4   SO Trail enters narrow, sandy section of
            canyon.
0.5 ▲   SO Exit narrow section.

▼ 0.6   SO Exit narrow section.
0.3 ▲   SO Trail enters narrow, sandy section of
            canyon.
        GPS: N 38°42.35′ W 109°48.49′

▼ 0.7   SO Track on left.
0.2 ▲   SO Track on right.

▼ 0.8   SO Loose, sandy climb out of wash.
0.1 ▲   SO Loose, sandy descent into wash.

▼ 0.9   Trail finishes at the junction with Trail
            #9: Bartlett Wash Trail. Turn left to
            return to Blue Hills Road, turn right to
            exit to the Dubinky Well Road.
0.0 ▲   Trail commences on Trail #9: Bartlett
            Wash Trail, 3.7 miles from the junction
            with Blue Hills Road. Zero trip meter
            and turn west on unmarked sandy
            track.
        GPS: N 38°42.33′ W 109°48.19′

Hidden Canyon Rim Trail

STARTING POINT Blue Hills Road, 3.9 miles
west of US 191
FINISHING POINT Hidden Canyon Rim; con-
nects to Trail #12: Hidden Canyon Rim
Escape Trail
TOTAL MILEAGE 4 miles
UNPAVED MILEAGE 4 miles
DRIVING TIME 1 hour
ELEVATION RANGE 4,600–5,100 feet
USUALLY OPEN Year-round
DIFFICULTY RATING 4
SCENIC RATING 9
REMOTENESS RATING +0

Driving along as the trail descends to Hidden Canyon viewpoint

Special Attractions
- Moderate, rocky trail with extensive slickrock.
- Spectacular views into Hidden Canyon.
- Can be treated either as a spur trail or combined with Trail #8: Hidden Canyon Rim Escape Trail to exit up to Bartlett Rim.

The white rocks or chimney pots can be found near the viewpoint

Description
This short trail travels out on the slickrock above a tributary of Hidden Canyon, swings around the head of the canyon, and drops down to end on a rock platform with a very pretty view. The first mile is easy going as you travel toward the edge of the first canyon; after that it is very slow going as you cross lumpy slickrock. Navigation in this second part requires a keen eye—some of the trail is marked with small cairns and other sections with boulders. However, there are long sections where the only indications that you are still on the correct trail are occasional black tire marks on the slickrock or tire prints in the infrequent sandy sections. It is easy to miss the trail here, so the route directions include more than the usual number of GPS coordinates to aid navigation.

The trail wraps around the head of the wash and then leaves the slickrock and follows a more defined sandy trail down to the viewpoint. It finishes on a rock platform right on the rim of Hidden Canyon. From here, you can also see multicolored slickrock domes around the edge and Trail #10: Hidden Canyon Wash Trail along the bottom.

Either treat this trail like a spur and retrace your route to Blue Hills Road or follow Trail #12: Hidden Canyon Rim Escape Trail, which connects with Trail #13: Bartlett Rim

Trail. The Escape trail is rated a 6 for difficulty, but it is the quickest and most exciting way out of the canyon.

Current Road Information
BLM Moab Field Office
82 East Dogwood, Suite M
Moab, UT 84532
(435) 259-2100

Map References
BLM   Moab (incomplete)
USGS 1:24,000   Jug Rock (incomplete)
       1:100,000 Moab (incomplete)
Maptech CD-ROM: Moab/Canyonlands
Trails Illustrated, #501
Utah Atlas & Gazetteer, p. 40
Other: Latitude 40—Moab West
       Canyon Country Off-Road Vehicle
       Trail Map—Island Area

Route Directions

▼ 0.0   From Blue Hills Road, 3.9 miles west of US 191, zero trip meter and turn south on unmarked, graded dirt trail.

1.2 ▲   Trail ends at intersection with Blue Hills Road. Turn right to exit to US 191.
    GPS: N 38°44.84' W 109°48.05'

▼ 0.3 TL Intersection. Ahead goes to Exclosure; track on right is alternative exit to Blue Hills Road. Turn and immediately cross through wash.

0.9 ▲ TR Cross through wash, then intersection. Left goes to Exclosure; track ahead is alternative exit to Blue Hills Road.
    GPS: N 38°44.61' W 109°48.19'

▼ 0.6 SO Cross through wash, then campsite on right.

0.6 ▲ SO Campsite on left, then cross through wash.

▼ 0.9 BR Track on left, then cattle guard, then track on right.

0.3 ▲ SO Track on left, then cattle guard, then track on right.
    GPS: N 38°44.08' W 109°47.99'

▼ 1.0 SO Cattletank on left.

0.2 ▲ SO Cattletank on right.
    GPS: N 38°44.01' W 109°48.06'

▼ 1.1 SO Brink Spring and tank on left. Trail is now ungraded and starts to climb.

0.1 ▲ SO Brink Spring and tank on right. Trail is now graded dirt.
    GPS: N 38°43.90' W 109°48.10'

▼ 1.2 BL Track on right is dead end. Over the hill on left are the remains of some old cabins (not visible from the trail). Zero trip meter.

0.0 ▲ Continue toward Blue Hills Road.
    GPS: N 38°43.88' W 109°48.17'

▼ 0.0   Continue toward Hidden Canyon.

Trail #11: Hidden Canyon Rim Trail

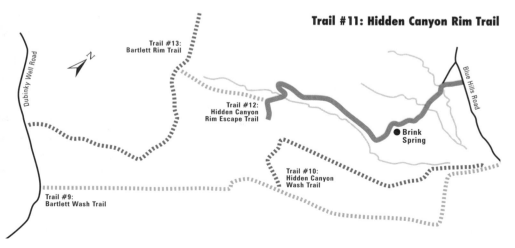

2.8 ▲	BR	Track on left is dead end. Over the hill on right are the remains of some old cabins (not visible from the trail). Zero trip meter.

▼ 0.2	SO	Start to cross slickrock. Track on left leaves through wire gate. Keep right toward the hill and look for cairns to mark the way.
2.6 ▲	SO	Follow around the hill, then track on right leaves through wire gate. End of slickrock.

GPS: N 38°43.71' W 109°48.03'

▼ 0.4	SO	Tributary of Hidden Canyon is on the left. Follow trail along rim.
2.4 ▲	SO	Trail follows the rim of a tributary of Hidden Canyon.

▼ 0.9	SO	Track on right.
1.9 ▲	SO	Track on left.

GPS: N 38°43.50' W 109°48.59'

▼ 1.4	BL	Bear southeast and cross over head of wash on slickrock, then continue straight for approximately 100 yards before bearing south. Trail is difficult to follow.
1.4 ▲	BR	Bear north before swinging left down to cross over head of wash on slickrock. Trail is difficult to follow.

GPS: N 38°43.38' W 109°49.00'

▼ 1.7	SO	Trail is more defined across the sandy section. Bear southwest.
1.1 ▲	SO	Trail leaves the defined sandy track and crosses slickrock. There are some cairns to mark the route.

GPS: N 38°43.17' W 109°49.20'

▼ 2.1	TL	Track continues straight on. Turn left, descend soft sandy trail to wash crossing.
0.7 ▲	TR	Cross through wash, then ascend sandy track and turn right at T-intersection.

GPS: N 38°42.98' W 109°49.57'

▼ 2.3	SO	Cross through wash, then exit up small ridge.
0.5 ▲	SO	Descend down small ridge and cross

through wash.

GPS: N 38°42.99' W 109°49.37'

▼ 2.6	SO	Track on right is Trail #12: Hidden Canyon Rim Escape Trail. Faint track on left.
0.2 ▲	SO	Track on left is Trail #12: Hidden Canyon Rim Escape Trail. Faint track on right.

GPS: N 38°42.78' W 109°49.44'

▼ 2.8	BL	Hidden Canyon Rim is directly ahead. Trail swings northeast along the rim, then descends to end on the rock platform directly above Hidden Canyon.
0.0 ▲		Return from Hidden Canyon overlook and exit either via Trail #12: Hidden Canyon Rim Escape Trail or by retracing your steps.

GPS: N 38°42.68' W 109°49.19'

MOAB REGION TRAIL #12

Hidden Canyon Rim Escape Trail

STARTING POINT Trail #11: Hidden Canyon Rim Trail
FINISHING POINT Trail #13: Bartlett Rim Trail
TOTAL MILEAGE 1.5 miles
UNPAVED MILEAGE 1.5 miles
DRIVING TIME 30 minutes
ELEVATION RANGE 5,000–5,400 feet
USUALLY OPEN Year-round
DIFFICULTY RATING 6
SCENIC RATING 9
REMOTENESS RATING +0

Special Attractions

■ Short challenging trail that links Hidden Canyon Rim Trail and Bartlett Rim Trail.

Description

This short trail is a quick and exciting route from Trail #11: Hidden Canyon Rim Trail up to Trail #13: Bartlett Rim Trail. The trail begins by climbing up a section of slickrock marked by a cairn. After the first section, it swings around to the southwest and climbs a second very steep, smooth slickrock face. This climb looks a lot worse than it is; most stock vehicles are able to tackle it. There are normally a couple of small cairns to show the way, but the most reliable indications of the best route are the black tire marks on the slickrock. The trail then climbs a very steep dirt and rock slope, and this middle section presents the real challenge. There are two alternate ways up, both steep; the left-hand one is probably slightly less steep, although it has a couple of small rock ledges near the top. The routes rejoin to traverse a narrow ridge with a steep drop on both sides. This is not difficult, but it can be a bit nerve-wracking and should not be attempted in wet weather!

After the ridge, there is another short rocky climb which has an alternate route that is about the same difficulty. The trail is now on top of the plateau and runs south to join Bartlett Rim Trail. There are some rocky sections, but the most difficult part is behind you. The trail finishes at the junction with Bartlett Rim Trail.

The Moab Jeep Safari held each Easter incorporates this climb into its 3D trail.

Current Road Information

BLM Moab Field Office
82 East Dogwood, Suite M
Moab, UT 84532
(435) 259-2100

Map References

BLM   Moab (incomplete)
USGS 1:24,000   Jug Rock (incomplete)
         1:100,000 Moab (incomplete)
Maptech CD-ROM: Moab/Canyonlands
Trails Illustrated, #501
Utah Atlas & Gazetteer, p. 40
Other: Latitude 40—Moab West

Route Directions

▼ 0.0   From Trail #11: Hidden Canyon Rim Trail, 0.2 miles before the end of the trail, turn southwest onto an unmarked sandy trail and zero trip meter.

1.5 ▲   Trail finishes at Trail #11: Hidden Canyon Rim Trail. Turn right to go to viewpoint of Hidden Canyon, turn left to exit to Blue Hills Road.
            GPS: N 38°42.78' W 109°49.44'

▼ 0.4   BR Faint track on left.

1.1 ▲   SO Faint track on right.
            GPS: N 38°42.54' W 109°49.77'

Driving up a steep section of the slickrock climb

Trail #12: Hidden Canyon Rim Escape

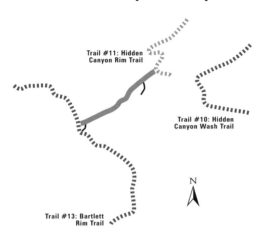

Trail #11: Hidden Canyon Rim Trail

Trail #10: Hidden Canyon Wash Trail

Trail #13: Bartlett Rim Trail

N

▼ 0.5 SO Trail climbs first slickrock hump, then swings right and climbs second steep slickrock section.

1.0 ▲ SO Trail descends steep slickrock section, then swings left and descends last slickrock hump.

GPS: N 38°42.47' W 109°49.84'

▼ 0.6 BL Straight ahead is the steeper alternative.

0.9 ▲ SO Alternative route rejoins.

GPS: N 38°42.44' W 109°49.85'

▼ 0.7 SO Alternative route rejoins to cross ridge with steep drops on either side.

0.8 ▲ BR Cross ridge with steep drops on either side, then alternative route forks. Right is the easier alternative.

▼ 0.8 BR Track straight on is alternative route, which rejoins almost immediately.

0.7 ▲ SO Track on right is alternative route, which rejoins almost immediately.

GPS: N 38°42.37' W 109°49.98'

▼ 0.9 SO Trail is on top of the plateau.

0.6 ▲ SO Trail starts to descend from plateau.

GPS: N 38°42.33' W 109°50.02'

▼ 1.4 BR Track on left also joins Trail #13: Bartlett Rim Trail.

0.1 ▲ BL Track on right rejoins Trail #13: Bartlett Rim Trail.

GPS: N 38°42.15' W 109°50.49'

▼ 1.5 Trail ends midway along Trail #13: Bartlett Rim Trail.

0.0 ▲ Trail commences on Trail #13: Bartlett Rim Trail, 3.7 miles from the northern end, 3.4 miles from the southern end. Turn northeast on unmarked trail and zero trip meter.

GPS: N 38°42.24' W 109°50.55'

MOAB REGION TRAIL #13

Bartlett Rim Trail

STARTING POINT Dubinky Well Road, 2.5 miles from junction with Spring Canyon Road and approximately 4 miles from Utah 313

FINISHING POINT Dubinky Well Road, 1.2 miles north of Dubinky Well

TOTAL MILEAGE 7.1 miles

UNPAVED MILEAGE 7.1 miles

DRIVING TIME 1.25 hours

ELEVATION RANGE 5,200–5,500 feet

USUALLY OPEN Year-round

DIFFICULTY RATING 4

SCENIC RATING 8

REMOTENESS RATING +0

Special Attractions

■ Panoramic views over The Needles and the Book Cliffs.

■ Views down into Bartlett Wash.

■ Short, moderate trail with many viewpoints.

Description

This short trail runs around the edge of the Bartlett Wash valley and then into one of the fingers of Hidden Canyon. There are several spur trails leading from it that go to viewpoints over the canyons, and there are fantastic views from the trail itself, especially along the northern end.

The trail is an ungraded dirt track, soft and sandy for a couple of miles at either end. The middle section is rocky and there is one

View of Bartlett Wash and the La Sal Mountains

moderate pinch in the middle of the trail that looks worse than it is. The trail is difficult in wet weather and may not be passable.

The northern end of the trail descends along a rise, providing views in all directions. To the north, you can see the Book Cliffs. The Needles, a large butte passed on Trail #16: Spring Canyon Point Trail, is to the south.

The trail ends back on the Dubinky Well Road, 3.7 miles to the north of where it started.

Current Road Information

BLM Moab Field Office
82 East Dogwood, Suite M
Moab, UT 84532
(435) 259-2100

Map References

BLM   Moab (incomplete)
USGS 1:24,000   Dubinky Wash, Jug
          Rock
          1:100,000 Moab (incomplete)
Maptech CD-ROM: Moab/Canyonlands
Trails Illustrated, #501 (incomplete)
Utah Atlas & Gazetteer, p. 40
Other: Latitude 40—Moab West
          Canyon Country Off-Road Vehicle
          Trail Map—Island Area

Route Directions

▼ 0.0   From Dubinky Well Road, 2.5 miles northwest of the junction with Spring Canyon Road, zero trip meter and turn northeast on an unmarked, ungraded sandy track.

3.4 ▲   Trail finishes back on Dubinky Well Road, 3.7 miles south of the start of the trail. Turn left to exit to Utah 313.

          GPS: N 38°40.13' W 109°51.15'

▼ 0.2   SO Pass through wire gate. Views to the right into Bartlett Wash.

3.2 ▲   SO Views to the left into Bartlett Wash. Pass through wire gate.

          GPS: N 38°40.30' W 109°51.04'

▼ 1.1   SO Track on right.

2.3 ▲   BR Track on left.

          GPS: N 38°40.81' W 109°50.27'

▼ 1.6   SO Cross short slickrock section.

1.8 ▲   SO Cross short slickrock section.

▼ 1.7   SO Faint track on right.

1.7 ▲   SO Faint track on left.

▼ 1.9   SO Views to the right into Bartlett

Trail #13: Bartlett Rim Trail

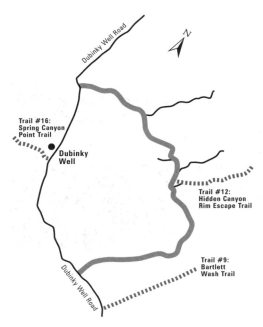

Canyon Rim Escape Trail. Also track on right.
GPS: N 38°42.13′ W 109°50.52′

▼ 3.4   SO   Track on right is Trail #12: Hidden Canyon Rim Escape Trail. Zero trip meter

0.0 ▲   Continue along Bartlett Rim.
GPS: N 38°42.24′ W 109°50.55′

▼ 0.0   Continue along Bartlett Rim.

3.7 ▲   BR   Track on left is Trail #12: Hidden Canyon Rim Escape Trail. Zero trip meter.

▼ 0.1   SO   Track on right passes viewpoint.

3.6 ▲   SO   Track on left passes viewpoint.
GPS: N 38°42.30′ W 109°50.58′

▼ 0.2   SO   Track on left.

3.5 ▲   SO   Track on right.

▼ 0.4   SO   Faint track on left.

3.3 ▲   SO   Faint track on right.

▼ 0.6   SO   Track on right, then faint track on left, then second track on right.

3.1 ▲   SO   Track on left, then faint track on right, then second track on left.
GPS: N 38°42.57′ W 109°50.93′

▼ 1.2   SO   Track on left and track on right.

2.5 ▲   SO   Track on right and track on left.
GPS: N 38°42.68′ W 109°51.52′

▼ 1.4   SO   Track on right goes to the pipeline and a great view.

2.3 ▲   SO   Track on left goes to the pipeline and a great view.

▼ 1.5   SO   Track on right.

2.2 ▲   BR   Track on left.

▼ 2.1   SO   Track on right.

1.6 ▲   BR   Track on left.
GPS: N 38°42.87′ W 109°52.55′

▼ 3.6   SO   Faint track on right.

0.1 ▲   SO   Faint track on left.

▼ 3.7   Trail ends at the junction with Dubinky

Wash—walk up the rise for the best view.

1.5 ▲   SO   Views to the left into Bartlett Wash— walk up the rise for the best view.
GPS: N 38°41.34′ W 109°49.70′

▼ 2.4   SO   Steep rocky pinch.

1.0 ▲   SO   Steep rocky pinch.
GPS: N 38°41.56′ W 109°49.74′

▼ 2.5   SO   Track on right.

0.9 ▲   SO   Track on left.
GPS: N 38°41.74′ W 109°49.94′

▼ 2.6   SO   Track on right.

0.8 ▲   BR   Track on left.

▼ 2.7   SO   Faint track on left.

0.7 ▲   BL   Faint track on right.

▼ 3.3   SO   Large rock cairn on right with a post in it. Track on right joins Trail #12: Hidden Canyon Rim Escape Trail. Also track on left.

0.1 ▲   SO   Large rock cairn on left with a post in it. Track on left joins Trail #12: Hidden

Well Road, 3.7 miles north of the start of the trail. Turn left to exit to Utah 313.

0.0 ▲ Trail commences on Dubinky Well Road, 1.2 miles north of Dubinky Well. Zero trip meter and turn northeast on unsigned, ungraded dirt track beside a rocky outcrop.
GPS: N 38°42.68' W 109°53.10'

Monitor and Merrimac Trail

STARTING POINT US 191, 0.2 miles north of mile marker 141
FINISHING POINT Same as starting point
TOTAL MILEAGE 12.1 miles
UNPAVED MILEAGE 12.1 miles
DRIVING TIME 2.5 hours
ELEVATION RANGE 4,400–5,100 feet
USUALLY OPEN Year-round
DIFFICULTY RATING 5
SCENIC RATING 10
REMOTENESS RATING +0

Special Attractions
- Monitor and Merrimac Buttes.
- Mill Canyon Dinosaur Trail.
- Historic sites of Mill Canyon Copper Mill and Halfway Stage Station.

History
The twin buttes of Monitor and Merrimac are both named after Civil War battleships.

The Halfway Stage Station near the end of the trail was also referred to as the Upper Courthouse Staging Station. It got the name Halfway Stage because it was at the halfway point for travelers between Moab and the railroad at Thompson.

The Denver & Rio Grande Western Railway was a boon to Moab when it opened in 1883, offering a more reliable connection with the outside world and attracting other settlers to the region. A trail developed between Moab and Thompson, and the most difficult section to cross was Courthouse Wash with its deep, soft sand. Heavily laden wagons were forced to go around to the west via the spring near Courthouse Rock, and a second staging station developed at this location. The trip took eight hours; stages with heavier loads needed two days to complete the journey.

Halfway Stage Station operated on a fairly primitive basis from the 1890s to 1903 until the grade around Courthouse Wash was improved, which eliminated the need to travel via Halfway. The Lower Courthouse Staging Station at the spring continued to operate until the 1920s. As the route gradually improved, and with the introduction of haulage trucks, the need for this staging station was also eliminated. The buildings of the Lower Courthouse Staging Station were demolished when the Potash Railroad was put through in the 1960s.

Copper mining began around the Courthouse Rock region about 1899, but the ore was of such poor quality that no milling process could make the mines profitable. The copper mill in Mill Canyon was abandoned not long after it started, possibly in 1902.

Description
This is a popular Moab area 4WD trail that is suitable for most high-clearance SUVs. It is a moderately challenging trail with a great variety of scenery and trail surfaces.

The trail leaves US 191 at the BLM sign for the Monitor and Merrimac Trail. It has signs sporadically along the route, so navigation should not be a problem. The BLM has posted a map and basic trail information at a parking area just off the highway.

The trail proper for 4WDs starts by going down the sandy Tusher Canyon Wash. It passes through a narrow section of canyon and then leaves the creek to swing around to the east and climb a sandy rise. After passing through a gap in the Entrada sandstone walls, it drops down and enters the equally sandy Courthouse Pasture. At this point, the trail passes right beside Determination Towers, large stand-alone buttes, and climbs

The Monitor stands on the right of the gap with the Merrimac to the left

steadily over slickrock pavements to their base. Just past the towers is the most difficult stretch of trail, a very short, steep pinch with some large boulders and deep gullies. Study the wheel placement before you start—the most obvious route will have larger vehicles tilting over toward a large rock on the left that could ding a panel.

After Determination Towers, the trail heads toward Monitor and Merrimac Buttes. You may want to take a short detour and fol-

low the BLM sign to view the infamous Wipe Out Hill, which is 0.1 miles from the trail. This extremely difficult short hill, a vertical drop down into the wash bottom, is popular with the extreme Jeep crowd, who will spend hours getting their vehicles down, and occasionally up, the hill. This is only recommended for groups with heavily modified vehicles who are not fazed by the likely possibility of vehicle damage; but if you are lucky enough to see someone having a go at the hill, stay to watch and marvel at what a fearless driver can accomplish!

The trail then passes directly underneath Merrimac Butte on the north side. Before swinging north to cross Courthouse Pasture, take the short spur trail south to a slickrock platform between the two buttes. This platform has great views to the south over Sevenmile Canyon and makes a great place for lunch.

A difficult 5-rated pinch along the Monitor and Merrimac Trail

The sandy trail across Courthouse Pasture is easier going, and the trail then drops into Mill Canyon and crosses Mill Canyon Wash several times. Some of these crossings can be tricky depending on recent weather, and the lower end of Mill Canyon Wash can be muddy and soft. The sparse remains of the copper mill are on the right as you exit the creek, just before the parking area for the Mill Canyon Dinosaur Trail on the left. This self-guided, 0.25-mile trail passes by several petrified dinosaur bones embedded in the rock. This is a rare opportunity to see the bones as they were found. Trail brochures available at the start explain in detail where to look.

From the Dinosaur Trail, the surface is a good, graded dirt road. A final detour at the end of the trail is down to the old Halfway Stage Stop, where there are substantial stone remains of the old station.

Current Road Information

BLM Moab Field Office
82 East Dogwood, Suite M
Moab, UT 84532
(435) 259-2100

Map References

BLM   Moab (incomplete)
USGS 1:24,000   Merrimac Butte, Jug
         Rock (incomplete)
         1:100,000 Moab (incomplete)
Maptech CD-ROM: Moab/Canyonlands
Trails Illustrated, #211; #501
Utah Atlas & Gazetteer, p. 40
Other: Latitude 40—Moab West
         Canyon Country Off-Road Vehicle
         Trail Map—Island Area

Route Directions

▼ 0.0   0.2 miles north of mile marker 141 on US 191, turn west on Mill Canyon Road, cross railroad and cattle guard and zero trip meter.
2.5 ▲   Trail finishes at intersection with US 191. Turn right for Moab, left for I-70.
           GPS: N 38°43.66′ W 109°43.29′

▼ 0.2   SO Information board on right; then cross through Courthouse Wash.
2.3 ▲   SO Cross through Courthouse Wash; information board on left.

▼ 0.5   SO Track on right.
2.0 ▲   SO Track on left.

▼ 0.6   BR Track on left is end of Monitor and Merrimac Trail. Follow the sign for Tusher Canyon.
1.9 ▲   BL Track on right is end of Monitor and Merrimac Trail.
           GPS: N 38°43.55′ W 109°43.90′

▼ 1.2   BL Track on right follows power lines.
1.3 ▲   BR Track on left follows power lines.

▼ 1.5   SO Track on left.
1.0 ▲   SO Track on right.

▼ 2.0   SO Cross through wash.
0.5 ▲   SO Cross through wash.

▼ 2.4   SO Track on right; then enter Tusher Wash and bear left.
0.1 ▲   SO Leave Tusher Wash; then track on left.
           GPS: N 38°43.22′ W 109°45.63′

▼ 2.5   TL Remain in wash. Track on right leaves wash. Zero trip meter.
0.0 ▲   Continue along wash.
           GPS: N 38°43.17′ W 109°45.71′

▼ 0.0   Continue in wash along Tusher Canyon. Two small tracks to the right.
3.0 ▲   TR Two faint tracks to the left, then track on left leaves wash. Zero trip meter.

▼ 0.7   SO Track on right leaves wash; track on left. Remain in wash.
2.3 ▲   SO Track on left leaves wash; track on right. Remain in wash.
           GPS: N 38°42.68′ W 109°45.49′

▼ 1.8   TL Leave the wash, following sign for the Monitor and Merrimac Trail.
1.2 ▲   TR Turn right and enter Tusher Canyon Wash.
           GPS: N 38°41.78′ W 109°45.79′

Trail #14: Monitor and Merrimac Trail

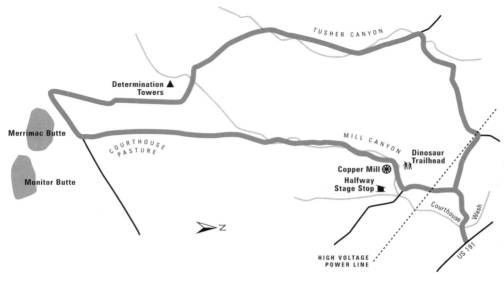

▼ 1.9   SO Enter wash.
1.1 ▲   SO Exit wash.

▼ 2.1   BL Tracks on right; follow sign for the Monitor and Merrimac Trail.
0.9 ▲   BR Tracks on left.
         GPS: N 38°41.53' W 109°45.65'

▼ 2.4   SO Exit wash.
0.6 ▲   SO Enter wash.

▼ 2.6   SO Pass through gap in cliffs. Determination Towers are ahead to the southeast.
0.4 ▲   SO Pass through gap in cliffs. Tusher Canyon is ahead.
         GPS: N 38°41.32' W 109°45.31'

▼ 2.8   TL Turn left and cross through wash.
0.2 ▲   TR Cross through wash and turn right.
         GPS: N 38°41.18' W 109°45.17'

▼ 3.0   TR Directly in front of Determination Towers, turn and climb up slickrock. Zero trip meter.
0.0 ▲   Continue toward Tusher Canyon. Trail heads generally north.
         GPS: N 38°41.10' W 109°44.94'

▼ 0.0   Continue toward Determination Towers.

1.9 ▲   TL T-intersection. Join sandy trail and zero trip meter.

▼ 0.2   SO Pass beside Determination Towers. Trail crosses slickrock and heads generally south. Many smaller trails to the right and left; remain on main trail and go in the direction of Monitor and Merrimac Buttes.
1.7 ▲   SO Many smaller trails to the left and right. Pass beside Determination Towers across slickrock. Trail leaves in a northerly direction.
         GPS: N 38°40.96' W 109°44.94'

▼ 0.7   SO Track on left.
1.2 ▲   SO Track on right.
         GPS: N 38°40.52' W 109°44.95'

▼ 0.8   SO Short, steep, difficult uphill pinch.
1.1 ▲   SO Short, steep, difficult downhill pinch.
         GPS: N 38°40.43' W 109°44.90'

▼ 0.9   SO Track on left.
1.0 ▲   SO Track on right.
         GPS: N 38°40.32' W 109°44.92'

▼ 1.2   SO Cross through small wash.
0.7 ▲   SO Cross through small wash.

▼ 1.4 TL Track straight on goes to Wipe Out Hill. Continue along north face of Merrimac Butte.

0.5 ▲ TR Track straight on goes to Wipe Out Hill.

GPS: N 38°39.90' W 109°45.06'

▼ 1.9 TL Crossroads. Track on right is spur that goes 0.8 miles to a slickrock platform between Monitor and Merrimac Buttes. Zero trip meter.

0.0 ▲ Continue along north face of Merrimac Butte.

GPS: N 38°40.18' W 109°44.53'

▼ 0.0 Continue north across Courthouse Pasture.

3.0 ▲ TR Crossroads. Straight ahead is a spur that goes 0.8 miles to a slickrock platform between Monitor and Merrimac Buttes. Zero trip meter.

▼ 0.5 SO Track on right.
2.5 ▲ SO Track on left.

▼ 0.8 SO Track on left.
2.2 ▲ SO Track on right.

GPS: N 38°40.95' W 109°44.58'

▼ 1.0 SO Track on left.
2.0 ▲ SO Track on right.

GPS: N 38°41.07' W 109°44.57'

▼ 1.1 SO Track on left.
1.9 ▲ SO Track on right.

GPS: N 38°41.25' W 109°44.56'

▼ 1.9 BL Track on right.
1.1 ▲ BR Track on left.

GPS: N 38°41.85' W 109°44.48'

▼ 2.0 SO Cross through Mill Canyon Wash.
1.0 ▲ SO Cross through Mill Canyon Wash.

▼ 2.1 SO Cross through Mill Canyon Wash; track on right goes to campsite.

0.9 ▲ SO Track on left goes to campsite; cross through Mill Canyon Wash.

▼ 2.2 SO Cross through Mill Canyon Wash.

0.8 ▲ SO Cross through Mill Canyon Wash.

GPS: N 38°42.13' W 109°44.43'

▼ 2.5 SO Enter Mill Canyon Wash.
0.5 ▲ SO Exit Mill Canyon Wash.

▼ 2.7 SO Pass through gate.
0.3 ▲ SO Pass through gate.

GPS: N 38°42.56' W 109°44.41'

▼ 2.9 SO Leave Mill Canyon Wash. Remains of copper mill are up on the bank to the right just after the wash exit.

0.1 ▲ SO Remains of copper mill are up on the bank to the left; enter Mill Canyon Wash.

▼ 3.0 SO Parking area for Mill Canyon Dinosaur Trail on the left. Zero trip meter.

0.0 ▲ Continue down to Mill Canyon Wash.

GPS: N 38°42.75' W 109°44.32'

▼ 0.0 Continue along graded dirt road.

0.6 ▲ SO Parking area for Mill Canyon Dinosaur Trail on the right. Zero trip meter.

▼ 0.1 SO Cross through small wash.
0.5 ▲ SO Cross through small wash.

▼ 0.4 SO Cross through small wash, then track on left.

0.2 ▲ SO Track on right, then cross through small wash.

▼ 0.6 BL Track on right goes 0.3 miles to Halfway Stage Station. Zero trip meter.

0.0 ▲ Continue on graded road.

GPS: N 38°43.07' W 109°43.89'

▼ 0.0 Continue toward US 191.

1.1 ▲ BR Track on left goes 0.3 miles to Halfway Stage Station. Zero trip meter.

▼ 0.1 SO Track on left.
1.0 ▲ SO Track on right.

▼ 0.5 TR Track to the left is the start of the loop.
0.6 ▲ TL Track to the right is the finish of the loop.

GPS: N 38°43.55' W 109°43.90'

▼ 0.6	SO	Track on left.
0.5 ▲	SO	Track on right.

▼ 0.9	SO	Cross through Courthouse Wash; information board on left.
0.2 ▲	SO	Information board on right; cross through Courthouse Wash.

▼ 1.1	Trail finishes at intersection with US 191. Turn right for Moab, left for I-70.
0.0 ▲	0.2 miles north of mile marker 141 on US 191, turn west on Mill Canyon Road, cross railroad and cattle guard and zero trip meter.

GPS: N 38°43.66' W 109°43.29'

MOAB REGION TRAIL #15

Klondike Bluffs Trail

STARTING POINT North of mile marker 142 on US 191

FINISHING POINT Klondike Bluffs

TOTAL MILEAGE 6.5 miles

UNPAVED MILEAGE 6.5 miles

DRIVING TIME 2.5 hours (one-way)

ELEVATION RANGE 4,500–5,200 feet

USUALLY OPEN Year-round

DIFFICULTY RATING 5

SCENIC RATING 9

REMOTENESS RATING +0

Special Attractions

- Moderately challenging 4WD trail, with the novelty of driving over expanses of slickrock.
- Far-ranging vistas to the west and south.
- Abandoned mine site and equipment.
- Dinosaur print.

Description

This interesting 4WD trail is perfect for those wanting a little driving excitement combined with fantastic scenery and historic interest. The Klondike Bluffs Trail is contained within BLM land to the east of US 191. The trail is used by mountain bikes

as well as vehicles. The first 2.7 miles are graded dirt road suitable for most vehicles. After crossing a fence line, the trail becomes loose sand, wraps around the edge of Little Valley, and crosses a wide, sandy creek. The next 0.7 miles can be the trickiest, especially for large vehicles or those with side steps or low hanging brush bars, as the trail twists along a narrow canyon. A couple of spots call for careful wheel placement to avoid underbody damage.

After 4 miles, the trail heads steadily up a large slab of tilted slickrock. Boulders and white painted lines on the rock show the direction, but keep your eyes open, as hidden gullies can catch the unwary.

Watch for the dinosaur print in the rocks, marked by informal rings of sticks or rocks. At the 5.4-mile mark, the trail reverts to dirt and rocks for the final section across the Klondike Bluffs plateau. A track on the right leads to the remains of a copper mine. The miners worked the poor-grade copper ore from the cliff behind and carried out the first stages of processing on the site. Hunt around to find the water source used—a hole drilled in solid sandstone reveals its location.

The trail is closed to vehicles shortly after the turn to the mine. Mountain bikes can continue on for another couple of hundred

Driving along the white colored slickrock of Klondike Bluffs Trail

Copper mine ruins can still be found near the end of Klondike Bluffs Trail

yards to the border of Arches National Park.

This trail becomes impassable for a day or two after light snow or heavy rain.

Current Road Information

BLM Moab Field Office
82 East Dogwood, Suite M
Moab, UT 84532
(435) 259-2100

Map References

BLM   Moab (incomplete)
USGS 1:24,000   Merrimac Butte,
        Klondike Bluffs
        1:100,000 Moab (incomplete)

Maptech CD-ROM: Moab/Canyonlands
Trails Illustrated, #211 (incomplete); #501
Utah Atlas & Gazetteer, p. 40
Utah Travel Council #5 (incomplete)
Other: Latitude 40—Moab West
       Canyon Country Off-Road Vehicle
       Trail Map—Arches Area

Route Directions

▼ 0.0   North of mile marker 142 on US 191, turn right through a gate. There is a small parking area, and a BLM sign points to Klondike Bluffs Trail.
           GPS: N 38°44.45' W 109°43.97'

▼ 0.9 SO Track on right.
▼ 2.0 SO Track on left.
▼ 2.4 BL Road forks.
           GPS: N 38°46.24' W 109°42.90'

▼ 2.6 BL Second leg of track enters on right.
▼ 2.7 SO Cross through fence line. Trail standard turns to 4WD.
▼ 3.1 SO Follow along the edge of Little Valley.
▼ 3.3 SO Faint track on left, swing right and cross sandy wash.
▼ 3.4 TR T-intersection. Follow route markers for Klondike Bluffs.
           GPS: N 38°46.98' W 109°43.04'

▼ 3.6 SO Track on left into canyon. Couple of places need care with wheel placement.

Trail #15: Klondike Bluffs Trail

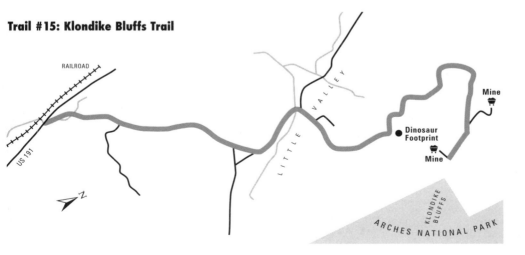

▼ 4.1   SO   Start gradual climb over slickrock.
▼ 4.6   SO   Faint bike track on left. Follow white painted trail markers on rock.
▼ 4.7   SO   Cross crevasse in slickrock that has been filled with rocks.
▼ 4.8   SO   Dinosaur footprint marked by branches on right of trail.
              GPS: N 38°47.58' W 109°42.34'

▼ 5.4   SO   Leave slickrock pavement. Trail is now packed dirt and rock.
▼ 5.8   SO   Track on left.
▼ 5.9   TR   Follow brown trail markers.
              GPS: N 38°48.66' W 109°42.22'

▼ 6.2   BL   Track on right.
▼ 6.5   Track on right goes to mining remains. Vehicle route ends here. Track continues and appears to climb bluff, but is blocked on first corner. National park boundary is 0.3 miles farther on. Foot travel only past this point.
              GPS: N 38°48.25' W 109°41.85'

Rock cairn along the Spring Canyon Point Trail

MOAB REGION TRAIL #16

Spring Canyon Point Trail

STARTING POINT Dubinky Well
FINISHING POINT Spring Canyon Point
TOTAL MILEAGE 12.9 miles
UNPAVED MILEAGE 12.9 miles
DRIVING TIME 1 hour (one-way)
ELEVATION RANGE 4,100–5,300 feet
USUALLY OPEN Year-round
DIFFICULTY RATING 2
SCENIC RATING 8
REMOTENESS RATING +0

Special Attractions

■ Views over the Green River.
■ Access to a network of 4WD trails.

History

Dubinky Spring, at the start of this trail, is named after Dubinky Anderson, whose parents settled the area in the 1920s. The Anderson family used to live in Valley City, several miles north on US 191. Albert Anderson, Dubinky's father, was notorious for distilling illicit moonshine, and one time he was caught and did six months in jail. A widely circulated tale tells of Dubinky seeing a ghost in an abandoned cabin in Valley City and taking flight barefoot. He was eventually found shivering and terrified many miles from Valley City at what is now called Dubinky Spring.

The well, named for the spring, was built in 1937 with the assistance of workers from the Dalton Wells Civilian Conservation Corps (located on US 191). In the ongoing battle between sheep herders and cattlemen, the sheep herders would damage the well when the cattlemen left the region in an attempt to get rid of the cattle. But cattle continued to be driven north to the railroad at Thompson and south to graze in the Island in the Sky region.

Description

This easy and scenic trail leads along sandy, graded roads to finish on a narrow-necked promontory high above the Green River. The trail surface makes it suitable for high-clearance vehicles in dry weather. It is predominantly graded sandy road, with sections of deep, powder-fine sand. There are great views all along this trail: Early on there are rocky red buttes and glimpses into Spring Canyon to the southeast and later, as you travel out onto the point, the

Green River dominates the view far below.

The trail leaves Dubinky Well Road immediately south of the old windmill and spring. It crosses the very start of Spring Canyon Wash and then passes directly underneath The Needles. These large red rock buttes are also known as Tombstone Rock. Around their bases are a couple of pleasant campsites, which are the best on the trail—ones farther down tend to be very exposed.

Many trails that lead off from this road are worth exploring if you have time. The main trail ends on Spring Canyon Point. Scramble over the rocks at the end for views of the river; the trail below goes to Hey Joe Canyon.

Current Road Information

BLM Moab Field Office
82 East Dogwood, Suite M
Moab, UT 84532
(435) 259-2100

Map References

BLM   Moab, San Rafael Desert
USGS 1:24,000 Dubinky Wash, Tenmile
         Point, Bowknot Bend
         1:100,000 Moab, San Rafael Desert
Maptech CD-ROM: Moab/Canyonlands;
        Central/San Rafael

Utah Atlas & Gazetteer, p. 40
Utah Travel Council #5 (incomplete)
Other: Latitude 40—Moab West
        Canyon Country Off-Road Vehicle
        Trail Map—Island Area

Route Directions

▼ 0.0   From Dubinky Well Road, 0.2 miles south of the windmill itself, zero trip meter and turn west onto unmarked graded sandy road.
        GPS: N 38°41.45′ W 109°52.87′

▼ 1.2 SO Cross through wash; this is start of Spring Canyon Wash.
▼ 1.3 SO Track on right.
▼ 1.4 SO Cattle guard.
▼ 1.9 SO Foot of The Needles. Small track on right, then track on left. Keep right around the base of The Needles. Continue to the northwest.
        GPS: N 38°41.05′ W 109°54.97′

▼ 2.0 SO Cattle guard, then track on right.
▼ 2.1 BL Track on right is Trail #17: Rainbow Rocks Trail. Zero trip meter.
        GPS: N 38°41.19′ W 109°55.15′

▼ 0.0   Continue along main trail.

The Needles rise up behind the Spring Canyon Wash crossing

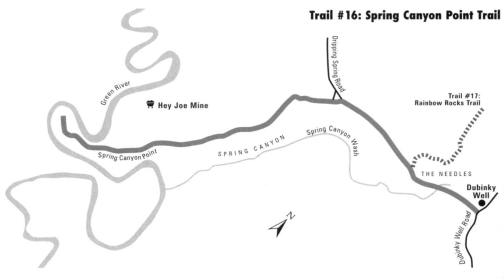

Trail #16: Spring Canyon Point Trail

▼ 0.7   SO   Track on left.
▼ 1.0   SO   Track on right.
▼ 1.2   SO   Track on left.
▼ 1.3   BL   Track on right goes to Dripping Spring. Zero trip meter.
            GPS: N 38°41.47′ W 109°56.54′

▼ 0.0   Continue toward Spring Canyon Point.
▼ 0.1   SO   Second entrance to Dripping Spring road on right.
▼ 0.7   SO   Pass through fence line.
▼ 0.9   SO   Track on left.
            GPS: N 38°41.33′ W 109°57.54′

▼ 1.7   SO   Track on right.
            GPS: N 38°41.13′ W 109°58.28′

▼ 1.9   SO   Track on left, then track on right goes to cairn.
▼ 3.2   SO   Cross through rocky wash.
▼ 3.4   BR   Cross through fence line, then track on left.
            GPS: N 38°40.07′ W 109°59.09′

▼ 4.2   SO   Track on right.
▼ 4.5   SO   Track on right.
▼ 5.4   SO   Track on left. Main trail runs out along the narrow Spring Canyon Point.
▼ 5.8   SO   Cross through fence line.
▼ 5.9   SO   Viewpoint on left.
▼ 6.6   SO   Track on right.
            GPS: N 38°37.77′ W 110°01.30′

▼ 6.7   SO   Track on left.
▼ 7.0   SO   Track on left.
▼ 9.4   SO   Oil drilling hole on left.
▼ 9.5   Trail ends at overlook for the Green River. Large turnaround area on promontory, with river views on three sides.
            GPS: N 38°36.91′ W 110°03.67′

MOAB REGION TRAIL #17

Rainbow Rocks Trail

STARTING POINT The Needles on Trail #16: Spring Canyon Point Trail
FINISHING POINT Trail #18: Levi Well Trail, 2.8 miles from western end
TOTAL MILEAGE 5.9 miles
UNPAVED MILEAGE 5.9 miles
DRIVING TIME 1 hour
ELEVATION RANGE 4,400–5,200 feet
USUALLY OPEN Year-round
DIFFICULTY RATING 5
SCENIC RATING 9
REMOTENESS RATING +0

Special Attractions

■ Multihued sandstone rock cliffs.
■ Interesting trail over a variety of surfaces.

Description

This short trail leaves immediately west of The Needles, the prominent Entrada sandstone butte near the start of Trail #16: Spring Canyon Point Trail. Initially, the ungraded trail is soft and sandy as it runs near the western side of The Needles. Then after a fork, it parallels the cliff more closely, the sand gives way to rocks and slickrock, and it crosses a slickrock pavement marked by small cairns.

After 1.5 miles, the trail crosses through a wash with a short, steep slickrock exit. Once the trail drops down onto the plain of Freckle Flat, it becomes very sandy and is subject to frequent washouts. Some of these ruts can be very deep; negotiating them takes careful wheel placement. If any washouts are too deep, a few minutes' work with a shovel in the sand can often make them passable. As the trail passes along Freckle Flat, you can see the multi-hued sandstone rocks that give the trail its name. The Entrada sandstone domes are banded with colors from white to pale pink to the deepest reds. The trail ends on the equally sandy Trail #18: Levi Well Trail—the shortest exit is to the left to Duma Point Road.

For campers, the best place to pitch a tent is at the start of the trail, around the face of the Needles. Otherwise the trail does not offer much in the way of campsites.

Current Road Information

BLM Moab Field Office
82 East Dogwood, Suite M
Moab, UT 84532
(435) 259-2100

Map References

BLM Moab (incomplete)
USGS 1:24,000 Dubinky Wash
      1:100,000 Moab (incomplete)
Maptech CD-ROM: Moab/Canyonlands
Utah Atlas & Gazetteer, p. 40
Other: Latitude 40—Moab West
      Canyon Country Off-Road Vehicle
      Trail Map—Island Area

Route Directions

▼ 0.0   From Trail #16: Spring Canyon Point Trail, 2.1 miles from the junction with Dubinky Well Road, turn north immediately past The Needles and zero trip meter.

5.9 ▲   Trail ends at the junction with Trail #16: Spring Canyon Point Trail at The Needles. Turn right to continue to

Cinder and lava protrusion found along Rainbow Rocks Trail

Spring Canyon Point; turn left to exit to
Dubinky Well Road.
GPS: N 38°41.19' W 109°55.13'

▼ 0.2 BR Track on left.
5.7 ▲ SO Track on right.

▼ 1.0 SO Cross slickrock pavement; small cairns
            show the route.
4.9 ▲ SO Leave slickrock pavement.

▼ 1.5 SO Cross through wash with short, steep
            slickrock exit.
4.4 ▲ SO Cross through wash with short, steep
            slickrock exit. Trail now crosses slick-
            rock; small cairns show the route.

▼ 2.2 BR Track on left.
3.7 ▲ BL Track on right.
            GPS: N 38°42.37' W 109°54.66'

▼ 2.4 SO Cross through rocky wash. Trail is now
            very sandy.
3.5 ▲ SO Cross through rocky wash.

**Climbing over a steep section of a wash crossing on the Rainbow
Rocks Trail**

Trail #17: Rainbow Rocks Trail

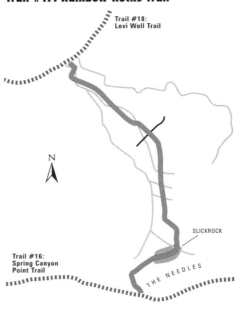

▼ 2.9 SO Cross through sandy wash.
3.0 ▲ SO Cross through sandy wash.

▼ 3.1 SO Cross through wash.
2.8 ▲ SO Cross through wash.

▼ 3.8 SO Tracks on right and left.
2.1 ▲ SO Tracks on right and left.
            GPS: N 38°43.79' W 109°55.01'

▼ 5.0 SO Enter wash.
0.9 ▲ SO Exit wash.
            GPS: N 38°44.40' W 109°55.93'

▼ 5.3 BL Exit wash up bank on left.
0.6 ▲ BR Enter wash.
            GPS: N 38°44.55' W 109°56.13'

▼ 5.4 BL Enter wash.
0.5 ▲ BR Exit wash on right.

▼ 5.5 SO Exit wash on right.
0.4 ▲ SO Enter wash.

▼ 5.9   Trail ends at the junction with Trail
            #18: Levi Well Trail. Turn left to exit
            via Duma Point Road; turn right to exit
            via Blue Hills Road.

0.0 ▲   Trail starts at the junction with Trail #18: Levi Well Trail, 0.1 miles east of a deep, sandy creek crossing and 2.8 miles from the western end of the trail. Zero trip meter and turn southeast on unmarked, small sandy track.

        GPS: N 38°44.94' W 109°56.63'

MOAB REGION TRAIL #18

Levi Well Trail

STARTING POINT   Blue Hills Road, 0.2 miles north of Dubinky Well Road

FINISHING POINT   Duma Point Road, 5.1 miles south of the junction with Blue Hills Road

TOTAL MILEAGE   8.8 miles

UNPAVED MILEAGE   8.8 miles

DRIVING TIME   1 hour

ELEVATION RANGE   4,300–4,500 feet

USUALLY OPEN   Year-round

DIFFICULTY RATING   4

SCENIC RATING   8

REMOTENESS RATING   +0

Special Attractions

- Beautiful Tenmile Canyon.
- Entrada buttes and the Blue Hills.
- Photo opportunities in the sand dunes.

Description

The difficulty with this trail is the loose, deep sand along most of its length, particularly the last 3 miles around Tenmile Canyon. The trail slants away from Blue Hills Road. The first section runs through the Blue Hills, close to the upper end of Tenmile Wash. This section can be extremely boggy when wet, as the remaining ruts testify. The trail passes out of the low Blue Hills and passes by Levi Well itself, which is just off the trail in a thicket of tamarisk. This is a free-flowing well that feeds a cattletank.

The trail rises slightly and runs along wide Tenmile Canyon. The surface is very loose in dry weather and, conversely, is often impassable in wet weather, as the deep sand traps turn to greasy mud! Just before the end of Trail #17: Rainbow Rocks Trail, there are some very photogenic sand dunes off the trail to the north, set against the backdrop of the Entrada sandstone buttes. There are further small

Entering Tenmile Canyon along the Levi Well Trail

dunes a short way along Rainbow Rocks Trail. After you pass the end of the Rainbow Rocks Trail, the worst of the sand starts, as the trail immediately drops down to cross a sandy creek, a tributary of Tenmile Canyon. The crossing itself is easy, but the exit is up a steep, washed out, loose sandy slope that may give you trouble in drier weather.

The main Tenmile Canyon is crossed a mile farther on, and this is a very wide, flat-bottomed sandy canyon, with the loosest and deepest sand of all and a tricky exit. The creek flows pretty much year-round, reducing to a trickle in the drier months. This canyon is very pretty, with large cottonwoods in the wash around Dripping Spring, just off the trail to the left.

From Tenmile Canyon, there are a couple more wash crossings; then the trail proceeds to join the Duma Point Road.

Current Road Information

BLM Moab Field Office
82 East Dogwood, Suite M
Moab, UT 84532
(435) 259-2100

Map References

BLM   Moab
USGS 1:24,000   Valley City, Dee Pass,
       Dubinky Wash
       1:100,000 Moab
Maptech CD-ROM: Moab/
       Canyonlands
Trails Illustrated, #501 (incomplete)
Utah Atlas & Gazetteer, p. 40
Other: Latitude 40—Moab West
       Canyon Country Off-Road Vehicle
       Trail Map—Island Area

Route Directions

▼ 0.0   From Blue Hills Road, 0.2 miles north of Dubinky Well Road, turn northwest onto unmarked track and zero trip meter.
1.6 ▲   Trail ends at the junction with Blue Hills Road, 0.2 miles north of junction with Dubinky Well Road. Turn right to join Dubinky Well Road.
          GPS: N 38°47.08' W 109°51.03'

▼ 0.5   SO   Track on left.
1.1 ▲   SO   Track on right.

▼ 0.8   SO   Faint track on left.
0.8 ▲   SO   Faint track on right.

▼ 1.0   SO   Pass through fence line.
0.6 ▲   SO   Pass through fence line.
          GPS: N 38°47.25' W 109°52.21'

▼ 1.3   SO   Cross through small wash, then track on left.
0.3 ▲   SO   Track on right, then cross through small wash.

▼ 1.6   SO   Track on right goes to Levi Well, just off the trail. Also track on left. Zero trip meter.
0.0 ▲   Continue to the east.
          GPS: N 38°47.02' W 109°52.75'

▼ 0.0   Continue to the west.
4.4 ▲   SO   Track on left goes to Levi Well, just off the trail. Also track on right. Zero trip meter.

▼ 0.1   SO   Cross through fence line.
4.3 ▲   SO   Cross through fence line.

▼ 0.4   SO   Small track on right.
4.0 ▲   SO   Small track on left.

▼ 1.1   BR   Track on left.
3.3 ▲   BL   Track on right.
          GPS: N 38°46.63' W 109°53.73'

▼ 2.5   SO   Track on right.
1.9 ▲   SO   Track on left.

▼ 3.2   SO   Cross through wash.
1.2 ▲   SO   Cross through wash.

▼ 3.7   SO   Sand dunes on right, just a short way from the track.
0.7 ▲   SO   Sand dunes on left, just a short way from the track.

▼ 3.9   SO   Cattle guard.
0.5 ▲   SO   Cattle guard.

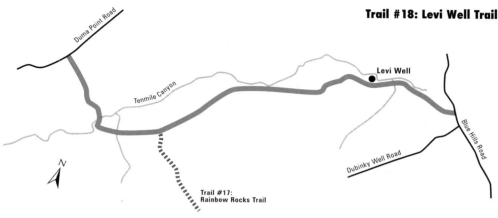

▼ 4.2   SO   Cross through wide, sandy wash; entrance often washes out and may require a detour.

0.2 ▲   SO   Cross through wide, sandy wash; exit often washes out and may require a detour.

▼ 4.4   SO   Track on left is start of Trail #17: Rainbow Rocks Trail. Zero trip meter.

0.0 ▲   Continue northeast.

             GPS: N 38°44.94' W 109°56.63'

▼ 0.0   Continue southwest.

2.8 ▲   SO   Track on right is start of Trail #17: Rainbow Rocks Trail. Zero trip meter.

▼ 0.1   SO   Cross through sandy creek; washed out steep, sandy exit.

2.7 ▲   SO   Cross through sandy creek; washed out steep, sandy entrance.

▼ 0.2   BR   Track on left, then track on right.

2.6 ▲   SO   Track on left, then track on right.

             GPS: N 38°44.84' W 109°56.76'

▼ 0.5   SO   Track on left, also track on right.

2.3 ▲   BL   Track on right, also track on left.

             GPS: N 38°44.73' W 109°57.09'

▼ 0.6   SO   Cross through slickrock wash.

2.2 ▲   SO   Cross through slickrock wash.

▼ 0.8   SO   Cross through wash.

2.0 ▲   SO   Cross through wash.

▼ 1.0   SO   Cross through wash, then track on left.

1.8 ▲   SO   Track on right, then cross through wash.

▼ 1.1   SO   Faint track on left.

1.7 ▲   SO   Faint track on right.

▼ 1.2   SO   Drop down to enter Tenmile Canyon.

1.6 ▲   SO   Leaving Tenmile Canyon.

▼ 1.3   SO   Cross through Tenmile Canyon wash, then creek. Track on left along wash and corral on right in wash.

1.5 ▲   SO   Cross through Tenmile Canyon creek, then wash. Track on right along wash and corral on left in wash.

             GPS: N 38°44.75' W 109°57.92'

▼ 1.5   SO   Track on left.

1.3 ▲   SO   Track on right.

▼ 1.6   BR   Track on left.

1.2 ▲   BL   Track on right.

▼ 1.7   SO   Cross through wash.

1.1 ▲   SO   Cross through wash.

▼ 2.2   BR   Track on left.

0.6 ▲   SO   Track on right.

             GPS: N 38°45.21' W 109°58.50'

▼ 2.8   Trail ends at intersection with the graded Duma Point Road. Turn right to exit via graded roads to US 191 and return to Moab. Turning right can also lead north to I-70.

0.0 ▲ Trail starts at intersection with the graded Duma Point Road, 5.1 miles from the junction with Blue Hills Road. Turn southeast onto dirt track and zero trip meter.
GPS: N 38°45.57' W 109°59.08'

Crystal Geyser Trail

STARTING POINT Utah 6 (Old Highway)
FINISHING POINT Ruby Ranch Road
TOTAL MILEAGE 21.7 miles
UNPAVED MILEAGE 20.9 miles
DRIVING TIME 3 hours
ELEVATION RANGE 4,000–4,400 feet
USUALLY OPEN Year-round
DIFFICULTY RATING 5
SCENIC RATING 8
REMOTENESS RATING +1

The trail winds along Green River with the San Rafael Reef in the distance

Special Attractions
- The Crystal Geyser and colorful mineral deposits.
- Views along the Green River.
- Moderately challenging remote route between Green River and Moab.

History
Crystal Geyser and four other geysers in the region are the unexpected results of oil drilling. Directly underneath Crystal Geyser is the sloping rock strata of the San Rafael Swell. Water runs down the strata, and where Crystal Geyser is located near the bottom, the water is under considerable pressure. Drillers searching for oil in the 1930s sunk a shaft that reached carbon dioxide pockets underneath the water. The geyser is the result of the gas pressure that builds until it shoots the water about 20 feet in the air at irregular intervals, roughly twice a day. These artificial geysers are the only cold water geysers on the continent.

The colorful deposits between the geyser and the Green River are calcite—calcium carbonate stained by various mineral impurities, creating hues from yellow and brown to vivid orange and rust red. The scalloped edges of the deposits act like tiny dams, and blue-green algae use them to immerse themselves in the mineral-rich waters. Tufa, the by-product of the algae's photosynthesis, gradually builds up over time, adding to the colorful runoff from the geyser.

The geyser's water, brought up from the underlying rock strata, is highly mineralized. Crystal Geyser alone is responsible for adding 3,000 tons of salts each year to the Green River and hence also to the Colorado River. The salt has consequences for both the river ecosystem and for users of the water. In the mid-1970s, Mexico claimed that the waters it received from the Colorado River were too highly mineralized for domestic or even agricultural use. A desalinization plant was built near the Colorado River in southern California to render the water acceptable to Mexico.

Description
This trail leaves the town of Green River, visits the cold water Crystal Geyser, then trav-

Difficult steep, rocky drop into the wash along the Crystal Geyser Trail

els farther along the Green River, crossing the desolate Morrison Formation on old mining trails, until it joins Salt Wash Road. The trail is moderately challenging—both for driving and route finding—but it is normally within the range of most stock high-clearance SUVs.

The route starts 4 miles east of the town of Green River along Utah 6, the Old Highway, which runs north of and parallel to I-70. For the first 5 miles to Crystal Geyser, the road is graded gravel. The geyser is particularly photogenic at sunset, when the setting sun intensifies the colors of the mineral deposits. From there, the trail parallels the Green River for a few more miles before bearing away on smaller, ungraded trails across the Morrison Formation. There are no route markings, so navigation can be tricky; this part of the trail is not on any map that we have seen. Therefore, we have provided additional GPS waypoints to help you navigate this difficult section. At times the correct trail is not the most used. There are a couple of short, steep sections with loose broken rock that will require careful wheel placement and maybe someone outside the vehicle to "spot," but most of the surface is easy going, with long sections of fairly smooth two-track. Interspersed with these are rougher rocky sections to keep the driver's attention on the trail! Some of the wash crossings are ditchy, which may catch longer rear overhangs.

Once the trail joins Salt Wash it becomes a graded dirt road; it follows above the wash before finishing on the graded gravel Ruby Ranch Road.

Current Road Information
BLM Moab Field Office
82 East Dogwood, Suite M
Moab, UT 84532
(435) 259-2100

Map References
BLM   San Rafael Desert, Moab (incomplete)
USGS 1:24,000   Green River NE, Green
       River, Green River SE, Dee Pass
       (incomplete)
       1:100,000 San Rafael Desert, Moab
       (incomplete)
Maptech CD-ROM: Moab/Canyonlands;
       Central/San Rafael
Utah Atlas & Gazetteer, pp. 39, 40
Utah Travel Council #5 (incomplete)
Other: Canyon Country Off-Road Vehicle
       Trail Map—Island Area

Route Directions

▼ 0.0   From the Old Highway, 4 miles east of
           Green River, 0.3 miles east of where it
           passes underneath the railroad, turn
           south on unmarked single lane paved
           road and zero trip meter.
4.8 ▲   Trail finishes on the Old Highway, 4
           miles east of Green River. Turn left for
           Green River and I-70.
           GPS: N 38°58.52' W 110°04.61'

▼ 0.6   SO Pass underneath I-70.
4.2 ▲   SO Pass underneath I-70.

▼ 0.7   SO Cattle guard.
4.1 ▲   SO Cattle guard.

▼ 0.8   SO Road is now graded gravel.
4.0 ▲   SO Road is now single lane and paved.

▼ 1.0   SO Track on left.
3.8 ▲   SO Track on right.

▼ 1.4   SO Pass underneath power lines, then
           intersection.

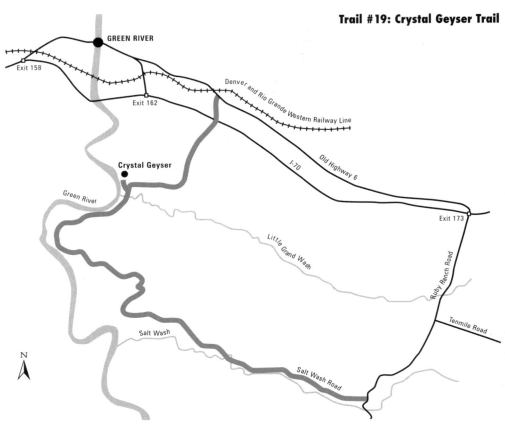

3.4 ▲ SO Intersection, then pass underneath power lines.
        GPS: N 38°57.39′ W 110°05.23′

▼ 2.7 SO Track on left.
2.1 ▲ SO Track on right.

▼ 3.0 SO Track on left.
1.8 ▲ SO Track on right.

▼ 4.6 SO Track on left.
0.2 ▲ SO Track on right.

▼ 4.8 BL Track on right goes 0.5 miles to Crystal Geyser. After visiting the geyser, return to this junction and continue on the left fork. Zero trip meter.
0.0 ▲ Continue toward I-70.
        GPS: N 38°56.08′ W 110°07.72′

▼ 0.0 Continue south toward the Green River.

2.9 ▲ SO Track on left goes 0.5 miles to Crystal Geyser. After visiting the geyser, return to this junction and continue straight ahead. Zero trip meter.

▼ 0.5 SO Track on left to corral, then second track on left at wash. Cross through Little Grand Wash.
2.4 ▲ SO Cross through Little Grand Wash. Track on right at wash, then second track on right to corral.
        GPS: N 38°55.69′ W 110°07.69′

▼ 0.6 SO Track on left. Main trail follows along the Green River.
2.3 ▲ SO Track on right.

▼ 1.4 SO Cattle guard.
1.5 ▲ SO Cattle guard.

▼ 1.6 SO Cross through wash.
1.3 ▲ SO Cross through wash.

▼ 2.2   SO   Track on right.
0.7 ▲   SO   Track on left.

GPS: N 38°55.19′ W 110°09.48′

▼ 2.8   BL   Track on right, then cross through wash.
0.1 ▲   SO   Cross through wash, then track on left.

GPS: N 38°55.07′ W 110°10.08′

▼ 2.9   BL   Track forks three ways; take left track. Middle track continues to river. Zero trip meter.
0.0 ▲   Continue to the northeast.

GPS: N 38°55.01′ W 110°10.14′

▼ 0.0   Continue to the southwest.
3.9 ▲   SO   Two tracks on left, continue straight ahead. First track on left goes to river.

▼ 0.1   SO   Track on left.
3.8 ▲   SO   Track on right.

▼ 0.5   SO   Small ditchy wash crossing.
3.4 ▲   SO   Small ditchy wash crossing.

▼ 0.7   SO   Track on right, then cross through fence line.
3.2 ▲   SO   Cross through fence line, then track on left.

GPS: N 38°54.35′ W 110°10.11′

▼ 0.9   BL   Track on right, followed by second track on right, and very faint track on left.
3.0 ▲   SO   Faint track on right, then track on left, followed by second track on left.

GPS: N 38°54.23′ W 110°10.01′

▼ 1.0   SO   Cross through wash.
2.9 ▲   SO   Cross through wash.

▼ 1.3   SO   Cross through small wash.
2.6 ▲   SO   Cross through small wash.

▼ 1.4   SO   Cross through small wash.
2.5 ▲   SO   Cross through small wash.

▼ 2.3   TL   T-intersection. Track on right goes to viewpoint and continues. Turn left over

ridge with views to both sides.
1.6 ▲   TR   Track straight on goes to viewpoint and continues.

GPS: N 38°53.87′ W 110°08.92′

▼ 2.5   SO   Descend from ridge.
1.4 ▲   SO   Top of ridge.

▼ 2.6   BL   At base of climb trail forks.
1.3 ▲   SO   Track on right. Trail climbs up ridge.

▼ 3.0   SO   Cross wash.
0.9 ▲   SO   Cross wash.

GPS: N 38°53.78′ W 110°08.19′

▼ 3.4   SO   Trail is wider and graded at this point.
0.5 ▲   SO   Trail is narrower and ungraded.

GPS: N 38°53.52′ W 110°07.80′

▼ 3.9   TR   Turn right onto faint track; larger trail bears left here. Zero trip meter.
0.0 ▲   Continue on larger, graded trail.

GPS: N 38°53.56′ W 110°07.22′

▼ 0.0   Continue on fainter trail.
7.8 ▲   TL   Track on right. Turn left onto wider graded trail. Zero trip meter.

▼ 0.1   TL   Intersection.
7.7 ▲   TR   Intersection.

GPS: N 38°53.46′ W 110°07.34′

▼ 0.5   SO   Trail crosses rocky area; route is marked by small cairns. Then short drop into wash.
7.3 ▲   SO   Short, steep climb out of wash, then cross rocky area marked by small cairns.

GPS: N 38°53.17′ W 110°07.19′

▼ 1.0   SO   Cross through fence line, then steep descent.
6.8 ▲   SO   Steep climb, then cross through fence line.

GPS: N 38°53.09′ W 110°07.49′

▼ 1.3   SO   Enter wash.
6.5 ▲   SO   Exit wash.

GPS: N 38°52.88′ W 110°07.68′

▼ 1.6   TL   T-intersection in small wash.
6.2 ▲   TR   Track on left in small wash.
         GPS: N 38°52.68' W 110°07.92'

▼ 1.8   SO   Faint track on left.
6.0 ▲   SO   Faint track on right.

▼ 1.9   BL   Track on right.
5.9 ▲   SO   Track on left.
         GPS: N 38°52.54' W 110°07.69'

▼ 2.0   TL   Track on right to viewpoint.
5.8 ▲   TR   Track on left to viewpoint.
         GPS: N 38°52.50' W 110°07.62'

▼ 2.1   BR   Two faint tracks ahead, cairn on right.
               Swing right and descend onto bench.
5.7 ▲   BL   Leave bench and swing left, cairn on
               left and two faint tracks on right.
         GPS: N 38°52.57' W 110°07.58'

▼ 2.2   SO   Cross gully, long vehicles watch rear.
5.6 ▲   SO   Cross gully, long vehicles watch rear.
         GPS: N 38°52.59' W 110°07.42'

▼ 2.5   SO   Wire gate, cross through fence line.
5.3 ▲   SO   Wire gate, cross through fence line.
         GPS: N 38°52.57' W 110°07.09'

▼ 2.7   SO   Cross through wash.
5.1 ▲   SO   Cross through wash.

▼ 2.9   SO   Track on right.
4.9 ▲   SO   Track on left.
         GPS: N 38°52.48' W 110°06.68'

▼ 3.7   SO   Cross through wash.
4.1 ▲   SO   Cross through wash.
         GPS: N 38°52.36' W 110°05.83'

▼ 3.8   SO   Tracks on left and right. Trail becomes
               easier.
4.0 ▲   SO   Tracks on left and right. Trail becomes
               rougher and narrower.
         GPS: N 38°52.28' W 110°05.67'

▼ 3.9   SO   Track on left.
3.9 ▲   SO   Track on right.

▼ 4.7   BL   Track on right. Salt Wash is on right.

3.1 ▲   BR   Track on left.
         GPS: N 38°51.76' W 110°05.26'

▼ 5.1   SO   Track on right.
2.7 ▲   SO   Track on left.
         GPS: N 38°51.58' W 110°04.82'

▼ 5.2   SO   Track on left.
2.6 ▲   SO   Track on right.

▼ 5.6   SO   Cross through wash.
2.2 ▲   SO   Cross through wash.

▼ 6.4   SO   Track on right.
1.4 ▲   SO   Track on left rejoins.
         GPS: N 38°50.99' W 110°03.56'

▼ 6.6   SO   Track on right rejoins. Enter Salt Wash.
1.2 ▲   SO   Track on left. Exit wash.

▼ 6.8   SO   Leave wash.
1.0 ▲   SO   Enter Salt Wash.

▼ 6.9   SO   Two faint tracks on left.
0.9 ▲   SO   Two faint tracks on right.

▼ 7.6   SO   Cross through wash.
0.2 ▲   SO   Cross through wash.

▼ 7.8   TR   T-intersection. Join graded dirt road
               and zero trip meter.
0.0 ▲   Continue on smaller, ungraded road.
         GPS: N 38°50.98' W 110°02.04'

▼ 0.0   Continue on graded road.
2.3 ▲   TL   Turn left onto smaller trail and zero trip
               meter.

▼ 1.0   SO   Corral against red rock on left.
1.3 ▲   SO   Corral against red rock on right.

▼ 2.1   SO   Cross through wash.
0.2 ▲   SO   Cross through wash.

▼ 2.2   SO   Cross through wash.
0.1 ▲   SO   Cross through wash.

▼ 2.3   Trail ends at junction with the graded
               gravel Ruby Ranch Road. Turn left
               for I-70.

0.0 ▲ Trail starts at the junction of the grad-
ed Ruby Ranch Road and Salt Wash
Road, 3.1 miles south of Tenmile Road.
Junction is unmarked. Zero trip meter
and turn west on graded dirt Salt
Wash Road.
GPS: N 38°50.19' W 109°59.68'

Yellow Cat Trail

STARTING POINT US 191, 0.7 miles north of
mile marker 152
FINISHING POINT Intersection with Utah 128
TOTAL MILEAGE 35.7 miles
UNPAVED MILEAGE 35.7 miles
DRIVING TIME 3.5 hours
ELEVATION RANGE 4,200–5,200 feet
USUALLY OPEN Year-round
DIFFICULTY RATING 3
SCENIC RATING 8
REMOTENESS RATING +1

Special Attractions

■ Uranium mining remains around The
Poison Strip.
■ Longer, more remote version of Trail #21:
Yellow Cat Road.
■ Access to many remote 4WD trails.

History

Uranium deposits around the Moab area first
attracted miners in the 1890s, but none of
the mines paid off until the Atomic Energy
Commission upped demand during the Cold
War in the 1950s. Fortune hunters came out
in droves, and there were many reasonably
profitable mines located around Yellow Cat
Flat and south of The Poison Strip. The area
had quite a collection of miners, prospectors,
and profiteers; as the old workings show,
there were some large adits tunneled into the
hillside. These mines were often abandoned
as quickly as they sprung up, leaving workings, ore hoppers, cabins, vehicles, and other
equipment to rust and rot.

One of the more famous miners to set up

a base on Yellow Cat Flat, hoping to strike it
rich, was Charlie Steen, who made his fortune when he founded the Mi Vida Mine
down in the Lisbon Valley. The Steen family
spent a winter in a small trailer on Yellow
Cat Flat in the early 1950s, staking many
small claims in the region.

Prior to uranium, Yellow Cat Flat yielded
another find. A scientific expedition in the
1920s discovered two tons of dinosaur bones
on the surface of Yellow Cat Flat.

The Poison Strip gained its name because
of arsenic in the soil, which killed the sheep
that grazed the area.

Description

This trail is the longer version of Trail #21:
Yellow Cat Road. It duplicates Yellow Cat
Road for a short stretch along The Poison
Strip, but it also includes some sections of
rougher trail at either end, and it passes by
other mines and points of interest. In dry
weather, this trail is suitable for a high-clearance vehicle, although some sections of the
trail can be very loose and sandy in extremely dry weather, making 4WD preferable.

The trail leaves US 191 along the Thompson Cutoff Road and passes the north end of
Trail #22: Salt Valley Road; then it crosses the
flat Little Valley and the desolate Yellow Cat

Timber supports line this adit near the eastern end of the trail

Flat. After 15 miles, it turns onto a smaller, ungraded trail that winds through the once-busy uranium mining district. A multitude of side trails are worth exploring; many of them lead to mining remains, adits, and workings.

The trail joins Mine Draw and swings north. This is the start of Trail #23: Salt Wash Overlook Trail, a short spur trail that passes more mining remains before finishing at an overlook above Salt Valley. The main trail goes north to join graded Trail #21: Yellow Cat Road, passing close to some of the more substantial uranium mine remains on the trail, the Parco Mines and the Little Eva Mines. These mines have tunnels so large you could drive a truck into them. It is possible, by cutting through the maze of smaller trails, to join Yellow Cat Road further to the east. A compass or GPS helps! These mines are private property and posted as the Lucky Strike, but they do not appear to be actively worked, and it is possible to see many of the old workings, adits, and old vehicles left abandoned. Remember that it is dangerous to enter adits or tunnels because of the buildup of deadly radon gas. Holes and diggings are also often unmarked, so exercise due care when exploring around the diggings.

The trail now joins the larger Yellow Cat Road, cuts through the gap of the blackstone incline, and then passes the substantial remains of an old ore hopper beside the trail. A maze of tracks to the right at this point leads back to the Parco Mines and the Little Eva Mines, and then you intersect the start of Trail #24: Dome Plateau Trail.

Remaining on The Poison Strip, the trail

CHARLES STEEN AND THE URANIUM MINING BOOM

Charles Steen was born in Caddo, Texas, in 1919. He studied geology at the Texas College of Mines and Metallurgy and received his degree in 1943. Steen worked in South America for the next couple of years before returning home, where he soon got married and took a job with the Standard Oil Company. However, he was soon fired for insubordination and was blacklisted from the industry.

Charles Steen

In 1949, the Atomic Energy Commission tried to vitalize domestic discovery and development of U.S. uranium mines. Previously, uranium was thought to be a useless byproduct of radium and vanadium mining, but soon old radium mines were being reopened to search for this newly valued element. Steen was one of many who packed up his family and moved to the Colorado Plateau. Though mocked for his conviction that the uranium could be found in much the same way as oil, Steen explored many different claims throughout the region. Just as he was about to give up he struck it rich near Moab, in southeastern Utah's Lisbon Valley. Not only did his Mi Vida Mine make him a millionaire, it proved that uranium was plentiful in the region. The Uranium Boom was on. Thousands of prospectors in old jeeps and jalopies combed the Utah countryside, eagerly waiting for their Geiger counters to point them to wealth and fortune. Moab's population quadrupled in less than five years.

Steen, soon dubbed the "Uranium King," became rich overnight and decided to live accordingly. Besides establishing his own mining company, he built mansions near Moab and Reno, Nevada. But the surest sign of his new status was the weekly flights he took to Salt Lake City for rhumba lessons.

In 1958, Steen was elected to the Utah State Senate, but he resigned in 1961 to work on expanding his business interests. Unfortunately, he soon found himself in over his head and was bankrupt by 1968. After his roller-coaster life had taken him full circle, Charles Steen moved to Colorado to work on his Cash Gold Mine, which represented the last of his once astonishing fortune.

continues east, just south of The Poison Strip ridge. The remains of the old Cactus Rat Mine are on both sides of the trail, but there is little here to see.

The trail leaves Yellow Cat Road 4.4 miles after joining it and continues along the plateau to the south. The trail standard drops to an ungraded dirt track again as it descends toward Owl Draw. This section has some of the prettiest scenery along the trail, as the multicolored sandstone domes appear. The surface is loose and sandy, and there can be washouts.

The Molly Hogans rise above the lake along Yellow Cat Trail

The trail, 7.6 miles after leaving Yellow Cat Road, passes two very solid log cabins built of railroad sleepers. There are mining remains and adits here, too, but the origin and the name of the mine are unknown.

The trail passes the northern end of Trail #29: Wood Road, which is marked on some maps as being the end of Yellow Cat Trail. The main trail, however, runs along Owl Draw to finish on Utah 128.

Current Road Information
BLM Moab Field Office
82 East Dogwood, Suite M
Moab, UT 84532
(435) 259-2100

Map References
BLM   Moab
USGS 1:24,000   Crescent Junction,
       Thompson Springs, Klondike Bluffs,
       Mollie Hogans, Cisco SW, Dewey
       1:100,000 Moab
Maptech CD-ROM: Moab/Canyonlands
Trails Illustrated, #501; #211
Utah Atlas & Gazetteer, pp. 40, 41
Utah Travel Council #5
Other: Latitude 40—Moab West
       Latitude 40—Moab East
       Canyon Country Off-Road Vehicle
       Trail Map—Arches Area

Route Directions

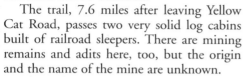

▼ 0.0   From US 191, 0.7 miles north of mile marker 152, turn northeast on graded dirt Thompson Cutoff Road. Turn is unsigned.
1.2 ▲   Trail ends at intersection with US 191. Turn right to join I-70, turn left for Moab.
          GPS: N 38°52.61' W 109°48.69'

▼ 0.2 SO Track on right.
1.0 ▲ SO Track on left.

▼ 1.1 SO Cross over wash on bridge.
0.1 ▲ SO Cross over wash on bridge.

▼ 1.2 TR Turn right onto unmarked, graded dirt road on right. Zero trip meter.
0.0 ▲   Continue to the southwest.
          GPS: N 38°53.55' W 109°47.99'

▼ 0.0   Continue to the southeast.
2.4 ▲ TL Turn left onto graded dirt Thompson Cutoff Road. To the right goes to Thompson. Zero trip meter.

▼ 0.2 SO Track on right.
2.2 ▲ SO Track on left.

▼ 1.4 SO Pass through gate.
1.0 ▲ SO Pass through gate.

▼ 2.1　SO　Track on left.
0.3 ▲　SO　Track on right.

▼ 2.2　SO　Cross through wash.
0.2 ▲　SO　Cross through wash.

▼ 2.4　TL　T-intersection. Track to the right is Trail #22: Salt Valley Road. Zero trip meter.
0.0 ▲　　　Continue to the northwest.
　　　　　GPS: N 38°52.87' W 109°45.59'

▼ 0.0　　　Continue to the east.
11.2 ▲　TR　Track on left is the Trail #22: Salt Valley Road. Zero trip meter.

▼ 1.1　SO　Track on left.
10.1 ▲　SO　Track on right.

▼ 1.4　SO　Track on right.
9.8 ▲　SO　Track on left.

▼ 1.8　SO　Track on right.
9.4 ▲　SO　Track on left.

▼ 3.3　SO　Track on right.
7.9 ▲　SO　Track on left.

▼ 3.6　SO　Track on right.
7.6 ▲　SO　Track on left.

▼ 4.4　SO　Track on right.
6.8 ▲　SO　Track on left.

▼ 6.7　SO　Track on right.
4.5 ▲　SO　Track on left.

▼ 7.7　SO　Track on right goes to brick ruin.
3.5 ▲　SO　Track on left goes to brick ruin.
　　　　　GPS: N 38°51.69' W 109°36.98'

▼ 8.5　SO　Track on left.
2.7 ▲　SO　Track on right.

▼ 9.3　BL　Track on right. Trail is now crossing Yellow Cat Flat.
1.9 ▲　BR　Track on left.
　　　　　GPS: N 38°50.90' W 109°36.37'

▼ 10.8　SO　Cattle guard.

0.4 ▲　SO　Cattle guard.

▼ 11.0　SO　Cross through wash.
0.2 ▲　SO　Cross through wash.

▼ 11.1　SO　Cross through wash.
0.1 ▲　SO　Cross through wash.

▼ 11.2　TR　Turn right onto smaller, ungraded track. Main track swings away to the left. Zero trip meter.
0.0 ▲　　　Continue to the west across Yellow Cat Flat.
　　　　　GPS: N 38°50.24' W 109°34.29'

▼ 0.0　　　Continue to the east.
2.2 ▲　TL　Turn left onto graded dirt road. Zero trip meter.

▼ 0.4　SO　Large dam on right.
1.8 ▲　SO　Large dam on left.
　　　　　GPS: N 38°50.25' W 109°33.83'

▼ 0.5　SO　Track on left.
1.7 ▲　SO　Track on right.

▼ 0.6　BL　Track on right.
1.6 ▲　SO　Track on left.
　　　　　GPS: N 38°50.11' W 109°33.72'

▼ 0.7　SO　Track on right.
1.5 ▲　SO　Track on left.

▼ 0.8　SO　Cross through wash.
1.4 ▲　SO　Cross through wash.

▼ 1.1　SO　Track on right.
1.1 ▲　SO　Track on left.
　　　　　GPS: N 38°49.92' W 109°33.26'

▼ 1.2　SO　Track on right.
1.0 ▲　SO　Track on left.

▼ 1.4　SO　Cross through wide wash.
0.8 ▲　SO　Cross through wide wash.

▼ 1.6　SO　Track on right.
0.6 ▲　SO　Track on left.
　　　　　GPS: N 38°50.04' W 109°32.95'

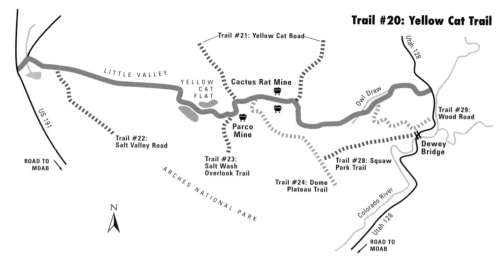

▼ 1.7   SO   Cross through wash, then fenced seep on left underneath rock ledge.

0.5 ▲   SO   Fenced seep on right underneath rock ledge, then cross through wash.

GPS: N 38°50.08' W 109°32.83'

▼ 1.8   SO   Track on left at wash.

0.4 ▲   SO   Track on right at wash.

▼ 1.9   SO   Mine workings on right.

0.3 ▲   SO   Mine workings on left.

▼ 2.0   SO   Two tracks on right go to mine workings.

0.2 ▲   SO   Two tracks on left go to mine workings.

▼ 2.1   SO   Cross through wash.

0.1 ▲   SO   Cross through wash.

▼ 2.2   SO   Unmarked track on the right is the start of Trail #23: Salt Wash Overlook Trail. Zero trip meter.

0.0 ▲   Continue to the west leaving Mine Draw.

GPS: N 38°50.02' W 109°32.35'

▼ 0.0   Continue on graded dirt road along Mine Draw.

1.3 ▲   BR   Turn onto ungraded dirt road. Track straight ahead is the start of Trail #23: Salt Wash Overlook Trail. Zero trip meter.

▼ 0.2   SO   Cross through wash. Many wash crossings along Mine Draw.

1.1 ▲   SO   Cross through wash.

▼ 0.3   SO   Track on right goes to the Parco Mine remains, then cross through wash.

1.0 ▲   SO   Cross through wash, then track on left goes to the Parco Mine remains.

GPS: N 38°50.21' W 109°32.09'

▼ 0.6   SO   Mine workings on right.

0.7 ▲   SO   Mine workings on left.

▼ 0.8   SO   Track on left, then track on right at wash.

0.5 ▲   SO   Track on left at wash, then track on right.

▼ 1.0   SO   Leaving Mine Draw.

0.3 ▲   SO   Entering Mine Draw. Many wash crossings along the draw.

▼ 1.3   BR   Yellow Cat Road comes in from the left. Turn right and join Trail #21: Yellow Cat Road along The Poison Strip. Zero trip meter.

0.0 ▲   Continue to the southwest.

GPS: N 38°50.94' W 109°32.12'

▼ 0.0   Continue east toward The Poison Strip.

1.4 ▲   BL   Track to the right is the continuation of Yellow Cat Road. Turn left, leaving Trail #21: Yellow Cat Road. Zero trip meter.

▼ 0.4 SO Old ore hopper on left, then track on right goes to the remains of the Little Eva and Parco Mines.
1.0 ▲ SO Track on left goes to the remains of the Little Eva and Parco Mines, then old ore hopper on right.
GPS: N 38°50.87′ W 109°31.68′

▼ 1.4 SO Graded road on right is Trail #24: Dome Plateau Trail. Zero trip meter.
0.0 ▲   Continue west along The Poison Strip.
GPS: N 38°51.04′ W 109°30.61′

▼ 0.0   Continue east along The Poison Strip.
3.0 ▲ SO Graded road on left is Trail #24: Dome Plateau Trail. Zero trip meter.

▼ 0.2 SO Faint track on left climbs up on top of The Poison Strip.
2.8 ▲ SO Faint track on right climbs up on top of The Poison Strip.

▼ 0.4 SO Faint track on right.
2.6 ▲ SO Faint track on left.

▼ 1.4 SO Site of the Cactus Rat Mine on both sides of the trail.
1.6 ▲ SO Site of the Cactus Rat Mine on both sides of the trail.
GPS: N 38°51.12′ W 109°29.10′

▼ 1.6 SO Track on right.
1.4 ▲ SO Track on left.

▼ 1.7 SO Track on left, then second entrance to same track on left.
1.3 ▲ SO Track on right, then second entrance to same track on right.

▼ 2.1 SO Dam on left.
0.9 ▲ SO Dam on right.

▼ 2.3 SO Cattle guard.
0.7 ▲ SO Cattle guard.
GPS: N 38°50.87′ W 109°28.29′

▼ 2.7 SO Cross over natural gas pipeline.
0.3 ▲ SO Cross over natural gas pipeline.

▼ 3.0 TR T-intersection. Track on left is the continuation of Trail #21: Yellow Cat Road. Zero trip meter.
0.0 ▲   Continue west along The Poison Strip.
GPS: N 38°50.90′ W 109°27.47′

▼ 0.0   Continue south; track on right.
3.6 ▲ TL Track on left, then track ahead is Yellow Cat Road going to join I-70. Turn left and join Trail #21: Yellow Cat Road along The Poison Strip.

▼ 0.6 SO Track on left.
3.0 ▲ SO Track on right.

▼ 0.7 SO Track on right.
2.9 ▲ SO Track on left.

▼ 2.4 BL Track on right connects to Trail #24: Dome Plateau Trail.
1.2 ▲ BR Track on left connects to Trail #24: Dome Plateau Trail.
GPS: N 38°49.25′ W 109°26.39′

▼ 2.6 SO Track on left goes to collapsed wooden structure.
1.0 ▲ SO Track on right goes to collapsed wooden structure.

▼ 2.7 SO Track on left.
0.9 ▲ SO Track on right.

▼ 3.3 SO Cattle guard.
0.3 ▲ SO Cattle guard.

▼ 3.6 SO Major graded track to the right goes to Auger Spring. Zero trip meter.
0.0 ▲   Continue on larger graded trail.
GPS: N 38°49.57′ W 109°25.20′

▼ 0.0   Continue on smaller graded trail.
5.0 ▲ SO Major graded track to the left goes to Auger Spring. Zero trip meter.

▼ 0.2 SO Track on left.
4.8 ▲ SO Track on right.

▼ 1.1 SO Faint track on right.
3.9 ▲ SO Faint track on left.

▼ 1.2   SO   Two tracks on left.
3.8 ▲   SO   Two tracks on right.

▼ 1.5   BR   Track on left. Trail starts to drop along escarpment.
3.5 ▲   SO   Track on right. Trail is now on top of escarpment.
     GPS: N 38°49.83' W 109°23.58'

▼ 2.0   SO   Track on right.
3.0 ▲   SO   Track on left.
     GPS: N 38°49.97' W 109°23.12'

▼ 2.8   BR   Track on left. Bear right and cross through Owl Draw.
2.2 ▲   BL   Cross through Owl Draw, then track on right.
     GPS: N 38°50.35' W 109°22.34'

▼ 2.9   SO   Cross through small wash.
2.1 ▲   SO   Cross through small wash.

▼ 3.4   SO   Track on right, then second track on right.
1.6 ▲   SO   Track on left, then second track on left.
     GPS: N 38°49.98' W 109°22.35'

▼ 3.9   SO   Track on left.
1.1 ▲   BL   Track on right.

▼ 4.0   SO   Two old timber cabins on left of trail, plus mining remains and adits.
1.0 ▲   SO   Two old timber cabins on right of trail, plus mining remains and adits.
     GPS: N 38°50.33' W 109°21.93'

▼ 4.9   BR   Faint track on left down wash, then cross through wash.
0.1 ▲   SO   Cross through wash, then faint track on right down wash.

▼ 5.0   SO   Track on right is the start of Trail #29: Wood Road. Zero trip meter.
0.0 ▲   Continue to the west.
     GPS: N 38°50.95' W 109°21.31'

▼ 0.0   Continue to the northeast.
4.4 ▲   BR   Track on left is the start of Trail #29: Wood Road. Zero trip meter.

▼ 0.1   SO   Faint track on left along draw. Trail

drops down and follows along Owl Draw, crossing through it often.
4.3 ▲   SO   Faint track on right along draw. Trail leaves Owl Draw.

▼ 1.2   SO   Pass through wire gate in Owl Draw.
3.2 ▲   SO   Pass through wire gate in Owl Draw.

▼ 1.3   SO   Leave Owl Draw and climb up alongside of canyon.
3.1 ▲   SO   Descend to enter Owl Draw, crossing through it often.

▼ 1.5   SO   Track on left.
2.9 ▲   SO   Track on right.
     GPS: N 38°51.76' W 109°20.18'

▼ 1.9   SO   Cross through Owl Draw.
2.5 ▲   SO   Cross through Owl Draw.

▼ 2.1   SO   Cattletank on left.
2.3 ▲   SO   Cattletank on right.

▼ 2.7   SO   Track on right.
1.7 ▲   SO   Track on left.

▼ 3.1   SO   Cross through wash.
1.3 ▲   SO   Cross through wash.

▼ 3.3   SO   Faint track on left.
1.1 ▲   SO   Faint track on right.

▼ 3.4   SO   Cross through wash.
1.0 ▲   SO   Cross through wash.

▼ 3.9   TL   Track on right is Kokopelli Trail for bikes and 4WDs.
0.5 ▲   TR   Track straight on is Kokopelli Trail for bikes and 4WDs.
     GPS: N 38°51.28' W 109°18.00'

▼ 4.4   Trail ends on Utah 128 at corral. Turn right for Moab, left for I-70.
0.0 ▲   Trail commences on Utah 128, 0.2 miles north of mile marker 34. Turn southwest just before a corral on graded dirt road at the BLM sign for the Kokopelli Trail.
     GPS: N 38°51.62' W 109°17.60'

Yellow Cat Road

STARTING POINT I-70, exit 190
FINISHING POINT I-70, exit 202
TOTAL MILEAGE 20.2 miles
UNPAVED MILEAGE 20.1 miles
DRIVING TIME 1 hour
ELEVATION RANGE 4,350–5,000 feet
USUALLY OPEN Year-round
DIFFICULTY RATING 1
SCENIC RATING 8
REMOTENESS RATING +0

Special Attractions

■ Uranium mining remains around The Poison Strip.
■ Shorter, easier version of Trail #20: Yellow Cat Trail.
■ Access to many remote area 4WD trails.

Description

This trail is a shorter, easier alternative to the full Trail #20: Yellow Cat Trail, yet it passes the same major points of interest. This route is graded gravel or dirt the entire length, and in dry weather is suitable for passenger vehicles. It starts and ends at I-70, making access to the trail easy. However, the trail can quickly become impassable in wet weather.

From I-70, you cross Sagers Flat to the southeast. As you get away from the freeway, the scenery is suprisingly varied and hilly. Once you reach the uranium mining area,

An old mining truck sits near an opening into the Parco Mines

Looking ahead at the road along The Poison Strip

just south of The Poison Strip, the road swings to the east and becomes graded dirt. Here it passes many sidetracks that lead to abandoned mines. The first is the Ringtail Mine; not too much remains there now, just some footings and tailings. A major track to the south is the longer Trail #20: Yellow Cat Trail. There are many remains to be seen just down this road, which for the first couple of miles is a good standard of graded dirt and suitable for passenger cars in dry weather. See Trail #20: Yellow Cat Trail for details.

As Yellow Cat Road continues, it cuts through the gap of the Blackstone incline and passes the substantial remains of an old ore hopper beside the trail. A maze of tracks to the right leads to the remains of what the topographical maps call the Parco Mines and the Little Eva Mines. These are private property and posted as the Lucky Strike, but they do not appear to be actively worked, and it is possible to see many of the old workings, adits, and old vehicles left abandoned. Remember that it is dangerous to enter adits or tunnels, because of the buildup of deadly radon gas. Holes and diggings are also often unmarked, so exercise due care when exploring around the diggings.

Remaining on The Poison Strip, the trail continues to the east just south of The Poison Strip ridge. You pass the start of Trail #24: Dome Plateau Trail and then the remains of the old Cactus Rat Mine on both sides of the trail, but there is little here to see. At a major fork in the road, the route bears left and follows the Pinto Draw road back to I-70. It winds through a gap in The Poison Strip, passing side trails to more adits and old workings. From here, the trail crosses back over Sagers Flats, Sagers Wash, and Pinto Draw before rejoining I-70, at the remains of the nearly ghost town of Cisco.

Current Road Information
BLM Moab Field Office
82 East Dogwood, Suite M
Moab, UT 84532
(435) 259-2100

Map References
BLM   Moab
USGS 1:24,000   Sagers Flat, Mollie
        Hogans, Cisco SW, White House
        1:100,000 Moab
Maptech CD-ROM: Moab/Canyonlands
Trails Illustrated, #501
Utah Atlas & Gazetteer, pp. 40, 41
Utah Travel Council #5
Other: Latitude 40—Moab West
        Latitude 40—Moab East
        Canyon Country Off-Road Vehicle
        Trail Map—Arches Area

Route Directions

▼ 0.0   From I-70, exit 190, turn south onto paved road. Zero trip meter at cattle guard.
7.4 ▲   Trail ends at I-70 at exit 190. Turn west for Moab, east for Grand Junction, Colorado.
           GPS: N 38°56.46' W 109°36.84'

▼ 0.1   SO Road is now graded gravel.
7.3 ▲   SO Road is now paved.

▼ 0.5   SO Track on left.
6.9 ▲   SO Track on right.

▼ 0.6   SO Track on right.
6.8 ▲   SO Track on left.

▼ 1.6   SO Corral on right.
5.8 ▲   SO Corral on left.

▼ 3.1   SO Track on right.
4.3 ▲   SO Track on left.

▼ 3.3   SO Track on left.
4.1 ▲   SO Track on right.

▼ 4.5   SO Track on left and right.
2.9 ▲   SO Track on left and right.

▼ 5.7   SO Track on left.
1.7 ▲   SO Track on right.

▼ 5.8   SO Graded road on right joins Trail #20: Yellow Cat Trail and gives access to the north end of Arches National Park.
1.6 ▲   SO Graded road on left joins Trail #20: Yellow Cat Trail and gives access to the north end of Arches National Park.
        GPS: N 38°52.06' W 109°32.96'

▼ 6.2   SO Track on left.
1.2 ▲   SO Track on right.

▼ 6.3   SO Cattle guard, then track on right.
1.1 ▲   SO Track on left, then cattle guard.

▼ 6.6   SO Track on right.
0.8 ▲   SO Track on left.

▼ 7.3   SO Track on right.
0.1 ▲   SO Track on left.

▼ 7.4   BL Smaller track on right goes to the remains of the Ringtail Mine, then road forks. Right fork is the Trail #20: Yellow Cat Trail, which also goes to Trail #23: Salt Wash Overlook Trail. Zero trip meter.
0.0 ▲   Continue up Yellow Cat Road to the northwest.
           GPS: N 38°50.94' W 109°32.12'

▼ 0.0   Continue east toward The Poison Strip.
1.4 ▲   BR First track to the left is the Trail #20: Yellow Cat Trail, which also goes to Trail #23: Salt Wash Overlook Trail. Second smaller track to the left goes to the remains of the Ringtail Mine.

Trail # 21: Yellow Cat Road

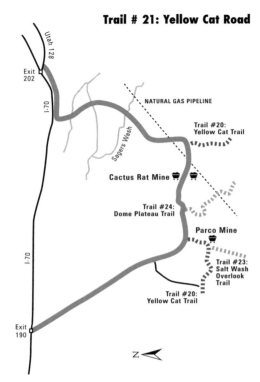

▼ 1.4 SO Site of the Cactus Rat Mine on both sides of the trail.

1.6 ▲ SO Site of the Cactus Rat Mine on both sides of the trail.

GPS: N 38°51.12′ W 109°29.10′

▼ 1.6 SO Track on right.

1.4 ▲ SO Track on left.

▼ 1.7 SO Track on left, then second entrance to same track on left.

1.3 ▲ SO Track on right, then second entrance to same track on right.

▼ 2.1 SO Dam on left.

0.9 ▲ SO Dam on right.

▼ 2.3 SO Cattle guard.

0.7 ▲ SO Cattle guard.

GPS: N 38°50.87′ W 109°28.29′

▼ 2.7 SO Cross over natural gas pipeline.

0.3 ▲ SO Cross over natural gas pipeline.

▼ 3.0 TL T-intersection. Track on right is Trail #20: Yellow Cat Trail and goes to The Highlands. Zero trip meter.

0.0 ▲ Continue west along The Poison Strip.

GPS: N 38°50.90′ W 109°27.47′

▼ 0.0 Continue toward I-70.

8.4 ▲ TR Straight on is Trail #20: Yellow Cat Trail to the Highlands. Zero trip meter.

▼ 0.2 SO Track on right.

8.2 ▲ SO Track on left.

▼ 0.5 SO Cross over natural gas pipeline and track on right along pipeline.

7.9 ▲ SO Cross over natural gas pipeline and track on left along pipeline.

▼ 0.7 SO Track on right goes to diggings, then track on left to adits.

7.7 ▲ SO Track on right goes to adits, then track on left to diggings.

GPS: N 38°51.41′ W 109°27.25′

▼ 0.8 SO Track on left.

▼ 0.4 SO Old ore hopper on left, then track on right goes to the remains of the Little Eva and Parco Mines.

1.0 ▲ SO Track on left goes to the remains of the Little Eva and Parco Mines, then old ore hopper on right.

GPS: N 38°50.87′ W 109°31.68′

▼ 1.4 SO Graded road on right is Trail #24: Dome Plateau Trail. Zero trip meter.

0.0 ▲ Continue west along The Poison Strip.

GPS: N 38°51.04′ W 109°30.61′

▼ 0.0 Continue east along The Poison Strip.

3.0 ▲ SO Graded road on left is Trail #24: Dome Plateau Trail. Zero trip meter.

▼ 0.2 SO Faint track on left climbs up on top of The Poison Strip.

2.8 ▲ SO Faint track on right climbs up on top of The Poison Strip.

▼ 0.4 SO Faint track on right.

2.6 ▲ SO Faint track on left.

7.6 ▲	SO	Track on right.

▼ 1.1	SO	Cross through wash.
7.3 ▲	SO	Cross through wash.

▼ 1.3	SO	Cattle guard.
7.1 ▲	SO	Cattle guard.

▼ 1.7	SO	Cross through wash.
6.7 ▲	SO	Cross through wash.

▼ 2.1	SO	Track on left goes to dam.
6.3 ▲	SO	Track on right goes to dam.

▼ 2.9	SO	Cross through wash.
5.5 ▲	SO	Cross through wash.

▼ 3.0	SO	Cross through wash.
5.4 ▲	SO	Cross through wash.

▼ 3.1	SO	Track on right, then track on left.
5.3 ▲	SO	Track on right, then track on left.

▼ 3.2	SO	Cross over Sagers Wash.
5.2 ▲	SO	Cross over Sagers Wash.

GPS: N 38°53.18′ W 109°25.98′

▼ 3.7	SO	Track on left goes to corral and track on right on top of the ridge.
4.7 ▲	SO	Track on right goes to corral and track on left on top of the ridge.

▼ 4.6	SO	Cross through wash.
3.8 ▲	SO	Cross through wash.

▼ 5.2	SO	Track on left.
3.2 ▲	SO	Track on right.

▼ 5.5	SO	Cross through wash.
2.9 ▲	SO	Cross through wash.

▼ 5.6	SO	Track on left.
2.8 ▲	SO	Track on right.

▼ 6.5	TR	T-intersection. Turn right and follow alongside I-70.
1.9 ▲	TL	Turn south and leave I-70 frontage road.

▼ 6.9	SO	Track on right.

1.5 ▲	SO	Track on left.

▼ 7.3	SO	Cross through wash on concrete ford.
1.1 ▲	SO	Cross through wash on concrete ford.

▼ 7.4	SO	Cattle guard.
1.0 ▲	SO	Cattle guard.

▼ 7.8	SO	Cross through wash on concrete ford.
0.6 ▲	SO	Cross through wash on concrete ford.

▼ 8.3	SO	Track on right leaves through gravel pit.
0.1 ▲	SO	Track on left leaves through gravel pit.

▼ 8.4		Trail ends at the junction with I-70, at exit 202, and Utah 128. Turn right to go to Moab via Utah 128, turn left to join I-70.
0.0 ▲		Trail starts at exit 202 on I-70 at the junction with Utah 128. Turn south on Utah 128, then immediately turn west on unsigned frontage road and zero trip meter.

GPS: N 38°56.22′ W 109°24.35′

MOAB REGION TRAIL #22

Salt Valley Road

STARTING POINT Trail #20: Yellow Cat Trail, 3.6 miles from US 191
FINISHING POINT Arches National Park
TOTAL MILEAGE 15 miles
UNPAVED MILEAGE 15 miles
DRIVING TIME 45 minutes
ELEVATION RANGE 4,600–5,200 feet
USUALLY OPEN Year-round
DIFFICULTY RATING 2
SCENIC RATING 9
REMOTENESS RATING +0

Special Attractions

- Alternative entrance to Arches National Park.
- Hiking trail to Tower Arch.
- Easy trail along a long and scenic valley.

History

The small settlement of Valley City, located along US 191 and Thompson Road, was abandoned by 1930. In 1908, the settlement was flooded by a burst reservoir, which is accessible from the top of the trail, and continued flooding caused the demise of the town.

Skyline Arch (upper left) in the distance

The reservoir was an important watering point for cattle driven from Dugout Ranch in the south up to the railroad at Thompson. The town charged a fee per head of cattle—the Valley City Reservoir was the last watering point before the railroad, and often 2,000 to 3,000 head of cattle were driven along the stock route.

Albert and Dubinky Anderson (of Dubinky Well fame), lived here for a while, and Valley City was reputed to be one of the sites of a bootleg liquor operation, for which Albert did jail time.

Description

This easy trail leads down a long pretty valley into the north end of Arches National Park. It is best suited for high-clearance vehicles, because of the long stretches of deep sand traps that can quickly bog down a regular vehicle. In wet weather this road quickly becomes impassable to even 4WD vehicles, and the National Park Service may close it temporarily in wet conditions.

The trail travels quickly down Salt Valley. The northern end of the valley is fairly enclosed, but as the trail enters Arches National Park, it widens out to a wide, grassy valley. The preferable direction for travel is north to south, as this way gives great views into the park, the La Sal Mountains, Klondike Bluffs, and Devil's Garden. Farther down the trail, Skyline Arch comes into view to the east. This natural arch doubled in size in 1940 when a large chunk fell out of the window.

The trail within the park sees a lot more use than the northern end, and this part of the road is washboardy as a result. Many park visitors travel the trail to the north to access the hiking trailhead to Tower Arch, or to travel Trail #25: Eye of the Whale Trail.

Camping within the national park is restricted to the Devil's Garden Campground, which can fill up by 10 A.M. during peak season.

Current Road Information

Arches National Park
PO Box 907
Moab, UT 84532
(435) 719-2299

BLM Moab Field Office
82 East Dogwood, Suite M
Moab, UT 84532
(435) 259-2100

Map References

BLM   Moab
USGS   1:24,000   Crescent Junction,
        Valley City, Klondike Bluffs, Mollie
        Hogans, The Windows Section
        1:100,000 Moab

Signpost along the Salt Valley Road

Maptech CD-ROM: Moab/Canyonlands
Trails Illustrated, #211 (incomplete); #501
Utah Atlas & Gazetteer, p. 40
Utah Travel Council #5
Other: Latitude 40—Moab West
Canyon Country Off-Road Vehicle
Trail Map—Arches Area

Route Directions

▼ 0.0   From Trail #20: Yellow Cat Trail, 3.6 miles from US 191, turn south on the unmarked, graded dirt Salt Valley Road and zero trip meter.

6.1 ▲   Trail ends at the junction with Trail #20: Yellow Cat Trail. Turn left to exit to US 191, turn right to continue along the Yellow Cat Trail.

GPS: N 38°52.86′ W 109°45.59′

▼ 0.4   SO   Cattle guard.
5.7 ▲   SO   Cattle guard.

▼ 0.6   SO   Track on right.
5.5 ▲   SO   Second entrance to track on left.

▼ 0.7   SO   Second entrance to track on right.
5.4 ▲   SO   Track on left.

GPS: N 38°52.28′ W 109°45.35′

▼ 0.9   SO   Track on left.
5.2 ▲   SO   Track on right.

▼ 1.2   SO   Track on left.
4.9 ▲   SO   Track on right.

▼ 1.4   SO   Track on left.
4.7 ▲   SO   Track on right.

GPS: N 38°51.75′ W 109°44.89′

▼ 1.7   SO   Faint track on left.
4.4 ▲   SO   Faint track on right.

▼ 6.0   SO   Track on right.
0.1 ▲   SO   Track on left.

▼ 6.1   SO   Track on left and track on right, then entering Arches National Park over cattle guard (fee area). Zero trip meter.
0.0 ▲   Continue out of the park.

GPS: N 38°48.90′ W 109°41.08′

▼ 0.0   Continue into Arches National Park. Klondike Bluffs are on the right.
2.0 ▲   SO   Leaving Arches National Park over cattle guard, then track on left and track on right outside park. Zero trip meter.

▼ 1.9   SO   Track on right goes to the Tower Arch hiking trailhead.
0.1 ▲   SO   Track on left goes to the Tower Arch hiking trailhead.

GPS: N 38°47.77′ W 109°39.48′

▼ 2.0   SO   Track on right is Trail #25: Eye of the Whale Trail. Zero trip meter.
0.0 ▲   Continue north along Salt Valley.

GPS: N 38°47.70′ W 109°39.42′

▼ 0.0   Continue south along Salt Valley.

Trail # 22: Salt Valley Road

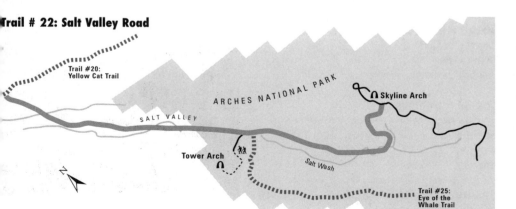

6.9 ▲	SO	Track on left is Trail #25: Eye of the Whale Trail. Zero trip meter.
▼ 3.6	SO	Enter Salt Wash.
3.3 ▲	SO	Exit Salt Wash.
▼ 4.6	SO	Exit Salt Wash.
2.3 ▲	SO	Enter Salt Wash.
▼ 5.0	SO	Skyline Arch is directly in front.
1.9 ▲	SO	Skyline Arch is directly behind.
▼ 6.9		Closure gate, then trail ends at the junction with the paved road in Arches National Park. Turn right to exit the park, turn left for Devil's Garden Campground.
0.0 ▲		Trail starts on the paved Arches National Park Road, just before Skyline Arch. The trail is unmarked. Turn south on graded gravel road through closure gate and zero trip meter.

GPS: N 38°46.11' W 109°35.28'

MOAB REGION TRAIL #23

Salt Wash Overlook Trail

STARTING POINT Trail #20: Yellow Cat Trail, 1.3 miles south of Trail #21: Yellow Cat Road

FINISHING POINT Salt Wash Overlook

TOTAL MILEAGE 3.3 miles

UNPAVED MILEAGE 3.3 miles

DRIVING TIME 45 minutes (one-way)

ELEVATION 4,500–4,700 feet

USUALLY OPEN Year-round

DIFFICULTY RATING 3

SCENIC RATING 10

REMOTENESS RATING +1

Special Attractions

■ Panoramic view over remote Salt Wash.
■ Remains of the Black A uranium mine.

History

Moab Garage Company Stage ran the mail route in the 1920s when Moab was the only place in southeastern Utah with a bank. The company shipped deposits for merchants from all over the county to Moab. The following day, the stage would do the run in reverse, delivering receipts and change back to the merchants. It is interesting to speculate how the stage ended up at Yellow Bird Mine!

Description

This short, sandy spur trail leads past some very interesting uranium mining remains, and it ends on a slickrock platform above picturesque Salt Wash. Salt Wash is a little-known area; it has no vehicle access and sees very little human activity of any kind.

The spur trail is short, but confusing, with many turns, all unmarked. To add further confusion, the trail often washes out and detours are pushed through. However, finding the correct route is normally relatively easy. Although Trail #21: Yellow Cat Road and Trail #20: Yellow Cat Trail see some 4WD traffic, this spur trail is rarely traveled.

After 0.8 miles, a track to the left travels 0.3 miles to the remains of Black A Mine, located out of sight up on the mesa. The original trail leading up to it washed out and has been blocked by fallen boulders, so you will need to park at the base of the mesa and walk the short distance to the mine. The hike is well worth your while, as there are numerous large adits, the remains of a tramway, loading points, and a sturdy timber cabin that even has carpet on the floor!

The trail deteriorates shortly after the Black A, as it leaves Mine Draw and heads out toward the viewpoint. There are frequent washouts along this section and large ruts.

You pass the remains of Yellow Bird Mine

Ruins of the Moab Garage Company Stage at Yellow Bird Mine

A large opening to the Black A Mine reveals its timber supports

after 2.5 miles, although the only things of note are the remains of the Moab Garage Company Stage vehicle, still with the writing on the side. Other than the stage, there are a few tailings piles and little else.

You reach the end of the trail 0.8 miles after the Yellow Bird, on the platform over Salt Wash. To your left is Cottonwood Wash, to the right is Mine Draw Canyon and Arches National Park. Salt Wash leads away in front of you, and the La Sal Mountains tower behind. Down in the bottom of Salt Wash, there is evidence of previous ranching activity if you look hard. Piles of timber are suggestive of old cattle troughs and fence lines.

There is a wonderful campsite near the end of the trail; although exposed, it has a breathtaking view.

Current Road Information

Arches National Park
PO Box 907
Moab, UT 84532
(435) 719-2299

BLM Moab Field Office
82 East Dogwood, Suite M
Moab, UT 84532
(435) 259-2100

Map References

BLM   Moab
USGS 1:24,000   Mollie Hogans
       1:100,000 Moab
Maptech CD-ROM: Moab/Canyonlands
Trails Illustrated, #211; #501
Utah Atlas & Gazetteer, p. 40
Other: Latitude 40—Moab East

Route Directions

▼ 0.0   Trail starts on Trail #20: Yellow Cat Trail, 1.3 miles south of the western junction with Trail #21: Yellow Cat Road. Zero trip meter, and turn southwest on the unmarked graded trail. Trail is following Mine Draw.
           GPS: N 38°50.02' W 109°32.35'

View over Salt Wash from the end of the trail

Trail #23: Salt Wash Overlook Trail

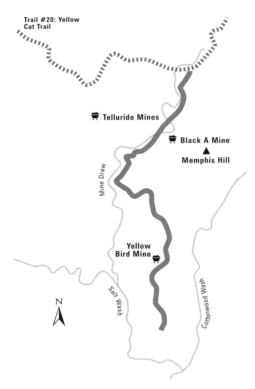

Trail #20: Yellow Cat Trail

Telluride Mines

Black A Mine

Memphis Hill

Mine Draw

Yellow Bird Mine

Salt Wash

Cottonwood Wash

N

▼ 0.4 SO Track on left.
▼ 0.8 SO Track on left goes to the remains of the Black A Mine.
GPS: N 38°49.48' W 109°32.73'

▼ 1.0 BL Track on right continues in the wash.
GPS: N 38°49.44' W 109°32.91'

▼ 1.1 BL Trail detours around a major washout.
▼ 1.2 SO Track on left at small wash, then track rejoins on the right.
▼ 1.5 BL Track on right.
GPS: N 38°49.15' W 109°33.09'

▼ 1.7 SO View right into Mine Draw.
GPS: N 38°49.03' W 109°32.93'

▼ 1.9 SO Cross through wash twice, then climb up ridge.
▼ 2.1 BR Track on left.
GPS: N 38°48.89' W 109°32.65'

▼ 2.4 SO Track on right.
▼ 2.5 SO Track on left goes to campsite, then remains of the Yellow Bird Mine on the right.
GPS: N 38°48.56' W 109°32.57'

▼ 3.1 SO Best viewpoint ahead into Salt Wash.
▼ 3.2 SO Campsite on left.
▼ 3.3   Trail ends on slickrock platform over Salt Wash.
GPS: N 38°48.02' W 109°32.61'

Dome Plateau Trail

STARTING POINT Trail #21: Yellow Cat Road, 1.4 miles east of intersection with Trail #20: Yellow Cat Trail
FINISHING POINT Dome Plateau
TOTAL MILEAGE 14.4 miles
UNPAVED MILEAGE 14.4 miles
DRIVING TIME 1.5 hours (including spur)
ELEVATION RANGE 4,700–5,800 feet
USUALLY OPEN Year-round
DIFFICULTY RATING 2
SCENIC RATING 8
REMOTENESS RATING +1

Special Attractions

■ Natural arch near trail.
■ Views over the Professor Valley and Arches National Park.
■ Access to many spur trails and viewpoints.

Description

The trail out to Dome Plateau is an easy trail that offers many vistas along its length. It leaves from Trail #21: Yellow Cat Road to the south and crosses the undulating terrain known as The Highlands. The graded trail can be sandy and loose in sections, but it is normally passable by high-clearance vehicles. Like most trails around here, it is one to avoid when it is wet.

The trail passes the spur trails to Lost Springs Canyon and Trail #27: Winter Camp Ridge Trail and gradually descends to

Dome Plateau. The views are fantastic! To the west, you can see Arches National Park; to the north are the Book Cliffs and The Highlands. Ahead to the south are the La Sal Mountains. Once on Dome Plateau, tracks to the left lead to other viewpoints, including a smaller trail used by the Moab Jeep Safari. The main trail runs west along the edge of Dome Plateau, giving glimpses into Fisher Valley, Professor Valley, and Castle Valley. The trail ends at a turning circle, with views to the west of Arches National Park.

Current Road Information

BLM Moab Field Office
82 East Dogwood, Suite M
Moab, UT 84532
(435) 259-2100

Map References

BLM   Moab
USGS 1:24,000   Mollie Hogans, Cisco
        SW, Big Bend
        1:100,000 Moab
Maptech CD-ROM: Moab/Canyonlands
Trails Illustrated, #211 (incomplete); #501
Utah Atlas & Gazetteer, pp. 40, 41
Utah Travel Council #5 (incomplete)
Other: Latitude 40—Moab East
        Canyon Country Off-Road Vehicle
        Trail Map—Arches Area

Route Directions

▼ 0.0   Trail commences on Trail #21: Yellow
           Cat Road, 1.4 miles east of the west-

The trail runs along the fence line on Dome Plateau

ern junction of Yellow Cat Road and Trail #20: Yellow Cat Trail. Turn south on unmarked graded dirt road and zero trip meter.

2.5 ▲   Trail ends at intersection with Trail #21: Yellow Cat Road, on The Poison Strip.

GPS: N 38°51.03' W 109°30.60'

▼ 0.6   SO Track on right.
1.9 ▲   SO Track on left.

▼ 0.9   SO Track on right.
1.6 ▲   SO Track on left.

▼ 1.3   SO Track on left, then cross through wash.
1.2 ▲   SO Cross through wash, then track on right.

▼ 1.7   SO Cross through wash.
0.8 ▲   SO Cross through wash.

View from atop Dome Plateau

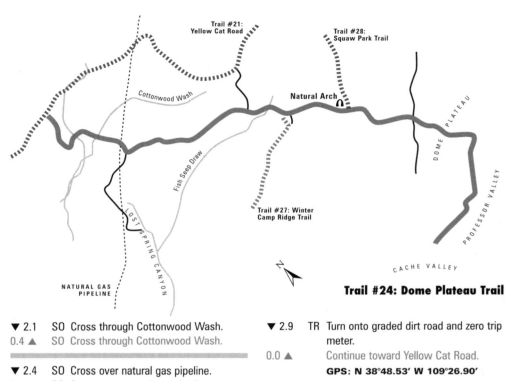

Trail #21:
Yellow Cat Road

Trail #28:
Squaw Park Trail

Cottonwood Wash

Natural Arch

DOME PLATEAU

Fish Seep Draw

PROFESSOR VALLEY

Trail #27: Winter
Camp Ridge Trail

LOST SPRING CANYON

NATURAL GAS
PIPELINE

N

CACHE VALLEY

Trail #24: Dome Plateau Trail

▼ 2.1   SO Cross through Cottonwood Wash.
0.4 ▲   SO Cross through Cottonwood Wash.

▼ 2.4   SO Cross over natural gas pipeline.
0.1 ▲   SO Cross over natural gas pipeline.

▼ 2.5   BL Track on right goes to Lost Spring
            Canyon. Zero trip meter.
0.0 ▲   Continue toward Yellow Cat Road.
            GPS: N 38°49.44′ W 109°29.74′

▼ 0.0   Continue toward Dome Plateau.
2.9 ▲   BR Track on left goes to Lost Spring
            Canyon. Zero trip meter.

▼ 0.3   SO Track on right.
2.6 ▲   SO Track on left.

▼ 0.4   BR Track on left.
2.5 ▲   SO Track on right.
            GPS: N 38°49.31 W 109°29.35′

▼ 1.0   SO Gate.
1.9 ▲   SO Gate.
            GPS: N 38°49.05′ W 109°28.87′

▼ 1.5   SO Track on left.
1.4 ▲   BR Track on right.

▼ 2.9   TR Turn onto graded dirt road and zero trip
            meter.
0.0 ▲   Continue toward Yellow Cat Road.
            GPS: N 38°48.53′ W 109°26.90′

▼ 0.0   Continue toward Dome Plateau.
1.2 ▲   TL T-intersection. Turn onto graded dirt
            road and zero trip meter.

▼ 0.1   SO Cross through fence line.
1.1 ▲   SO Cross through fence line.

▼ 0.4   SO Track on right.
0.8 ▲   SO Track on left.

▼ 0.7   SO Cross through Fish Seep Draw.
0.5 ▲   SO Cross through Fish Seep Draw.

▼ 1.2   SO Track on right is Trail #27: Winter
            Camp Ridge Trail. Zero trip meter.
0.0 ▲   Continue toward Yellow Cat Road.
            GPS: N 38°47.86′ W 109°26.08′

▼ 0.0   Continue toward Dome Plateau.
1.4 ▲   SO Track on left is Trail #27: Winter Camp
            Ridge Trail. Zero trip meter.

▼ 0.1   SO Track on right joins Trail #27: Winter
            Camp Ridge Trail.

1.3 ▲   BR   Track on left joins Trail #27: Winter Camp Ridge Trail.
GPS: N 38°47.83′ W 109°25.89′

▼ 0.3   SO   Track on left.
1.1 ▲   SO   Track on right.

▼ 0.7   SO   Track on left.
0.7 ▲   SO   Track on right.
GPS: N 38°47.64′ W 109°25.39′

▼ 1.2   SO   Track on right.
0.2 ▲   SO   Track on left.

▼ 1.3   SO   Pass through gate, then track on right along fence, then track on left.
0.1 ▲   BL   Track on right and track on left along fence, then pass through gate.
GPS: N 38°47.20′ W 109°25.03′

▼ 1.4   SO   Track on left is Trail #28: Squaw Park Trail. A natural arch is just before the junction on the left. Zero trip meter.
0.0 ▲   Continue toward Yellow Cat Road.
GPS: N 38°47.18′ W 109°24.94′

▼ 0.0   Continue toward Dome Plateau.
▼ 0.2   SO   Track on left.
▼ 0.4   SO   Faint track on left.
▼ 0.6   BL   Track on right.
GPS: N 38°46.73′ W 109°24.69′

▼ 0.8   SO   Track on right.
▼ 1.6   SO   Track on left and track on right.
GPS: N 38°46.31′ W 109°23.86′

▼ 1.7   BR   Track on left.
▼ 2.0   BL   Fence line leaves trail on right.
GPS: N 38°46.01′ W 109°23.87′

▼ 2.4   SO   Cross through wash.
▼ 2.7   BR   Track on left.
GPS: N 38°45.69′ W 109°23.31′

▼ 3.3   SO   Two tracks on left.
GPS: N 38°45.22′ W 109°23.07′

▼ 3.6   SO   Fence line. Track on left and track on right along fence, then second track on right after fence.

GPS: N 38°45.12′ W 109°23.26′

▼ 3.7   SO   Small track on right.
▼ 3.8   SO   Cross through wash, then track on left goes to viewpoint.
▼ 3.9   SO   Track on left.
▼ 4.2   SO   Cross through wash.
▼ 6.3   BR   Small track on right, then trail forks.
GPS: N 38°44.09′ W 109°25.67′

▼ 6.4   Trail ends at turning circle.
GPS: N 38°44.08′ W 109°25.73′

MOAB REGION TRAIL #25

Eye of the Whale Trail

STARTING POINT Trail #22: Salt Valley Road, 6.9 miles north of Arches National Park Road

FINISHING POINT Willow Flats Road, Arches National Park

TOTAL MILEAGE 10.9 miles

UNPAVED MILEAGE 10.9 miles

DRIVING TIME 3 hours

ELEVATION RANGE 4,600–5,200 feet

USUALLY OPEN Year-round

DIFFICULTY RATING 6

SCENIC RATING 10

REMOTENESS RATING +0

Special Attractions

- Only 4WD trail completely within Arches National Park.
- Challenging 4WD trail with spectacular scenery along its length.
- Eye of the Whale Arch.

Description

This spectacular trail is contained within Arches National Park near Moab. Exceptional scenery, a remote backcountry feel, and a challenging trail combine to make this an unforgettable driving experience. A parks permit is required to enter the park, although no special permit is required for the backcountry 4WD trail. The National Park Service recommended direction for travel to

The start of the 4WD section of the trail with Klondike Bluffs in the background

reduce environmental impact is counter-clockwise, from north to south. In summer this is the only possible direction, so as to descend the long stretch of loose sand. The trail commences on Trail #22: Salt Valley Road, 6.9 miles from the southern end. Turn west at the sign for the 4WD road to Balanced Rock. This first part of the trail is the most difficult; a very rocky climb and descent has several large rocks and ruts necessitating careful wheel placement to avoid scraping the underbody of your vehicle. The rocks show the scrape marks of those who were not so careful—use a spotter outside the vehicle to assist. The views north to the Marching

Men and Klondike Bluffs ensure that cameras will be clicking.

After 1.7 miles, a dead-end trail heads for Klondike Bluffs, with a rewarding short hiking trail at the end to Tower Arch. The main trail becomes very sandy, and you travel for a while in the creek wash. This is still a challenging drive, as you cross many loose sandy sections, short steep drops over slickrock, washouts, and off-camber sections. The trail then runs along the valley, crossing and recrossing the creek and undulating through sagebrush to the parking area for the Eye of the Whale Arch.

The trail ends at the junction with Willow Flats Road. Turn left to rejoin the paved road

Trail #25: Eye of the Whale Trail

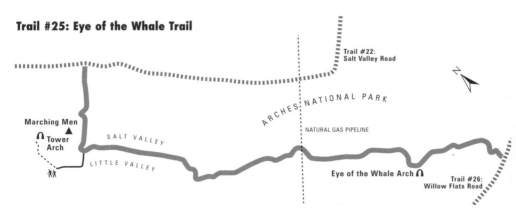

through the park, or turn right to exit the park via the scenic Trail #26: Willow Flats Road.

Current Road Information

Arches National Park
PO Box 907
Moab, UT 84532
(435) 719-2299

Map References

BLM   Moab (incomplete)
USGS 1:24,000   Mollie Hogans, The
        Windows Section, Klondike Bluffs,
        Merrimac Butte
        1:100,000 Moab (incomplete)
Maptech CD-ROM: Moab/Canyonlands
Trails Illustrated, #211; #501
Utah Atlas & Gazetteer, p. 40
Utah Travel Council #5 (incomplete)
Other: Latitude 40—Moab West
        Canyon Country Off-Road Vehicle
        Trail Map—Arches Area

Route Directions

▼ 0.0   From Trail #22: Salt Valley Road, zero
          trip meter and turn (at sign for
          Balanced Rock) onto trail heading
          southwest.
          GPS: N 38°47.70' W 109°39.42'

▼ 0.8   SO Start of rocky climb, care with wheel
          placement needed. Marching Men for-
          mation is to the right.
▼ 1.2   SO Top of climb. Trail descends over rock
          ledges.
▼ 1.7   TL Ahead leads to Tower Arch (1.3 miles).
          Trail is now predominately soft sand.
          GPS: N 38°46.74' W 109°40.63'

▼ 3.4   SO Tricky descent over slickrock into
          wash.
▼ 4.8   SO Trail exits wash.
▼ 6.4   SO Cross natural gas pipeline.
▼ 8.8   SO Track is now predominantly dirt and
          rock base.
▼ 9.1   SO Eye of the Whale Arch on right. Small
          parking area and hiking trail to arch.
          GPS: N 38°42.92' W 109°36.06'

▼ 10.9   End at intersection with Trail #26:
          Willow Flats Road. Turn left to return to
          main national park road. Turn right to
          exit park via Willow Flats Road.
          GPS: N 38°42.08' W 109°34.76'

MOAB REGION TRAIL #26

Willow Flats Road

STARTING POINT Junction of Arches National
   Park Road and Willow Flats Road
FINISHING POINT US 191
TOTAL MILEAGE 8 miles
UNPAVED MILEAGE 8 miles
DRIVING TIME 1 hour
ELEVATION RANGE 4,300–4,500 feet
USUALLY OPEN Year-round
DIFFICULTY RATING 4
SCENIC RATING 8
REMOTENESS RATING +0

Special Attractions

■ One of the few 4WD trails in Arches
  National Park.
■ Desert scenery and vegetation.
■ Moderately challenging alternative exit
  from Arches National Park.

Description

This less-traveled alternative route out of Arches National Park undulates through dry desert scenery and descends to cross several sandy washes and gullies before joining US 191. There are rewarding views east into Arches National Park and distant views of the La Sal Mountains to the southeast.

The trail begins at the Balanced Rock parking area in the national park and heads west. The trail surface at this stage is graded gravel and dirt. After passing the southern end of Trail #25: Eye of the Whale Trail, the surface becomes rougher and crosses a couple of rocky washes. After 4.2 miles the trail leaves the national park and enters public lands. It continues to undulate through junipers, yuccas, prickly pears, and

View down the track of Willow Flats Road

shinnery oaks until it ends at US 191.

There are some interesting driving sections on this trail, mainly rocky or sandy washes and some fairly deep washouts that call for careful wheel placement. It should be easily managed by most stock high-clearance SUVs. The National Park Service may close this trail following light snow or heavy rain.

You must pay an entrance fee into Arches National Park, but no special backcountry driving permit is required. There is no camping allowed on Willow Flats Road within Arches National Park.

Current Road Information

Arches National Park
PO Box 907
Moab, UT 84532
(435) 719-2299

Map References

BLM Moab (incomplete)
USGS 1:24,000 The Windows Section,
    Merrimac Butte
    1:100,000 Moab (incomplete)
Maptech CD-ROM: Moab/Canyonlands
Trails Illustrated, # 211; #501
Utah Atlas & Gazetteer, p. 40
Utah Travel Council #5
Other: Latitude 40—Moab West
    Canyon Country Off-Road Vehicle
    Trail Map—Arches Area

Route Directions

▼ 0.0   Turn west onto Willow Flats Road opposite the Balanced Rock parking area. Zero trip meter.

8.0 ▲   Trail ends at the Balanced Rock park-

Trail #26: Willow Flats Road

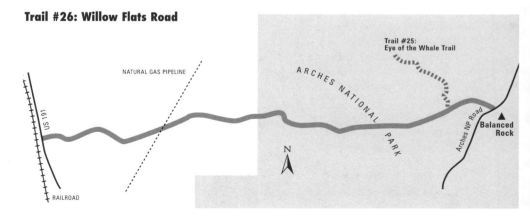

ing area on the main Arches National Park road. Turn right for the park entrance.

GPS: N 38°42.12' W 109°33.95'

▼ 0.1   SO   Picnic tables and pit toilet.
7.9 ▲   SO   Picnic tables and pit toilet.

▼ 0.2   SO   Track on left to parks work area.
7.8 ▲   SO   Track on right to parks work area.

▼ 0.8   SO   Track on right to Trail #25: Eye of the Whale Trail. Trail turns to dirt.
7.2 ▲   SO   Track on left to Trail #25: Eye of the Whale Trail. Trail turns to gravel road.

GPS: N 38°42.08' W 109°34.76'

▼ 3.3   SO   Trail crosses slickrock wash.
4.7 ▲   SO   Trail crosses slickrock wash.

▼ 3.6   SO   Trail dips into rocky wash.
4.4 ▲   SO   Views ahead to the La Sal Mountains. Trail dips into rocky wash.

▼ 4.2   SO   Leaving Arches National Park and entering state lands.
3.8 ▲   SO   Leaving state lands and entering Arches National Park (fee area).

GPS: N 38°42.09' W 109°38.06'

▼ 4.7   SO   Gate.
3.3 ▲   SO   Gate.

▼ 4.9   SO   Fork. Trails meet up in 0.1 miles. Choose your route.
3.1 ▲   SO   Trails rejoin.

▼ 5.0   SO   Trails rejoin.
3.0 ▲   SO   Fork. Trails meet up in 0.1 miles. Choose your route.

▼ 5.4   SO   Track on right.
2.6 ▲   SO   Track on left.

▼ 6.0   SO   Cross natural gas pipeline, past hut for generator. Track on left.
2.0 ▲   SO   Track on right, then cross natural gas pipeline, past hut for generator.

GPS: N 38°41.90' W 109°39.81'

▼ 6.4   SO   Cross small wash; care needed with wheel placement. Track on right.
1.6 ▲   SO   Track on left, then cross small wash, care needed with wheel placement.

▼ 6.6   SO   Cross wide sandy wash.
1.4 ▲   SO   Cross wide sandy wash.

▼ 6.8   TR   Turn right at T-intersection.
1.2 ▲   TL   Turn left.

▼ 7.6   SO   Track on left.
0.4 ▲   SO   Track on right.

▼ 8.0   Exit through a gate onto US 191. Turn left for Moab.
0.0 ▲   Trail commences 0.6 miles north of mile marker 138 on US 191. Turn east through a gate entering state lands and zero trip meter.

GPS: N 38°41.80' W 109°41.89'

Winter Camp Ridge Trail

STARTING POINT Trail #24: Dome Plateau Trail, 6.6 miles south of Trail #21: Yellow Cat Road

FINISHING POINT Boundary of Arches National Park

TOTAL MILEAGE 4.3 miles

UNPAVED MILEAGE 4.3 miles

DRIVING TIME 45 minutes (one-way)

ELEVATION RANGE 4,900–5,300 feet

USUALLY OPEN Year-round

DIFFICULTY RATING 3

SCENIC RATING 9

REMOTENESS RATING +1

Special Attractions

- Short spur trail can be done in conjunction with Trail #24: Dome Plateau Trail.
- Views into Arches National Park.
- Sandy trail is fun to drive.

A hazy view of Arches National Park seen along the Winter Camp Ridge Trail

Description
This short trail is a spur leading off from Trail #24: Dome Plateau Trail. It begins along an unmarked, roughly graded sandy trail that runs along the top of Winter Camp Ridge. The trail gradually descends the ridge top, offering some great views ahead into Arches National Park and south over Winter Camp Wash, Dome Plateau, and the La Sal Mountains. To the north you can see The Poison Strip, and farther to the north are the Book Cliffs. The difficulty factor of the trail comes from the very soft, deep, fine sand traps found along its entire length. There are no great grades to be negotiated; the trail gradually drops until it finishes at the boundary of Arches National Park. Directly ahead at the end of the trail is a jumble of red rocks that contains the distinctive Delicate Arch, although the arch itself is not visible. Behind them you can see the Windows Section of the park. There are a couple of nice campsites toward the end of the trail.

Current Road Information
Arches National Park
PO Box 907
Moab, UT 84532
(435) 719-2299

BLM Moab Field Office
82 East Dogwood, Suite M
Moab, UT 84532
(435) 259-2100

Map References
BLM   Moab
USGS 1:24,000   Cisco SW, Mollie Hogans
      1:100,000 Moab
Maptech CD-ROM: Moab/Canyonlands
Trails Illustrated, #501; #211
Utah Atlas & Gazetteer, p. 40
Utah Travel Council #5
Other: Latitude 40—Moab East
       Canyon Country Off-Road Vehicle
       Trail Map—Arches Area

Route Directions

▼ 0.0   From Trail #24: Dome Plateau Trail, 6.6 miles south of the junction with Trail #21: Yellow Cat Road, turn west on an unmarked formed track and zero trip meter.
          GPS: N 38°47.86' W 109°26.08'

▼ 0.1 SO Track on left is second entrance from Dome Plateau Trail.
▼ 1.4 BL Track on right.

Trail #27: Winter Camp Ridge Trail

▼ 1.8 BR Track on left.
GPS: N 38°47.17' W 109°27.79'

▼ 2.1 SO Track on left.
▼ 2.3 SO Track on left.
▼ 2.8 SO Cross through wash.
▼ 2.9 SO Pass through gate, then faint track on left.
GPS: N 38°46.76' W 109°28.87'

▼ 3.1 SO Track on right.
▼ 3.4 BR Track on left.
▼ 3.6 SO Faint track on left.
GPS: N 38°46.33' W 109°29.29'

▼ 4.3 Graded track ends at national park boundary. Trail swings right along fence line but does not continue.
GPS: N 38°45.66' W 109°29.47'

View of old Dewey Bridge

MOAB REGION TRAIL #28

Squaw Park Trail

STARTING POINT Dewey Bridge on Utah 128
FINISHING POINT Junction with Trail #24: Dome Plateau Trail
TOTAL MILEAGE 8.4 miles
UNPAVED MILEAGE 8.0 miles
DRIVING TIME 1 hour
ELEVATION RANGE 4,200–5,200 feet
USUALLY OPEN Year-round
DIFFICULTY RATING 5
SCENIC RATING 9
REMOTENESS RATING +0

Special Attractions
■ Historic Dewey Bridge.
■ Moderately challenging trail through a beautiful open valley.
■ Access to a network of 4WD trails.

History
Dewey Bridge, at the start of this trail, has the distinction of being both the longest suspension bridge and the longest clear span bridge in the state of Utah. Built in 1916, it allowed the communities in southeast Utah to access the markets in western Colorado to sell their produce and buy supplies. The old bridge, now being restored through the use of grants and public donations, sits next to the modern concrete highway bridge, which was built in the 1980s.

There is some debate as to whether the name for the settlement of Dewey comes from a prospector who used to live in the area, Dewey Smith, or from a ferry that transported goods downriver, which in turn was named after Admiral Dewey. Samuel King set up a ferry here in the 1880s, and this in turn led to a small settlement that was referred to as Kings Ferry.

Yellow Jacket wash gets its name from the number of wasps in the area!

Description
You begin in the Rio Colorado subdivision immediately north of Dewey Bridge on Utah 128. Follow small BLM signs for the Kokopelli Trail through the subdivision to the start of the trail itself, which swiftly leaves the subdivision behind. The first mile of the ungraded sand and rock trail is the hardest, with a series of rock ledges leading up to the gate. There are great views from the gate back to Dewey Bridge and the Colorado

One of the more difficult sections of the Squaw Park Trail

River. From here, the trail is smoother as it runs alongside Yellow Jacket Canyon. This is a fun trail to drive, as the surface is firm and smooth, but there are several dips and off-camber sections to keep the driver watching the trail.

After the junction where the Kokopelli Trail leaves to the right, there is a crossing of Yellow Jacket wash that is interesting to negotiate. There are two ways down to the wash, both steep and loose. One has some large ledges at the bottom that would be difficult to climb in the other direction. The rocky pour-off from the wash crossing has some pretty views into Yellow Jacket Canyon. From here, the trail is an easy and smooth drive as it crosses Squaw Park. It climbs a ridge, with Yellow Jacket Canyon on the right, and winds through the juniper trees to the junction with Trail #24: Dome Plateau Trail. A natural arch is on the right at the end of the trail, though it is hard to see, as it is low down on the cliff face. Some of the smaller tracks to the right just before the trail ends lead down toward the arch.

Current Road Information
BLM Moab Field Office
82 East Dogwood, Suite M
Moab, UT 84532
(435) 259-2100

Map References
BLM   Moab (incomplete)
USGS 1:24,000   Dewey, Cisco SW
      (incomplete)
      1:100,000 Moab (incomplete)
Maptech CD-ROM: Moab/Canyonlands
Trails Illustrated, #501
Utah Atlas & Gazetteer, p. 41
Other: Latitude 40—Moab East
       Canyon Country Off-Road Vehicle
       Trail Map—Arches Area

Route Directions

▼ 0.0   Immediately north of Dewey Bridge on Utah 128, turn west into the Rio Colorado subdivision and zero trip meter. Immediately turn right at the first intersection.

3.7 ▲   Turn left, then trail ends at the junction with Utah 128 at Dewey Bridge. Turn right for Moab, turn left for I-70.
               GPS: N 38°48.82′ W 109°18.13′

▼ 0.4   TR   Cross through concrete ford, then immediately turn right on ungraded dirt track.

3.3 ▲   TL   Turn onto paved road in the Rio Colorado subdivision and cross through concrete ford.
               GPS: N 38°48.88′ W 109°18.54′

▼ 0.7   SO   Cross through wash, then cross through second wash and track on left.

3.0 ▲   SO   Track on right and cross through wash, then cross through second wash.

▼ 1.0   SO   Pass through gate in old fence line.

2.7 ▲   SO   Pass through gate in old fence line.
               GPS: N 38°48.80′ W 109°19.01′

▼ 1.5   SO   Cross through wash.

2.2 ▲   SO   Cross through wash.

▼ 1.6   SO   Cross through wash.
2.1 ▲   SO   Cross through wash.

▼ 2.1   SO   Track on left.
1.6 ▲   SO   Track on right.
         GPS: N 38°48.78′ W 109°19.65′

▼ 2.3   SO   Cross through wash.
1.4 ▲   SO   Cross through wash.

▼ 2.7   SO   Track on right then cross through
            wash. Trail is traveling alongside
            Yellow Jacket Canyon.
1.0 ▲   SO   Cross through wash, then track on left.
         GPS: N 38°48.98′ W 109°20.26′

▼ 3.0   SO   Cross through wash.
0.7 ▲   SO   Cross through wash.

▼ 3.1   SO   Rock arch to the right, high up on the
            sandstone escarpment.
0.6 ▲   SO   Rock arch to the left, high up on the
            sandstone escarpment.
         GPS: N 38°49.06′ W 109°20.72′

▼ 3.7   TL   Turn left at T-intersection. There is a
            hard-to-spot arch on the right at the
            junction. Zero trip meter.
0.0 ▲   Continue to the east.
         GPS: N 38°49.30′ W 109°21.26′

▼ 0.0   Continue to the west.

4.7 ▲   TR   There is a hard-to-spot arch on the left
            at the junction. Zero trip meter.

▼ 0.1   BR   Trail divides and descends to cross
            Yellow Jacket wash. Both descents
            are steep; the right-hand one is usually
            easier.
4.6 ▲   BL   Trails rejoin.

▼ 0.2   SO   Cross through Yellow Jacket wash.
            Tracks rejoin.
4.5 ▲   SO   Cross through Yellow Jacket wash, then
            trail divides. Both ascents are steep;
            the left-hand one is usually easier.
         GPS: N 38°49.29′ W 109°21.46′

▼ 0.5   SO   Cross through wash. Trail crosses
            Squaw Park.
4.2 ▲   SO   Cross through wash.

▼ 1.5   SO   Cross through wash, then track on left.
3.2 ▲   SO   Track on right, then cross through wash.
         GPS: N 38°48.82′ W 109°22.76′

▼ 1.6   SO   Track on right and faint track on left.
3.1 ▲   SO   Track on left and faint track on right.
         GPS: N 38°48.76′ W 109°22.87′

▼ 1.8   SO   Cross through wash.
2.9 ▲   SO   Cross through wash.

▼ 1.9   SO   Cross through wash.

Trail #28: Squaw Park Trail

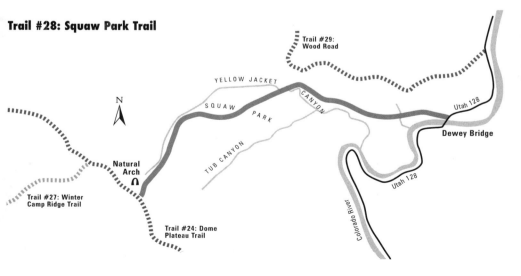

2.8 ▲	SO	Cross through wash.

▼ 2.1	SO	Cross through wash.
2.6 ▲	SO	Cross through wash.

▼ 2.2	SO	Cross through wash.
2.5 ▲	SO	Cross through wash.

▼ 2.3	SO	Cross through wash, then track on left is alternative route.
2.4 ▲	SO	Alternative route rejoins to the right, then cross through wash. Trail crosses Squaw Park.

▼ 2.5	SO	Alternative route rejoins to the left.
2.2 ▲	BL	Track on right is alternative route.
		GPS: N 38°48.78′ W 109°23.69′

▼ 2.7	SO	Cross through wash.
2.0 ▲	SO	Cross through wash. Trail runs alongside Yellow Jacket Canyon.

▼ 4.1	SO	Crossroads.
0.6 ▲	SO	Crossroads.
		GPS: N 38°47.68′ W 109°24.62′

▼ 4.2	BL	Track on right, then second track on right.
0.5 ▲	SO	Track on left, then second track on left.

▼ 4.4	BL	Track on right.
0.3 ▲	SO	Track on left.
		GPS: N 38°47.40′ W 109°24.80′

▼ 4.6	SO	Track on right.
0.1 ▲	SO	Track on left.

▼ 4.7		Trail ends at the graded Trail #24: Dome Plateau Trail. Faint trail continues on ahead. Turn left for Dome Plateau, turn right to exit 8 miles to Trail #21: Yellow Cat Road. A natural arch is on the right at the junction.
0.0 ▲		Trail starts along Trail #24: Dome Plateau Trail, 8 miles from Trail #21: Yellow Cat Road. Turn northeast on ungraded dirt trail just east of a natural arch and zero trip meter.
		GPS: N 38°47.18′ W 109°24.94′

Wood Road

STARTING POINT Utah 128, 0.1 miles north of mile marker 32

FINISHING POINT Trail #20: Yellow Cat Trail, 4.4 miles west of Utah 128

TOTAL MILEAGE 6.4 miles

UNPAVED MILEAGE 6.4 miles

DRIVING TIME 1.25 hours

ELEVATION RANGE 4,200–4,900 feet

USUALLY OPEN Year-round

DIFFICULTY RATING 4

SCENIC RATING 10

REMOTENESS RATING +0

Special Attractions

- Interesting driving over a variety of trail surfaces.
- Fantastic views along the rim over Fisher and Professor Valleys and into Squaw Park.
- Connects with the Kokopelli Trail and other 4WD trails.

Description

This moderate trail climbs up on the rim over Squaw Park and gives great views to the south, first over Professor Valley and the La Sal Mountains, and then later over Fisher Valley and Fisher Towers. Directly below is Trail #28: Squaw Park Trail running through Yellow Jacket Canyon.

The trail surface is predominantly rocky, with a couple of sections of slickrock pavement and some sand. The trail leaves Utah 128 north of Dewey Bridge and climbs up gradually to the rim overlooking Squaw Park. The major mountain bike trail, the Kokopelli Trail, follows the route for most of a mile before it diverges and continues down into Squaw Park. The trail crosses a section of sloping slickrock as it climbs to a small saddle and then swings sharp right and climbs a further steep section to the ridge. The best views are here at the top of the climb.

The final part of the trail is easier and sandy as it makes its way down to join Trail #20: Yellow Cat Trail near Owl Draw. From here, the quickest way out is to follow the last couple of miles of the Yellow Cat Trail northeast to Utah 128.

This trail is shown on some maps as the eastern end of Yellow Cat Trail. However, this trail is considerably more difficult than Yellow Cat.

Current Road Information
BLM Moab Field Office
82 East Dogwood, Suite M
Moab, UT 84532
(435) 259-2100

Map References
BLM   Moab (incomplete)
USGS   1:24,000   Dewey
        1:100,000 Moab (incomplete)
Maptech CD-ROM: Moab/Canyonlands
Trails Illustrated, #501
Utah Atlas & Gazetteer, p. 41
Other: Latitude 40—Moab East

Route Directions

▼ 0.0   From Utah 128, 0.1 miles north of mile marker 32, turn west off the highway

at a turnout. The trail climbs up the embankment above the highway to the north, then swings around to the southwest. Zero trip meter.

3.3 ▲   Trail finishes at the junction with Utah 128. Turn right for Dewey Bridge and Moab, turn left for I-70.
      GPS: N 38°49.96′ W 109°17.20′

▼ 0.1 SO Pass through wire gate.
3.2 ▲ SO Pass through wire gate.

▼ 0.6 BL Track on right.
2.7 ▲ SO Track on left.

▼ 1.0 SO Two tracks on left to viewpoints.
2.3 ▲ SO Two tracks on right to viewpoints.

▼ 1.2 SO Track on right.
2.1 ▲ SO Track on left.
      GPS: N 38°49.56′ W 109°18.24′

▼ 1.3 SO Track on left.
2.0 ▲ SO Track on right.

▼ 1.5 SO Cross through wash.
1.8 ▲ SO Cross through wash.

The landscape from a viewpoint along Wood Road

Looking back at a short, steep descent along Wood Road

▼ 1.6   SO   Cross through wash.
1.7 ▲   SO   Cross through wash.

▼ 1.9   BR   Track on left.
1.4 ▲   SO   Track on right.
        GPS: N 38°49.33' W 109°18.86'

▼ 2.2   SO   Track on left and views to the south
             toward Ninemile Bottom.
1.1 ▲   SO   Track on right and views to the south
             toward Ninemile Bottom.

▼ 2.3   SO   Track on right. Trail runs along the
             edge of the escarpment.
1.0 ▲   SO   Track on left.

▼ 2.8   SO   Cross through wash.
0.5 ▲   SO   Cross through wash.

▼ 3.0   SO   Walk to the edge for a great view into
             Squaw Park, Yellow Jacket Canyon,
             and the top end of the Professor

Valley—no formal turnout.
0.3 ▲   SO   Walk to the edge for a great view into
             Squaw Park, Yellow Jacket Canyon,
             and the top end of the Professor
             Valley—no formal turnout.
        GPS: N 38°49.42' W 109°20.15'

▼ 3.3   BL   Track on right is the Kokopelli Trail,
             which joins the main trail at this point.
             Zero trip meter.
0.0 ▲   Leave the Kokopelli Trail.
        GPS: N 38°49.50' W 109°20.33'

▼ 0.0   Continue along the Kokopelli Trail.
0.8 ▲   BR   Kokopelli Trail leaves to the left. Zero
             trip meter.

▼ 0.1   SO   Track on left goes to viewpoint.
0.7 ▲   SO   Track on right goes to viewpoint.

▼ 0.4   TL   Follow the sign for the Kokopelli Trail to
             the left.
0.4 ▲   TR   Follow the sign for the Kokopelli Trail to
             the right.
        GPS: N 38°49.70' W 109°20.65'

▼ 0.5   SO   Trail crosses slickrock pavement and is
             marked with Kokopelli route markers.

Trail #29: Wood Road

0.3 ▲	SO	End of slickrock section.
▼ 0.7	SO	End of slickrock section.
0.1 ▲	SO	Trail crosses slickrock pavement and is marked with Kokopelli route markers.
▼ 0.8	SO	Intersection. Kokopelli Trail leaves to the left. Zero trip meter.
0.0 ▲		Leave slickrock and continue straight. **GPS: N 38°49.83' W 109°21.00'**
▼ 0.0		Trail crosses slickrock pavement. Keep to the right.
2.3 ▲	SO	Intersection. Track to the right is the Kokopelli Trail, which joins the main trail at this point. Zero trip meter.
▼ 0.4	SO	Trail leaves slickrock and climbs to small saddle.
1.9 ▲	SO	Trail crosses slickrock pavement. Keep to the left.
▼ 0.6	TR	Swing hard right at saddle and climb steep short pinch to top of ridge.
1.7 ▲	TL	Swing hard left at saddle. **GPS: N 38°49.72' W 109°21.70'**
▼ 0.7	SO	Top of ridge. Great views!
1.6 ▲	SO	Descend steep short pinch to saddle.
▼ 1.5	BL	Track on right.
0.8 ▲	SO	Track on left. **GPS: N 38°50.35' W 109°21.41'**
▼ 1.7	SO	Track on right.
0.6 ▲	SO	Track on left. **GPS: N 38°50.45' W 109°21.42'**
▼ 2.3		Cross through wash, then trail ends at intersection with Trail #20: Yellow Cat Trail, 4.4 miles from Utah 128.
0.0 ▲		Trail commences at Trail #20: Yellow Cat Trail, 4.4 miles west from Utah 128. Zero trip meter, and turn south on unmarked, ungraded sandy trail. **GPS: N 38°50.93' W 109°21.28'**

Cache Valley Trail

STARTING POINT Arches National Park
FINISHING POINT Cache Valley
TOTAL MILEAGE 3.6 miles
UNPAVED MILEAGE 3.6 miles
DRIVING TIME 45 minutes (one-way)
ELEVATION RANGE 4,400–5,000 feet
USUALLY OPEN Year-round
DIFFICULTY RATING 4
SCENIC RATING 8
REMOTENESS RATING +0

Special Attractions

■ Views along the wide Cache Valley.
■ View of Delicate Arch.
■ Interesting side trail to add to a day in Arches National Park.

Description

This short spur trail is an enjoyable side trip to a day in Arches National Park. It leaves from the end of the paved road to Delicate Arch and descends to Cache Valley Wash running along Cache Valley. It runs along the wash, crossing it frequently. The trail then turns to the south and climbs toward Dry Mesa. This route finishes on a ridge with a great view back along Cache Valley to Arches National Park. The trail does continue up onto the mesa, but it is very steep and because it is so difficult, it is well beyond the scope of this book.

It is possible to continue along the wash in Cache Valley for another mile before it becomes too narrow for vehicles.

Current Road Information

Arches National Park
PO Box 907
Moab, UT 84532
(435) 719-2299

Map References

BLM Moab
USGS 1:24,000 The Windows Section, Big Bend
1:100,000 Moab

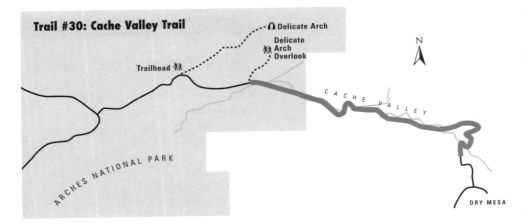

Trail #30: Cache Valley Trail

Maptech CD-ROM: Moab/Canyonlands
Trails Illustrated, #211; 501
Utah Atlas & Gazetteer, p. 40
Utah Travel Council #5 (incomplete)
Other: Latitude 40—Moab East

Route Directions

▼ 0.0   From the end of the paved road to Delicate Arch, zero trip meter and continue on the ungraded dirt Cache Valley Road.
    GPS: N 38°44.01′ W 109°30.05′

▼ 0.1 SO Cross through small wash. View of Delicate Arch to the left.
    GPS: N 38°44.00′ W 109°29.91′

▼ 0.4 SO Trail enters wash and runs alongside or in it, crossing it frequently, for the next 1.3 miles.

▼ 0.6 SO Pass through gate, please keep closed. Boundary of Arches National Park.
    GPS: N 38°43.87′ W 109°29.42′

▼ 1.7 SO Leave wash and follow south side of Cache Valley.

▼ 2.1 SO Cross through small tributary wash.

▼ 2.6 BL Trail forks around washed-out section.

▼ 2.7 SO Alternative routes rejoin.

▼ 2.9 SO Track to the left continues along the wash for another mile before becoming too narrow for vehicles. Zero trip meter.
    GPS: N 38°43.53′ W 109°27.21′

▼ 0.0   Continue along Cache Valley.

▼ 0.5 BR Enter wash and swing right, then swing left out of wash along trail.

Sandstone spires along the snowy trail

Some vehicles go straight across, which is harder. Look back to see a cave or mine, with a short dead-end tunnel in the cliff.

▼ 0.7   Harder trail rejoins on left. Trail continues and climbs very steeply up to Dry Mesa. The extremely difficult climb has very large ledges and deep holes and gullies that take it beyond the scope of the book. Turn around at this viewpoint over Cache Valley and retrace your steps back to Delicate Arch.

GPS: N 38°43.26′ W 109°27.27′

The Wine Glass Arch

MOAB REGION TRAIL #31

Anticline Overlook Trail

STARTING POINT Needles Overlook Road (CR 133), 14.5 miles from US 191
FINISHING POINT Anticline Overlook
TOTAL MILEAGE 15.6 miles
UNPAVED MILEAGE 15.6 miles
DRIVING TIME 1 hour (one-way)
ELEVATION RANGE 5,500–6,300 feet
USUALLY OPEN Year-round
DIFFICULTY RATING 1
SCENIC RATING 10
REMOTENESS RATING +0

Special Attractions
- Easy trail to spectacular viewpoint at the Anticline Overlook.
- Access to a number of 4WD trails and backcountry campsites.
- Wine Glass Arch.

History
In 1881, Alonzo Hatch settled near a spring in the northwest section of Dry Valley and gave his name to Hatch Point, Hatch Wash, and Hatch Rock. Hatch Wash was also known as Hudson Wash after a local character called Spud Hudson, who always carried a potato in his pocket!

The Dave Minor Overlook near the end of the trail was named by Fran Barnes after a recreation officer in the BLM.

Description
This easy trail follows a graded gravel road to the panoramic Anticline Overlook. The trail, which is suitable for passenger vehicles, gradually descends over the sagebrush benches of Hatch Point to the overlook. The views are not confined to the overlook at the end of the trail. From the start, you get glimpses into Lockhart Basin and of the Henry Mountains beyond; a couple of marked turnouts farther on have spectacular views of the deep Dripping Spring Canyon and the Colorado River. To the north of the trail, the La Sal Mountains rise up in direct contrast to the jumbled boulders of the Behind The Rocks area.

Halfway along the trail is the BLM's Hatch Point Campground. This small campground has several sites scattered along an escarpment just off the trail. There is limited shade, but it is a pleasant place to camp (fee required).

The Anticline Overlook itself has some scattered picnic tables in the small juniper trees. A short scramble leads to the fenced overlook and its staggering views. To the west, you can see Trail #50: Chicken Corners Trail far below, as well as the Colorado River with the Island in the Sky district of Canyonlands National Park and Dead

Horse Point rising up behind. To the north, the view stretches over the lower reaches of Kane Springs Canyon through The Portal in the Moab Rim to Arches National Park. Moab can be glimpsed through The Portal. Trail #49: Hurrah Pass Trail can clearly be seen. To the east is Kane Springs Canyon and the La Sal Mountains.

For an easily accessible, awe-inspiring viewpoint, this one is hard to beat!

Current Road Information
BLM Moab Field Office
82 East Dogwood, Suite M
Moab, UT 84532
(435) 259-2100

Map References
BLM   La Sal
USGS 1:24,000   Eightmile Rock, Shafer
       Basin, Trough Springs Canyon
       1:100,000 La Sal
Maptech CD-ROM: Moab/Canyonlands
Trails Illustrated, #501 (incomplete)
Utah Atlas & Gazetteer, p. 30
Utah Travel Council #5
Other: Latitude 40—Moab West
       (incomplete)
       Canyon Country Off-Road Vehicle
       Trail Map—Canyon Rims &
       Needles Areas

Route Directions

▼ 0.0   From the Needles Overlook Road (CR 133), 14.5 miles from US 191, turn northwest onto graded gravel road and zero trip meter.
         GPS: N 38°15.45' W 109°34.84'

▼ 0.1   SO Track on right is Trail #32: Eightmile Road.
▼ 1.1   SO Faint track on right.
▼ 2.3   SO Track on left.
         GPS: N 38°17.44' W 109°35.08'

▼ 2.7   SO Faint track on left.
▼ 2.8   SO Faint track on left.
▼ 3.2   SO Track on left.
▼ 3.5   SO Track on left.
▼ 4.0   SO Track on right goes to corral, then track on left.
▼ 4.5   SO Cattle guard.
         GPS: N 38°19.35' W 109°35.95'

▼ 4.8   SO Views on left into Lockhart Basin.
         GPS: N 38°19.64' W 109°36.06'

▼ 4.9   SO Track on right.
▼ 5.7   SO Track on right.
▼ 6.7   SO Track on right.
▼ 7.8   SO Track on right and track on left.
         GPS: N 38°22.19' W 109°37.05'

The view from the Dave Minor Overlook encompasses the Colorado River, Dripping Springs Canyon, and Chicken Corners Trail

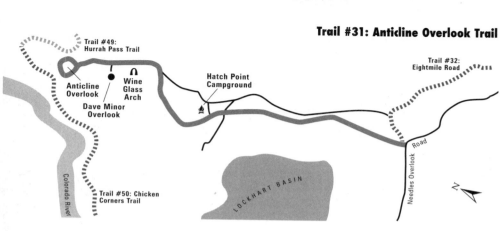

▼ 8.0	SO	Track on right goes to Hatch Point Campground (fee area). Zero trip meter. **GPS: N 38°22.35' W 109°37.23'**

▼ 0.0		Continue to the Anticline Overlook.
▼ 0.9	SO	Track on left, then track on right.
▼ 1.8	SO	Track on left.
▼ 2.8	SO	Track on left, then second gravel track on left goes to Dripping Spring Canyon overlook; potash works are on far side of Colorado River.
▼ 3.7	SO	Track on right is Trough Springs track. **GPS: N 38°24.72' W 109°36.25**

▼ 3.9	SO	Cattle guard.
▼ 4.0	SO	Track on right.
▼ 4.7	SO	Track on right.
▼ 4.9	SO	Track on right.
▼ 5.2	SO	Track on right, then the Wine Glass Arch is on the left. **GPS: N 38°25.93' W 109°36.50'**

▼ 5.9	SO	Graded gravel road on left goes short distance to the Dave Minor Overlook. Zero trip meter. **GPS: N 38°26.50' W 109°36.77'**

▼ 0.0		Continue to Anticline Overlook.
▼ 1.4	SO	Cattle guard.
▼ 1.6	BR	Start of loop at end of overlook.
▼ 1.7		End of trail at start of hiking trail out to the overlook. **GPS: N 38°27.91' W 109°37.60'**

MOAB REGION TRAIL #32

Eightmile Road

STARTING POINT CR 171, 0.1 miles along Trail #31: Anticline Overlook Trail
FINISHING POINT US 191
TOTAL MILEAGE 16.5 miles
UNPAVED MILEAGE 16.5 miles
DRIVING TIME 1 hour
ELEVATION RANGE 5,600–6,300 feet
USUALLY OPEN Year-round
DIFFICULTY RATING 2
SCENIC RATING 8
REMOTENESS RATING +0

Special Attractions
- Large arch in Looking Glass Rock.
- Rock dwellings in Eightmile Rock and Hatch Rock.
- Access to numerous 4WD spur trails over Hatch Wash.

History
Hatch Rock, like Hatch Point and Hatch Wash, was named for Alonzo Hatch, whose small ranch stood just west of Hatch Rock in the 1880s. The rock was also used as a navigation point by the Macomb Expedition of 1859.

As you approach the rock, it appears there are several "houses" set right up against it. As you get closer, however, you will see that the doors and windows are actually in the rock,

Looking along the face of dugout dwellings in Eightmile Rock

which is now home to a small alternative community called Rocklands Ranch, a group founded by Bob Foster in 1974. The inhabitants live in dwellings dug, tunneled, and dynamited into Hatch Rock. The government has granted the group a 50-year lease for dwelling purposes. The community has well water, propane for cooking, and solar units for heating.

Description

This trail follows county roads from the beginning of Trail #31: Anticline Overlook Trail east to US 191. Eightmile Road first leaves the Anticline Overlook Trail and follows the graded dirt road (CR 171) to the northeast. After a mile, it passes Eightmile Rock. To the left at this point are some dwellings tunneled into the rock. One digging is used as a small cabin; the others are used as feed storage for cattle.

The road descends the bench, crossing many small washes. The surface is graded dirt, easily passable when dry by a high-clearance vehicle, but add moisture and the surface deteriorates to sticky mud and is often impassable. There are many spur trails as the road travels along Hatch Point; many leading northeast go to overlooks of Hatch Wash.

After 7.8 miles, the road (CR 132) swings east, where it meets another graded county road (CR 135) from the south. On the left is Hatch Rock and the community of Rocklands Ranch. The trail follows Wind Whistle Draw until it joins in with the larger Hatch Wash.

The next major feature on the trail is the large Looking Glass Rock, which has a large arch on the southeast corner. A short loop track takes you to the base of the arch, and it

View of the moon and adventurer through Looking Glass Rock

is an easy scramble over the slickrock to the window. There is a long drop on the far side! The trail finishes 1.8 miles farther on, at the junction with US 191.

Current Road Information
BLM Moab Field Office
82 East Dogwood, Suite M
Moab, UT 84532
(435) 259-2100

Map References
BLM   La Sal
USGS 1:24,000   Eightmile Rock, Harts
          Point North, Hatch Rock, La Sal
          Junction
          1:100,000 La Sal
Maptech CD-ROM: Moab/Canyonlands
Trails Illustrated, #501 (incomplete)
Utah Atlas & Gazetteer, pp. 30, 31
Utah Travel Council #5
Other: Latitude 40—Moab West
          (incomplete)
          Latitude 40—Moab East
          (incomplete)
          Canyon Country Off-Road Vehicle
          Trail Map—Canyon Rims &
          Needles Area

Route Directions

▼ 0.0   0.1 miles from the start of Trail #31: Anticline Overlook Trail, turn northeast on graded dirt road (CR 171), following the sign for Eightmile Rock, and zero trip meter.

7.8 ▲   Trail finishes 0.1 miles from the start of Trail #31: Anticline Overlook Trail. Turn right to continue to the Anticline Overlook. Turn left on CR 133 to reach US 191.
          GPS: N 38°15.52' W 109°34.92'

▼ 0.5   SO Track on right.
7.3 ▲   SO Track on left.

▼ 1.1   BR Track on left at Eightmile Rock. Small cabin and farm sheds set into the rock itself, just up the track on the left.
6.7 ▲   SO Track on right at Eightmile Rock. Small cabin and farm sheds set into the rock itself, just up the track on the left.
          GPS: N 38°16.29' W 109°34.08'

▼ 1.6   SO Track on right.
6.2 ▲   SO Track on left.

Trail #32: Eightmile Road

▼ 2.4   SO Track on left and faint track on right.
5.4 ▲   SO Track on right and faint track on left.

▼ 2.6   SO Track on left.
5.2 ▲   SO Track on right.

▼ 2.8   SO Track on right and track on left.
5.0 ▲   SO Track on left and track on right.

▼ 3.6   SO Track on right, then cross through
            Threemile Creek.
4.2 ▲   SO Cross through Threemile Creek, then
            track on left.
            GPS: N 38°15.06' W 109°31.75'

▼ 4.6   SO Track on left.
3.2 ▲   SO Track on right.

▼ 4.7   SO Track on right and corral on left.
3.1 ▲   SO Track on left and corral on right.
            GPS: N 38°14.43' W 109°30.81'

▼ 5.1   SO Cross over Little Water Creek.
2.7 ▲   SO Cross over Little Water Creek.

▼ 5.9   SO Track on left.
1.9 ▲   SO Track on right.

▼ 6.8   SO Track on left goes to Little Rock Reservoir.
1.0 ▲   SO Track on right goes to Little Rock
            Reservoir.
            GPS: N 38°13.31' W 109°29.14'

▼ 7.0   SO Cattle guard.
0.8 ▲   SO Cattle guard.

▼ 7.6   SO Cross over creek.
0.2 ▲   SO Cross over creek.

▼ 7.8   SO Track on right is CR 135. Zero trip meter.
0.0 ▲   Continue toward Eightmile Rock.
            GPS: N 38°12.78' W 109°28.32'

▼ 0.0   Continue toward Hatch Rock.
6.9 ▲   BR Track on left is CR 135. Zero trip meter.

▼ 0.3   SO Track on left goes to Hatch Rock and
            Rocklands Ranch community.
6.6 ▲   SO Track on right goes to Hatch Rock and
            Rocklands Ranch community.

GPS: N 38°12.91' W 109°27.98'

▼ 1.2   SO Track on left.
5.7 ▲   SO Track on right.

▼ 2.1   SO Trail runs alongside Hatch Wash.
4.8 ▲   SO Trail runs alongside Hatch Wash.

▼ 3.0   SO Cross through wash.
3.9 ▲   SO Cross through wash.

▼ 3.9   SO Track on right. Trail is now CR 131.
3.0 ▲   SO Track on left. Trail is now CR 132.
            GPS: N 38°14.18' W 109°25.50'

▼ 6.6   SO Cattle guard. Looking Glass Rock on right.
0.3 ▲   SO Cattle guard. Looking Glass Rock on left.

▼ 6.8   SO Track on right goes to base of Looking
            Glass Rock and arch.
0.1 ▲   SO Track on left goes to base of Looking
            Glass Rock and arch.

▼ 6.9   SO Graded track on right goes to Looking
            Glass Rock and arch. Zero trip meter.
0.0 ▲   Continue toward Hatch Rock.
            GPS: N 38°16.59' W 109°24.38'

▼ 0.0   Continue toward US 191.
1.8 ▲   BR Graded track on left goes to Looking
            Glass Rock and arch. Zero trip meter.

▼ 0.4   SO Track on right, then cross pipeline.
1.4 ▲   SO Cross pipeline, then track on left.

▼ 0.8   SO Track on right.
1.0 ▲   SO Track on left.

▼ 1.1   SO Track on left through gate.
0.7 ▲   SO Track on right through gate.

▼ 1.8   Cross cattle guard, then trail ends at
            intersection with US 191, 0.6 miles
            south of La Sal Junction.
0.0 ▲   From US 191, at the sign for Looking
            Glass Road, 0.6 miles south of La Sal
            Junction, turn southwest on graded CR
            131 and zero trip meter.
            GPS: N 38°18.11' W 109°23.67'

Elephant Hill Loop

STARTING POINT Elephant Hill Trailhead, Canyonlands National Park

FINISHING POINT Elephant Hill Trailhead, Canyonlands National Park

TOTAL MILEAGE 7.3 miles

UNPAVED MILEAGE 7.3 miles

DRIVING TIME 6 hours (entire loop)

ELEVATION RANGE 5,000–5,400 feet

USUALLY OPEN Year-round

DIFFICULTY RATING 7

SCENIC RATING 9

REMOTENESS RATING +0

Special Attractions

- Extremely challenging and technical trail.
- Canyonlands National Park.
- Spectacular red rock scenery along Devil's Lane.

History

Elephant Hill was originally a cattle trail forged to gain grazing access to Chesler Park and the Grabens. In the 1940s Al Scorup of the Dugout Ranch contracted a bulldozer to improve the cattle trail over Elephant Hill. The trail passes along "grabens," which are down-dropped sections between elevated fault lines. The trail took its name from the rounded formations on the many sides of the hill, which reminded the stockmen of the tops of elephant heads. The Silver Stairs farther along the trail were named because of the silvery color of the ledges in certain light.

The Moab Jeep Safari, held every Easter, has special permission from the National Park Service to include this trail in their program.

Description

This extremely challenging and difficult trail is nevertheless passable for an experienced driver in a high-clearance stock SUV with good tires. The trail is short, but it will still take the best part of a day to drive, especially if you take the side trail to the confluence

of the Colorado and Green Rivers. Elephant Hill is one trail on which you want to have a camera or better still a video—most people will be amazed at what their vehicle can do!

The hills provide the challenge on this trail, and Elephant Hill itself is only the first. These hills are very steep and extremely rocky, with large rocks, ledges, and holes to negotiate. The National Park Service has filled in the worst of the trail with concrete so that park vehicles can get over it, but do not underestimate the trail—it is still extremely difficult. Although the NPS uses a modified Jeep Wrangler, most robust 4WDs will be able to handle it. However, extra clearance is a definite advantage; low-hanging winch bars or side steps will increase the difficulty. Careful wheel placement is needed all along this trail to avoid scraping the undercarriage. The "Squeezeplay," where the trail passes through an extremely narrow crevice in the rock for about 100 yards, is very tight for larger vehicles. We drove through in a Land Rover Discovery, but not before we had first measured the widest part of the vehicle against the width of the gap. We estimated the Land Rover needed 77

A narrow section of the Elephant Hill Loop

Jeep trail sign at the top of the hill

inches, not including mirrors, to fit through, and we only had a scant couple of inches to spare on each side. The narrowness is made worse by the fact that the trail is seriously off-camber in the gap, tilting a vehicle over and effectively increasing its width. There are no alternate routes around this or any of the obstacles along the trail.

The trail lets you know immediately what you are in for, as it leaves the Elephant Hill parking area and climbs steeply. The first switchback has been modified by the NPS into a flat concrete turning area, so the first turn is easy. Continue up the hill. At the top of Elephant Hill, a small Jeep sign points the way down. The descent is far steeper, rockier, and more difficult than the ascent—and remember, you have to come back up it at the end! In fact, the ascent on the return trip is possibly the most difficult section on the entire trail. Stop at the top and take a look down before committing yourself. If you are unsure about your own or your vehicle's ability to return back up this hill, there is still time to turn around. The stretch to study is from the top down to the first "Pull Up and Back Down" sign. The park service says that towing fees for vehicles stranded here typically exceed $1,500! The "Pull In and Back

Up" sign, at the halfway point, marks the notorious stretch where the switchback is too tight for a vehicle to make the turn. Vehicles are required to pull up and then back down for approximately 100 yards, then back up and continue on in the normal forward manner! Returning vehicles must make the same maneuver. Luckily the section of trail you have to back along is flatter, wider, and easier than the rest, but it's still an interesting challenge.

Once past Elephant Hill, the trail is easy and sandy as it runs along in spectacular country. It passes the end of the loop and becomes one-way only as it follows a small creek, crossing the creek bed a couple of times; there are plenty of interesting sections here but nothing terribly difficult until the next hill. This hill is again steep and has very large boulders that must be climbed and deep holes to be avoided. It is also extremely loose. At the top it passes underneath a rocky overhang before descending again.

All along the Elephant Hill Loop, previous drivers have stacked rocks to help ease their vehicles up or down the worst of the rock ledges. Most drivers will need to adjust these rocks to best fit the wheel placement

Looking up at Elephant Hill from the first switchback

of their vehicle—so having a passenger to "spot" for you and move some rocks around is a definite advantage! In between the obstacles there are some long sections of easy sand driving.

Half a mile after this second difficult hill, you reach the Squeezeplay. Note that the far end is very off camber and can catch the unwary—wider vehicles will need to watch the roofline on the rock on the right.

Just past the Squeezeplay is the farthest point of the loop and the junction with Trail #34: Bobby's Hole and Ruin Park Trail.

The return trip along the second half of the loop is a lot easier than the way out. The trail runs along Devil's Lane before squeezing through another narrow canyon in the rock, although this looks like a freeway after the Squeezeplay! The Silver Stairs is a wide descent over some rock ledges, but there is a good line and the ledges are small and should not cause anyone any trouble who has made it this far. Next you reach the junction with the Confluence Overlook Trail, a 3-mile spur trail that goes to an overlook at the confluence of the Green and Colorado Rivers. The return section of the loop follows in or alongside a sandy wash for most of its way; there is only one other hill that is tricky, and it appears just after the Confluence Overlook Trail. The trail descends over steep slickrock before wrapping around to descend a loose ledgy hill. Again, this hill is easier than the ones encountered so far.

At the end of the loop, turn left to retrace your path over Elephant Hill and back to the trailhead.

The National Park Service does not allow pets on the trail, even in a vehicle, and an overnight permit is required if you are planning to camp at the campground at Devil's Kitchen. The trail can be open year-round, but may be closed due to snow for short periods. If in doubt, check ahead.

Current Road Information

Canyonlands National Park
Needles Ranger District
(435) 259-4711

Map References

BLM   La Sal
USGS 1:24,000   The Loop
          1:100,000 La Sal
Maptech CD-ROM: Moab/Canyonlands
Trails Illustrated, #210
Utah Atlas & Gazetteer, p. 30
Utah Travel Council #5 (incomplete)
Other: Canyon Country Off-Road Vehicle
          Trail Map—Canyon Rims &
          Needles Areas

Route Directions

▼ 0.0   Follow the park signs for Elephant Hill from The Needles visitor center to Elephant Hill Trailhead and picnic area. Zero trip meter at the picnic area, and proceed to climb up the 4WD trail.
GPS: N 38°08.51' W 109°49.64'

▼ 0.1   BR Sharp switchback with turning area straight ahead.

▼ 0.3   SO Top of Elephant Hill. Trail is sandy dirt as it runs along the top.
GPS: N 38°08.52' W 109°49.75'

▼ 0.5   SO Descent of Elephant Hill is marked by small Jeep marker.
GPS: N 38°08.66' W 109°49.98'

▼ 0.6   SO "Pull Up and Back Down" sign—pull forward and then reverse down the trail for approximately 100 yards.
GPS: N 38°08.72' W 109°50.00'

▼ 0.7   SO "Pull In and Back Up" sign—drive forward from this point. If approaching, pull in and back up trail approximately 100 yards.
GPS: N 38°08.73' W 109°49.99'

▼ 0.8   SO End of descent from Elephant Hill.
GPS: N 38°08.74' W 109°50.02'

▼ 1.1   SO Cross through wash.
▼ 1.2   SO Cross through wash.
▼ 1.4   SO Track on right is end of loop. Trail is now one-way. Zero trip meter.
GPS: N 38°09.10' W 109°50.52'

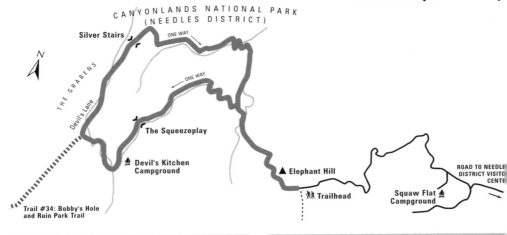

▼ 0.0   Continue along trail to the northwest.
▼ 0.7   SO   Cross through wash.
▼ 1.1   SO   Start of second difficult hill climb.
▼ 1.7   SO   The Squeezeplay.
          GPS: N 38°08.24' W 109°51.64'

▼ 1.8   TR   Track on left goes into Devil's Kitchen Campground, permit required. Trail is now two-way.
          GPS: N 38°08.22' W 109°51.65'

▼ 2.4   TR   T-intersection with Devil's Lane. Track on left is Trail #34: Bobby's Hole and Ruin Park Trail. Zero trip meter.
          GPS: N 38°08.44' W 109°52.05'

▼ 0.0   Continue northeast along Devil's Lane.
▼ 0.7   SO   Enter narrow passage of sandstone.
▼ 0.8   SO   Exit narrow passage of sandstone.
▼ 1.3   SO   Top of the Silver Stairs.
          GPS: N 38°09.40' W 109°51.81'

▼ 1.4   SO   Bottom of the Silver Stairs.
▼ 1.5   TR   Trail straight on is the Confluence Overlook Trail. Zero trip meter.
          GPS: N 38°09.52' W 109°51.68'

▼ 0.0   Continue toward the end of the loop. Trail is now one-way.
▼ 0.2   SO   Descend rocky hill.
▼ 0.3   SO   End of descent. For the next 1.7 miles the trail crosses the wash many times.
          GPS: N 38°09.38' W 109°51.51'

▼ 2.0   TL   End of loop, turn left to retrace your steps over Elephant Hill toward trailhead.
          GPS: N 38°09.10' W 109°50.52'

MOAB REGION TRAIL #34

Bobby's Hole and Ruin Park Trail

STARTING POINT Canyonlands National Park, Trail #33: Elephant Hill Loop
FINISHING POINT Junction with Trail #36: Beef Basin Trail
TOTAL MILEAGE 16.3 miles
UNPAVED MILEAGE 16.3 miles
DRIVING TIME 3 hours
ELEVATION RANGE 5,200–6,600 feet
USUALLY OPEN May to November
DIFFICULTY RATING 7
SCENIC RATING 9
REMOTENESS RATING +1

Special Attractions

- 4WD trail within the Needles district of Canyonlands National Park.
- Ancient pictographs and Anasazi ruins in Ruin Park.
- Extremely challenging stretch of trail at Bobby's Hole.

History

Evidence of early Native Americans abounds on this trail. The handprint pictographs under the rock overhang near the start of the trail are from the Fremont Indians and are about two thousand years old. There are two sorts of prints, both dating from the same time period. In one, the hand was held against the rock and color was blown through a reed to make an outline of the hand. In the other, the hand was dipped in paint and pressed against the rock to make a solid print.

The lack of year-round water and the difficult access has kept the human presence in the region low. Along with those on nearby Elephant Hill, today's 4WD access routes were once cow trails used by cattle ranchers as early as the mid-1880s. Chesler Park, now within the national park, was used as winter pasture by settler Tom Trout, an ex-Texan then residing in nearby Indian Creek.

Various other settlers came, improved, and sold out until the main name in the region was the S&S Co., the Somerville and Scorup Cattle Company. Under the direction of Al Scorup, the more difficult sections of the trails were bulldozed through in the 1940s. Chesler Park was apparently used as an airstrip for ease of access during the bulldozing operations.

The ancient Anasazi tower in Ruin Park, like others in the region, was sometimes referred to as a "castle" by the early European explorers. Whether the tower was used as a fort, an observation point, a granary, a ceremonial chamber, or for other purposes is not known. Those with sufficient time may like to explore the side trails in Ruin Park. Many of them lead to other Anasazi ruins.

Today, Bobby's Hole and Ruin Park are the winter pastures for cattle from Dugout Ranch, near Cottonwood Canyon.

Description

This trail provides a connection between Trail #33: Elephant Hill Loop in the Needles district of Canyonlands National Park and Trail #36: Beef Basin Trail, which leads to Trail #35: Cottonwood Canyon Trail. However, although most of the trail is relatively easy, there is an extremely difficult, 7-rated climb out of Bobby's Hole into Ruin Park that may be impassable. If you wish, approach this spot from the moderate, 3-rated Beef Basin Trail. Though still difficult, the descent of the loose, steep hill into Bobby's Hole from Ruin Park should not cause too many problems. However, drivers who choose to come this way solve one problem only to confront another: they must be prepared to exit via the equally difficult, 7-rated Elephant Hill Loop, because they may find it impossible to turn around and climb back out of Bobby's Hole. See Trail #33: Elephant Hill Loop for a description of and warnings about this extremely technical trail. Those who wish to visit Ruin Park without confronting the difficult driving at Bobby's Hole (from either di-

The Bobby's Hole and Ruin Park Trail winds along the jagged terrain of Devil's Lane

Rock formations of Devil's Lane

rection) can approach via Trail #36: Beef Basin Trail and then proceed along the Bobby's Hole and Ruin Park Trail, turning back before the descent into Bobby's Hole.

A final word of caution—the minimum towing charge in this region is in excess of $1,500, so it pays to know the limits of your driving and your vehicle's ability before you go.

Warnings aside, this is a lovely, scenic, historic trail. The trail starts at the farthest point of the Elephant Hill Loop in The Needles district of Canyonlands National Park. The sandy track runs along Devil's Lane, a row of jagged sandstone spires. Just before a difficult zigzag hill, there is a series of pictographs under an overhang to the right of the trail. These are mainly handprints, both solid and silhouette on the rock.

The trail crosses many sandy washes as it goes toward the park boundary. It passes by the primitive national park campgrounds at Bobby Jo and Horsehoof Arch and crosses Chesler Park. This section is mainly easy going, although there is one very nasty, axle-twisting, off-camber turn over large rocks and loose sand.

Bobby's Hole is reached 1.6 miles after leaving the national park. The difficult section can clearly be seen as you climb steeply out of the basin. It is advisable to walk it first to see firsthand the current condition of the trail. This climb has very loose, deep sand washouts, and a steep grade. Just when your vehicle will be bogging down and losing traction near the top, there are large rock ledges to negotiate, very loose rubble, and then a sharp turn to the left! If you still have forward motion at this point—relax, you've made it! At the top of the climb there is a sign warning vehicles traveling in the other direction about the difficulties of the trail. If you are traveling in the other direction, from Beef Basin Trail, and do not want to tackle Elephant Hill—this is your signal to turn back.

Once out of Bobby's Hole, the route is an easier 3-rated trail. It runs along open Ruin Park, where many tracks lead right and left to pleasant campsites and to numerous Anasazi ruins in the area. It is worth taking the time to explore some of these trails.

The well-known landmark of the Anasazi tower is to the right of the trail, at the edge of the trees. The trail gets easier until it finishes at the well-marked junction with the Beef Basin Trail. Travelers who have come through from Elephant Hill in wet weather should be aware that the exit through the Manti-La Sal National Forest travels over some graded dirt shelf road that is extremely greasy, if not impassable, after rain.

An alternative name for this trail on some maps is Hushaby Road, or CR 119.

Current Road Information

Canyonlands National Park
Needles Ranger District
(435) 259-4711

Map References

BLM   La Sal, Blanding
USGS 1:24,000   House Park Butte, Druid
           Arch, Cross Canyon, Spanish
           Bottom, The Loop
           1:100,000 La Sal, Blanding
Maptech CD-ROM: Moab/Canyonlands
Trails Illustrated, #210
Utah Atlas & Gazetteer, p. 30
Other: Canyon Country Off-Road Vehicle
        Trail Map—Canyon Rims &
        Needles Areas

0.0		At the farthest point of Trail #33: Elephant Hill Loop, turn southwest along Devil's Lane, following the sign for Chesler Park. Zero trip meter.
0 ▲		Trail ends at the farthest point along Trail #33: Elephant Hill Loop. Continue straight ahead for the Elephant Hill Loop.

GPS: N 38°08.44' W 109°52.05'

0.8	SO	Pull in to the right to view handprint pictographs under the overhang.
2 ▲	SO	Pull in to the left to view handprint pictographs under the overhang.

GPS: N 38°07.72' W 109°52.52'

0.9	SO	Short zigzag hill through gap. Vehicles may need to back up to turn.
1 ▲	SO	Short zigzag hill through gap. Vehicles may need to back up to turn.

1.6	SO	Cross through wash. Many sandy wash crossings in the next 1.2 miles.
4 ▲	SO	End of wash crossings.

2.5	SO	Devil's Kitchen hiking trail on left.

4.5 ▲	SO	Devil's Kitchen hiking trail on right.

GPS: N 38°06.68' W 109°52.14'

▼ 2.8	BR	Chesler Park hiking trail on left. Follow sign to Beef Basin and cross wash.
4.2 ▲	BL	Cross wash, then Chesler Park hiking trail on right. Many sandy wash crossings in the next 1.2 miles.

GPS: N 38°06.52' W 109°52.26'

▼ 3.5	SO	Difficult off-camber section.
3.5 ▲	SO	Difficult off-camber section.

▼ 4.0	SO	Bobby Jo Campground on right.
3.0 ▲	SO	Bobby Jo Campground on left.

GPS: N 38°05.56' W 109°52.82'

▼ 4.1	SO	Horsehoof Arch hiking trail and campground on right.
2.9 ▲	SO	Horsehoof Arch hiking trail and campground on left.

GPS: N 38°05.53' W 109°52.86'

▼ 4.3	SO	Cross through wash.
2.7 ▲	SO	Cross through wash.

▼ 5.7	SO	Cross through wash.
1.3 ▲	SO	Cross through wash.

Trail #34: Bobby's Hole and Ruin Park Trail

Trail #33: Elephant Hill Loop

CHESLER CANYON

Butler Wash

Pictographs ●

Bobby Jo Campground

Horsehoof Arch Campground

CANYONLANDS NATIONAL PARK (NEEDLES DISTRICT)

Trail #36: Beef Basin Trail

RUIN PARK

BEEF BASIN

▲ Anasazi Tower

BOBBY'S HOLE

N

▼ 7.0   SO Gate. Leaving Canyonlands National Park, entering BLM land. Zero trip meter.

0.0 ▲   Continue into the national park.

GPS: N 38°03.69′ W 109°54.99′

▼ 0.0   Continue toward Bobby's Hole.

6.6 ▲   SO Gate. Entering Canyonlands National Park. Camping is restricted to campgrounds and requires a backcountry permit. Zero trip meter.

▼ 0.5   SO Track on left goes to campsite.

6.1 ▲   SO Track on right goes to campsite.

▼ 1.1   SO Corral on right. Entering Bobby's Hole.

5.5 ▲   SO Corral on left. Leaving Bobby's Hole.

▼ 1.2   SO Track on right.

5.4 ▲   SO Track on left.

▼ 1.6   BL Track on right. Trail swings left and climbs steeply out of Bobby's Hole. This climb may be impassable to 4WD vehicles.

5.0 ▲   BR End of descent. Track on left at bottom of hill.

GPS: N 38°02.59′ W 109°56.22′

▼ 1.8   SO Top of climb.

4.8 ▲   SO Final warning sign and start of difficult descent into Bobby's Hole. Vehicles that continue past this point must be prepared to exit via Elephant Hill. See Trail #33: Elephant Hill Loop.

GPS: N 38°02.43′ W 109°56.24′

▼ 2.0   SO Track on left.

4.6 ▲   SO Track on right.

▼ 2.5   SO Campsite on right. Trail standard is now easier.

4.1 ▲   SO Campsite on left. Trail is getting harder. First warning sign about continuing on trail.

GPS: N 38°02.05′ W 109°56.36′

▼ 3.0   BR Track on left.

3.6 ▲   BL Track on right.

GPS: N 38°02.14′ W 109°55.85′

▼ 3.2   SO Entering Ruin Park.

3.4 ▲   SO Leaving Ruin Park.

▼ 3.4   SO Cross through wash.

3.2 ▲   SO Cross through wash.

▼ 3.9   SO Track on right goes to small ruin.

2.7 ▲   SO Track on left goes to small ruin.

▼ 4.5   SO Cross through wash.

2.1 ▲   SO Cross through wash.

▼ 5.0   SO Track on right goes to campsite.

1.6 ▲   SO Track on left goes to campsite.

GPS: N 38°01.14′ W 109°54.74′

▼ 5.6   SO Track on right.

1.0 ▲   SO Track on left.

GPS: N 38°00.67′ W 109°54.53′

▼ 6.0   SO Track on right.

0.6 ▲   SO Track on left.

▼ 6.6   SO Track on right goes to Anasazi tower. Zero trip meter.

0.0 ▲   Continue toward Bobby's Hole.

GPS: N 38°00.39′ W 109°53.84′

▼ 0.0   Continue toward Beef Basin.

2.7 ▲   SO Track on left goes to Anasazi tower. Zero trip meter.

▼ 0.7   SO Track on left.

2.0 ▲   SO Track on right.

▼ 1.0   SO Track on right.

1.7 ▲   SO Track on left.

▼ 1.2   SO Two tracks on left.

1.5 ▲   SO Two tracks on right.

▼ 1.9   SO Track on left.

0.8 ▲   BL Track on right.

GPS: N 37°59.52′ W 109°52.26′

▼ 2.1   SO Faint track on left.

0.6 ▲   SO Faint track on right.

▼ 2.2   SO Track on right.

0.5 ▲   SO Track on left.

▼ 2.6   SO   Track on right.
0.1 ▲   SO   Track on left.

▼ 2.7   Trail ends at intersection with Trail #36: Beef Basin Trail (CR 104). Turn right to continue around the Beef Basin Loop, turn left to exit via the Manti-La Sal National Forest.
0.0 ▲   Trail starts at intersection with Trail #36: Beef Basin Trail (CR 104). Turn north on graded dirt road (CR 119) following sign for Canyonlands National Park. Zero trip meter.
            GPS: N 37°58.82' W 109°52.36'

MOAB REGION TRAIL #35

Cottonwood Canyon Trail

STARTING POINT Junction Utah 211 and CR 104
FINISHING POINT Junction of Trail #38: North and South Elk Ridge Trail (FR 088) and Trail #39: Blue Mountains Road (FR 095/CR 225)
TOTAL MILEAGE 29.6 miles
UNPAVED MILEAGE 29.6 miles
DRIVING TIME 3.5 hours
ELEVATION RANGE 5,200–8,200 feet
USUALLY OPEN April to November
DIFFICULTY RATING 2
SCENIC RATING 8
REMOTENESS RATING +0

Special Attractions
- Varied scenery from canyon floor to alpine forest.
- Access to backcountry campsites.
- Little-used backcountry road provides access to a number of 4WD trails.

Description
This long and highly scenic trail commences at the junction of Utah 211 and CR 104 (Beef Basin Road), 7.5 miles northwest of Newspaper Rock State Park. The first few miles pass through private property before the trail enters public land. It proceeds up a valley, with the jagged Bridger Jack Mesa to the west, crosses several small washes, and then runs alongside the deepening North Cottonwood Creek canyon before swinging away to run around the north side of Cathedral Butte.

The trail climbs out of the deep valley to enter the Manti-La Sal National Forest. The vegetation changes from the dry sagebrush and junipers of the valley floor to the ponderosa pines and aspens of the alpine life zone. The trail connects with Trail #36: Beef Basin Trail, which leads to Beef Basin proper; then it connects with Trail #37: North Long Point Trail and, after crossing grassy alpine meadows, finishes at Sego Flat at the junction with FR 095. This is an endpoint for both Trail #38: North and South Elk Ridge Trail and Trail #39: Blue Mountains Road.

View of Cottonwood Canyon Trail near Cathedral Butte

There are good backcountry campsites along this road at all elevations.

The trail is a graded dirt road for its entire length. However, sections of it can be rough, requiring high clearance, and there can be washouts, especially in North Cottonwood Creek valley. This trail is suitable for high-clearance 2WD vehicles in dry weather, but after rain it can become impassable, even for 4WD vehicles, as the red soil turns to thick mud. It should be attempted in dry weather only to avoid track damage.

Dugout Ranch at the north end of the trail has been used as the location for many movies, but it is private property and cannot be visited.

Current Road Information

Canyonlands National Park
Needles Ranger District
(435) 259-4711

Manti-La Sal National Forest
Monticello Ranger District
496 East Central; PO Box 820
Monticello, UT 84535
(435) 587-2041

Map References

BLM   La Sal, Blanding
USGS   1:24,000   Harts Point South, Shay
Mt., Cathedral Butte, House Park
Butte, Poison Canyon
1:100,000 La Sal, Blanding
Maptech CD-ROM: Moab/Canyonlands
Trails Illustrated, #703
Utah Atlas & Gazetteer, p. 30
Utah Travel Council #5
Other: Canyon Country Off-Road Vehicle
Trail Map—Canyon Rims &
Needles Areas

Route Directions

▼ 0.0   From Utah 211, turn south on CR 104, following sign for Beef Basin Road, and zero trip meter. Cross cattle guard. Trail is crossing private property.

16.5 ▲   End at intersection with Utah 211. Canyonlands National Park is to the left.

Monticello and Moab are to the right.
GPS: N 38°05.02' W 109°34.08'

▼ 0.2   SO   Mine dugout in rock on left, old building on right.
16.3 ▲   SO   Mine dugout in rock on right, old building on left.

▼ 0.4   SO   Old wooden aqueduct on right.
16.1 ▲   SO   Old wooden aqueduct on left.

▼ 0.5   SO   Cross Indian Creek on stony-bottomed ford.
16.0 ▲   SO   Cross Indian Creek on stony-bottomed ford.

▼ 0.8   SO   Cattle guard, then track on right.
15.7 ▲   SO   Track on left, then cattle guard.

▼ 1.4   SO   Track on left. Trail swings south up North Cottonwood Creek valley. Bridger Jack Mesa on right.
15.1 ▲   SO   Track on right.

▼ 4.1   SO   Cattle guard, then track on left. Entering public lands.
12.4 ▲   SO   Track on right, then cattle guard. Leaving public lands.

▼ 4.6   SO   CR 104A to the left. Continue on CR 104.
11.9 ▲   SO   CR 104A to the right. Continue on CR 104.

▼ 8.2   SO   Wire gate, please close.
8.3 ▲   SO   Wire gate, please close.
GPS: N 37°59.21' W 109°37.43'

▼ 8.8   SO   Track on left. North Cottonwood Canyon is to the left.
7.7 ▲   SO   Track on right. North Cottonwood Canyon is to the right.
GPS: N 37°58.92' W 109°36.99'

▼ 10.5   SO   Track on left to campsite.
6.0 ▲   SO   Track on right to campsite.

▼ 13.1   BR   Track on left. Continue on main trail. View of Cathedral Butte on left.
3.4 ▲   SO   Track on right. Continue on main trail.

Trail #35: Cottonwood Canyon Trail

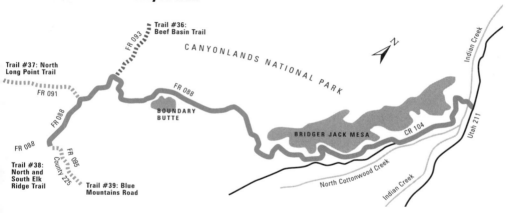

View of Cathedral Butte on right.

▼ 13.7 SO Track on right.
2.8 ▲   SO Track on left.

▼ 14.1 SO Track on left.
2.4 ▲   SO Track on right.

▼ 14.5 SO Track on right.
2.0 ▲   SO Track on left.

▼ 14.9 SO Small track on right.
1.6 ▲   SO Small track on left.

▼ 15.3 SO Track on left to campsite overlooking
             Cathedral Butte.
1.2 ▲   SO Track on right to campsite overlooking
             Cathedral Butte.

▼ 15.9 SO Track on right.
0.6 ▲   SO Track on left.

▼ 16.0 SO Track on left.
0.5 ▲   SO Track on right.

▼ 16.4 SO Track on right to viewpoint over the
             eroded sandstone of East Fork Salt
             Creek.
0.1 ▲   SO Track on left to viewpoint over the
             eroded sandstone of East Fork Salt
             Creek.

▼ 16.5 SO Bright Angel hiking trailhead on right.
             Parking area and campsite with shade
             and views. Track on left to campsites.

Zero trip meter.

0.0 ▲   Continue to the northeast.
        GPS: N 37°57.01' W 109°42.25'

▼ 0.0   Continue along trail, heading south-
           west.
7.5 ▲ SO Track on right to campsites. Bright
           Angel hiking trailhead on left. Parking
           area and campsite with shade and
           views. Zero trip meter.

▼ 1.0 SO Track on right and left. Many small
           tracks to campsites for the next 1.7
           miles.
6.5 ▲ SO Track on left and right.

▼ 1.3 SO Fence line, views on left to Davis
           Canyon.
6.2 ▲ SO Fence line, views on right to Davis
           Canyon.

▼ 2.7 SO Entering Manti-La Sal National Forest
           over cattle guard, then track on right
           along fence line. Trail becomes FR 088,
           skirts Boundary Butte on left and Salt
           Creek Canyon on right.
4.8 ▲ SO Track on left along fence line, then trail
           leaves Manti-La Sal National Forest and
           enters public land over cattle guard. Trail
           becomes CR 104. Many small tracks to
           campsites for the next 1.7 miles.
           GPS: N 37°55.86' W 109°44.79

▼ 4.6 BR Track on left.
2.9 ▲ BL Track on right.

▼ 5.5   SO   Salt Creek Canyon viewpoint on right, then hiking trail on left.

2.0 ▲   SO   Hiking trail on right, then Salt Creek Canyon viewpoint on left.

▼ 6.1   SO   Views back over Salt Creek Canyon and Boundary Butte.

1.4 ▲   SO   Views ahead over Salt Creek Canyon and Boundary Butte.

▼ 7.5   SO   Intersection with Trail #36: Beef Basin Trail (FR 093/CR 104) to the right. Zero trip meter.

0.0 ▲   Continue along FR 088.

    GPS: N 37°54.37' W 109°47.40'

▼ 0.0   SO   Continue south on FR 088.

2.4 ▲   SO   Trail #36: Beef Basin Trail (FR 093/CR 104) on left. Ahead is FR 088. Zero trip meter.

▼ 2.0   SO   ATV trail #423 on right.

0.4 ▲   SO   ATV trail #423 on left.

▼ 2.4   SO   Track on right is FR 091 (CR 221), Trail #37: North Long Point Trail. Zero trip meter.

0.0 ▲   Continue straight, signed to Dugout Ranch and Beef Basin.

    GPS: N 37°52.74' W 109°47.48'

▼ 0.0   Continue straight, signed to Gooseberry Guard Station.

3.2 ▲   SO   Track on left is FR 091 (CR 221), Trail #37: North Long Point Trail. Zero trip meter.

▼ 1.1   SO   Track on right to corral.

2.1 ▲   SO   Track on left to corral.

▼ 1.3   SO   ATV trail #444 on left, followed by FR 144 on right.

1.8 ▲   SO   FR 144 on left, followed by ATV trail #444 on right.

▼ 2.9   SO   Track on right.

0.3 ▲   SO   Track on left.

▼ 3.2   End at intersection with FR 095 (CR 225). Right is Trail #38: North and

South Elk Ridge Trail and goes to Blanding; left is Trail #39: Blue Mountains Road and goes to Monticello

0.0 ▲   From the junction of FR 095 (CR 225) and FR 088 (CR 104), zero trip meter and proceed north on FR 088 toward Beef Basin.

    GPS: N 37°50.42' W 109°46.39'

Beef Basin Trail

STARTING POINT Junction of FR 088 and FR 093, along Trail #35: Cottonwood Canyon Trail

FINISHING POINT Beef Basin

TOTAL MILEAGE 13.7 miles

UNPAVED MILEAGE 13.7 miles

DRIVING TIME 1 hour

ELEVATION RANGE 6,100–8,200 feet

USUALLY OPEN May to November

DIFFICULTY RATING 3

SCENIC RATING 9

REMOTENESS RATING +0

Special Attractions

■ Ruins and cliff dwellings in Beef Basin.

■ Views over Butler Wash Wilderness Study Area.

History

The many ruins in Ruin Park, House Park, and Beef Basin date back to the time of the Anasazi. Some of the ancient buildings are unusual in that they were built out in the open instead of being tucked under a cliff face. Other dwellings and granaries are built under the cliff overhang.

The Somerville and Scorup Cattle Company, the largest in the area in the 1930s, held its cattle in the basin until the roundup was complete. It would then take seven to eight days to drive the cattle north across the Colorado River to the railroad at Thompson. Today, Beef Basin is the winter pasture for cattle from the Dugout Ranch, located on Utah 211.

Description

This route leads off Trail #35: Cottonwood Canyon Trail and descends into the large bowl of Beef Basin. The trail is a mixture of sandy sections and rock, and conditions can change quickly depending on recent weather. The first section of the trail, where it leaves Trail #35, is impassable when wet. We saw tire tracks that went straight through the mud, missing the bend, and into a tree. Snow in the Manti-La Sal National Forest restricts access to Beef Basin along this road from November to May. You can also approach this area from Canyonlands National Park, using Trail #33: Elephant Hill Loop and Trail #34: Bobby's Hole and Ruin Park Trail. However, this route is extremely difficult; make sure you have the experience and the right vehicle to tackle the notorious Bobby's Hole and Elephant Hill.

A driver repairs part of the Beef Basin Trail before passing through

The trail often washes out after heavy rains, and it can take weeks or even months for the county grader to reach the area and make the road passable again.

After the trail descends into the flat open area of House Park, there are many side trails leading to ancient ruins. The spur trail down Ruin Canyon is particularly good.

The short loop described goes through Beef Basin. If you have more time, a longer loop is possible, and sidetracks off both loops lead to numerous small ruins. Another option is to combine this route with the southern part of Trail #34: Bobby's Hole and Ruin Park Trail to visit Ruin Park.

Current Road Information

Canyonlands National Park
Needles Ranger District
(435) 259-4711

Manti-La Sal National Forest
Monticello Ranger District
496 East Central; PO Box 820
Monticello, UT 84535
(435) 587-2041

Looking toward Beef Basin

THE ANASAZI INDIANS

Current scholars have no idea what the Anasazi called themselves. The name Anasazi is actually derived from a Navajo word that can be translated as "ancient tribe," "ancient ones," or "enemy ancestors." Similarly, it is not known why the Anasazi disappeared around 1300, abandoning their villages and the sprawling pueblos carved into the faces of cliffs.

The construction of the Anasazi villages can be dated through tree trunks found in their remains. Tree ring width varies with rainfall, thereby creating a record of annual rainfall. This dating method has been very helpful in showing past droughts, and suggests that a prolonged dry spell **Anasazi kiva** could have compelled the tribe to leave the area. Alternatively, the Anasazi may have been driven out by, or assimilated into, the Ute or Navajo cultures, which were then moving into the area. Or the disappearance of the Anasazi may have come about because of both scenarios. Interestingly, there is evidence that some Anasazi settlements were burned shortly after the tribe's departure, although scholars are not certain who burned them or why.

What scholars do know is that the Anasazi were an advanced people. They were excellent craftsmen, especially when it came to baskets, pottery, and sandals. Moving away from a hunter-gatherer lifestyle, they developed an agricultural system that relied heavily on dry-farming techniques—a method that requires direct rainfall. The Anasazi employed stone masonry to create flat-roofed rooms, subterranean living quarters, and communal structures of ranging sizes. Subterranean ceremonial rooms called kivas appeared later in their culture as did middens—large trash areas that not only contained garbage, but the tribe's dead as well. Much evidence of this fascinating culture can still be seen in the ruins scattered across southeast Utah, and throughout the Four Corners region.

Map References

BLM   Blanding
USFS   Manti-La Sal National Forest
USGS   1:24,000   House Park Butte, Fable
       Valley
       1:100,000 Blanding
Maptech CD-ROM: Moab/Canyonlands
Trails Illustrated, #703; #210 (incomplete)
Utah Atlas & Gazetteer, p. 30
Utah Travel Council #5
Other: Canyon Country Off-Road Vehicle
       Trail Map—Canyon Rims &
       Needles Areas

Route Directions

▼ 0.0   From Trail #35: Cottonwood Canyon
         Trail, at junction of FR 088 and FR

093 (CR 104), turn north onto FR 093
and zero trip meter.

8.7 ▲   Trail ends at intersection with FR
         088. Turn left to follow Trail #35:
         Cottonwood Canyon Trail to Utah
         211; turn right to follow Trail #38:
         North and South Elk Ridge Trail to
         Blanding.
         GPS: N 37°54.37' W 109°47.40'

▼ 0.8   SO Trail runs around shelf road as it
         descends to Beef Basin.
7.9 ▲   SO Shelf road ends.

▼ 2.6   SO Cattle guard, entering BLM land.
         Stay on established road, road is now
         CR 104.
6.1 ▲   SO Cattle guard, entering Manti-La Sal

National Forest; road is now FR 093.
GPS: N 37°56.08' W 109°47.76'

▼ 3.1　SO　Tracks on right and left.
5.6 ▲　SO　Tracks on right and left.

▼ 3.8　SO　Track on right.
4.9 ▲　SO　Track on left.

▼ 4.5　SO　Cross through rocky wash.
4.2 ▲　SO　Cross through rocky wash.

▼ 5.3　SO　Cattle guard.
3.4 ▲　SO　Cattle guard.

▼ 5.7　SO　Campsite on right.
3.0 ▲　SO　Campsite on left.

▼ 5.9　BR　Track on left.
2.8 ▲　SO　Track on right.
GPS: N 37°58.35' W 109°49.61'

▼ 6.2　SO　Descending shelf road, with wilderness study area on right.
2.5 ▲　SO　End of shelf road.

▼ 6.7　SO　Entering House Park.
2.0 ▲　SO　Start of shelf road with wilderness study area on left. Leaving House Park.

▼ 7.4　SO　Track on left.
1.4 ▲　SO　Track on right.
GPS: N 37°58.55' W 109°50.95'

▼ 7.6　SO　Track on left.
1.1 ▲　SO　Track on right.

▼ 8.1　SO　Track on right.
0.6 ▲　SO　Track on left.

▼ 8.7　SO　Crossroads. Zero trip meter. To the right, Trail #34: Bobby's Hole and Ruin Park Trail (CR 119) leads to Canyonlands National Park; track on left goes to campsite.
0.0 ▲　　　Continue toward the Manti-La Sal National Forest Boundary.
GPS: N 37°58.84' W 109°52.33'

▼ 0.0　　　Continue toward Beef Basin.
1.4 ▲　SO　Crossroads. Zero trip meter at intersection. To the left, Trail #34: Bobby's Hole and Ruin Park Trail (CR 119) leads to Canyonlands National Park; track on right goes to campsite.

▼ 0.2　SO　Cross through sandy wash.

Trail #36: Beef Basin Trail

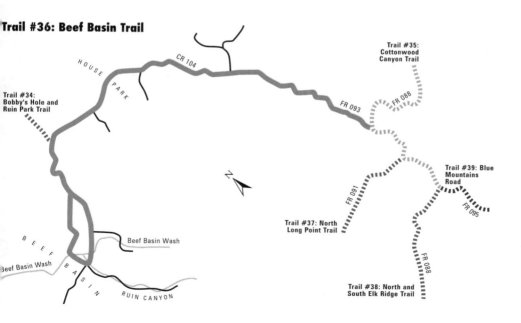

1.2 ▲	SO	Cross through sandy wash.

▼ 0.6	SO	Two campsite on left.
0.8 ▲	SO	Two campsites on right.

▼ 0.9	SO	Cattle guard, entering Beef Basin.
0.5 ▲	SO	Cattle guard, leaving Beef Basin.

▼ 1.4	SO	Track on right is end of short loop. Zero trip meter and commence the loop.
		GPS: N 37°57.85' W 109°53.03'

▼ 0.0		Continue around short loop.
▼ 0.1	SO	Cross through wash.
▼ 0.2	SO	Cattle guard, then track on left.
▼ 0.4	SO	Water trough on right, then cattle guard.
▼ 0.5	BR	Track on left, then cross through Beef Basin Wash.
		GPS: N 37°57.44' W 109°53.03'

▼ 0.6	SO	Cross through two washes.
▼ 0.7	SO	Cross through wash.
▼ 0.9	BR	Track on left goes to Calf Canyon.
		GPS: N 38°57.15' W 109°53.44'

▼ 1.5	SO	Cross through Beef Basin Wash; this often washes out and may require a detour.
▼ 1.7	TR	Five-way junction. Take first right to continue around small loop. First left goes to small ruin. Second left goes to Ruin Canyon. Straight on is a longer loop around Beef Basin. Zero trip meter.
		GPS: N 37°56.79' W 109°54.09'

▼ 0.0		Continue around small loop.
▼ 0.3	SO	Cross through Beef Basin Wash.
▼ 0.5	SO	Track on left, then campsite on right.
▼ 0.6	SO	Cross through fence line, then track on left.
		GPS: N 37°57.25' W 109°54.00'

▼ 1.3	SO	Cross through fence line.
▼ 1.8	BR	Track on left.
▼ 1.9		End of loop. Turn left to exit Beef Basin.
		GPS: N 37°57.86' W 109°53.02'

North Long Point Trail

STARTING POINT Junction of Trail #35: Cottonwood Canyon Trail (FR 088) and FR 091
FINISHING POINT Middle Point, Dark Canyon Primitive Area
TOTAL MILEAGE 27.2 miles
UNPAVED MILEAGE 27.2 miles
DRIVING TIME 3 hours (one-way)
ELEVATION RANGE 6,100–8,600 feet
USUALLY OPEN May to November
DIFFICULTY RATING 2
SCENIC RATING 8
REMOTENESS RATING +1

Special Attractions

- Diversity of life zones from alpine to arid desert plateau.
- Good selection of backcountry campsites.
- Very remote, little-traveled trail.

Description

This spur trail commences at the junctions of FR 088 and FR 091, near the south end of Trail #35: Cottonwood Canyon Trail. The turnoff is well marked, and in dry weather the trail is accessible by high-clearance 2WDs as far as North Long Point. Snowfall is erratic in this region, so the trail may be open longer than the stated dates. This diverse trail winds down through the Manti-La Sal National Forest through stands of aspen and ponderosa pine. A couple of spur trails lead to natural springs in the area. After 6 miles, you reach North Long Point, with its far-reaching views over Dark Canyon Plateau and Canyonlands National Park.

The trail descends onto the arid Dark Canyon Plateau, where the vegetation changes to sagebrush, junipers, and pinyon pines. The surface is graded dirt and clay on the upper portions of track, while farther down on Dark Canyon Plateau it becomes predominantly sandy. This route is impassable to 4WDs in wet weather. After 11 miles, you reach the Sweet Alice Hills. A short spur goes 0.5 miles to the Sweet Alice Spring. The trail winds through increasingly arid land until it finishes on Middle Point in the Dark Canyon Primitive Area. Trails continue on from here, but they are mainly used by ATVs and are very narrow and twisty. The end of the trail has panoramic views over the Glen Canyon National Recreation Area and the Henry Mountains to the west and north toward Canyonlands National Park.

Current Road Information
Manti-La Sal National Forest
Monticello Ranger District
496 East Central; PO Box 820
Monticello, UT 84535
(435) 587-2041

Map References
BLM Blanding, Hite Crossing
USFS Manti-La Sal National Forest
USGS 1:24,000 House Park Butte, Poison Canyon, Warren Canyon, Fable Valley, Bowdie Canyon East, Bowdie Canyon West
1:100,000 Blanding, Hite Crossing
Maptech CD-ROM: Moab/Canyonlands
Trails Illustrated, #703
Utah Atlas & Gazetteer, p. 30
Utah Travel Council #5

Route Directions

▼ 0.0   At the intersection of FR 088 and FR 091, along Trail #35: Cottonwood Canyon Trail, zero trip meter and turn

Driving through a muddy section of the North Long Point Trail

         west onto FR 091, North Long Point Road.
         GPS: N 37°52.74′ W 109°47.48′

▼ 0.6   SO   Cattle guard followed by track on left.
▼ 0.7   SO   Track on right to Crystal Spring. Main trail travels through semi-open areas of aspen and ponderosa pine. Numerous camps on right and left.
         GPS: N 37°52.57′ W 109°48.66′

▼ 3.1   SO   Track on right and campsite.
▼ 4.3   BR   Track on left to Big Spring. Views over Poison Canyon and the Dark Canyon Wilderness to the left.
▼ 5.7   SO   Track on right.
▼ 6.1   BR   North Long Point. Views of Dark

Trail #37: North Long Point Trail

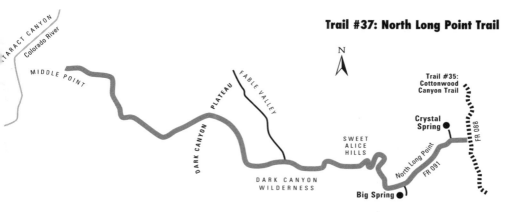

Canyon Plateau and Sweet Alice Hills. Track starts to descend.

GPS: N 37°51.40' W 109°52.38'

▼ 7.5	SO	ATV trail #425 on right.
▼ 8.2	SO	Finish descent. Trail Canyon hiking trailhead on left at edge of Dark Canyon Wilderness.
▼ 8.3	SO	Leaving Manti-La Sal National Forest over cattle guard; entering Dark Canyon Primitive Area. Corral on right. Zero trip meter.

GPS: N 37°51.89' W 109°52.80'

▼ 0.0		Continue into primitive area.
▼ 1.9	SO	Sweet Alice Hills on right.
▼ 2.7	SO	Corral on left.
▼ 2.8	SO	CR 223 on right, immediately followed by CR 222 on right to Sweet Alice Spring. Faint track on left.

GPS: N 37°51.64' W 109°55.44'

▼ 5.4	SO	Trail follows the plateau, views ahead to the Henry Mountains, right over Fable Valley, and left over Dark Canyon.
▼ 6.0	SO	Fable Valley trail on right. Zero trip meter.

GPS: N 37°51.68' W 109°58.74'

▼ 0.0		Continue west.
▼ 0.2	SO	Little-used track on left.
▼ 1.0	SO	Fence line, followed by track on left. Trail runs over open plateau.
▼ 3.5	SO	Track on left, corral, and dam.
▼ 3.6	BL	Track on right.
▼ 8.1	BR	Faint track on left.

GPS: N 37°53.82' W 110°05.45'

▼ 10.1	SO	Track on right to campsite and view over Bowdie Canyon.
▼ 11.6	SO	Oil drill hole on left.
▼ 12.0	SO	End of county road maintenance. Track narrows and twists down through the small trees.
▼ 12.9		End at rocky area with180-degree views to Glen Canyon National Recreation Area and the Henry Mountains. Trail continues but is used mainly by ATVs.

GPS: N 37°55.98' W 110°08.61'

North and South Elk Ridge Trail

STARTING POINT Junction Trail #35: Cottonwood Canyon Trail (FR 088) and Trail #39: Blue Mountains Road (FR 095)

FINISHING POINT Junction CR 228 and CR 227, midpoint Trail #40: Cottonwood Wash Trail

TOTAL MILEAGE 26 miles

UNPAVED MILEAGE 26 miles

DRIVING TIME 2 hours

ELEVATION RANGE 5,600–8,700 feet

USUALLY OPEN May to November

DIFFICULTY RATING 2

SCENIC RATING 8

REMOTENESS RATING +0

Special Attractions

- Access to a network of 4WD trails.
- The Notch Viewpoint.
- Duck Lake.

Description

This wonderfully scenic drive in the Manti-La Sal National Forest also provides access to wilderness areas and some great viewpoints. This trail can be combined with either Trail #35: Cottonwood Canyon Trail or Trail #39: Blue Mountains Road and Trail #40: Cottonwood Wash Trail to create a loop drive from Monticello.

The trail travels along the top of North Elk Ridge and is graded dirt its entire length. In dry weather, passenger cars can handle the drive without too much difficulty, although a high-clearance vehicle is preferred. In wet weather, the trail becomes very muddy and impassable even to 4WDs, as do most of the trails in the area.

The trail picks up at the end of Trail #35: Cottonwood Canyon Trail, following FR 088 south from the junction with Trail #39: Blue Mountains Road (FR 095) at Sego Flats. For most of its length it travels

Tall aspens rise above the North and South Elk Ridge Trail

through stands of ponderosa pines and aspens, interspersed with wide, grassy meadows. It passes by the Gooseberry Guard Station and, at the 2-mile mark, Duck Lake. This small natural lake is popular with waterfowl and offers some very pretty campsites along its shores.

After 6.4 miles, the trail runs around the rim of Dark Canyon, offering some spectacular views back to the northwest. Then it descends a series of tight switchbacks to the Notch, where there are views over Notch Canyon to the east as well as over the Dark Canyon Wilderness Area to the west. The best view, however, is slightly to the north of the actual Notch viewpoint—trees obscure the view west at the Notch itself.

After 12.5 miles, a vehicle trail to the northwest leads down into Kigalia Canyon, one of the rare vehicle trails that penetrates a wilderness area. The vehicle trail is a narrow corridor through the wilderness area.

At the 14-mile point, the trail passes

through a logging area. Bark beetles have infested the trees in the Manti-La Sal National Forest, and the logging is part of an effort to contain the spread of the beetles, encouraging the healthy trees to grow, and salvaging the timber from the infested trees.

The trail ends at the junction with the Cottonwood Wash Road (CR 227), midway along Trail #40: Cottonwood Wash Trail. Head north to follow the Cottonwood Wash Trail back into the Manti-La Sal National Forest; continue straight to go to Blanding via Trail #40: Cottonwood Wash Trail as it heads south before turning east onto Utah 95.

Current Road Information

Manti-La Sal National Forest
Monticello Ranger District
496 East Central; PO Box 820
Monticello, UT 84535
(435) 587-2041

Map References

BLM   Blanding
USFS Manti-La Sal National Forest
USGS 1:24,000 Poison Canyon, Kigalia
         Point, Cream Pots
         1:100,000 Blanding
Maptech CD-ROM: Moab/Canyonlands
Trails Illustrated, #703
Utah Atlas & Gazetteer, pp. 30, 22
Utah Travel Council #5

Route Directions

▼ 0.0   At the junction of Trail #35: Cottonwood Canyon Trail (FR 088) and Trail #39: Blue Mountains Road (FR 095/CR 225), zero trip meter and head south on FR 088 following the sign to Gooseberry Guard Station.

7.1 ▲   End at the junction of Trail #35: Cottonwood Canyon Trail (FR 088) and Trail #39: Blue Mountains Road (FR 095/CR 225). Bear right for Monticello; turn left for Utah 211.
         GPS: N 37°50.41' W 109°46.41'

▼ 0.2 SO Cattle guard.

6.9 ▲	SO	Cattle guard.

▼ 0.6	SO	Tracks right and left are FR 048.
6.5 ▲	SO	Tracks right and left are FR 048.

▼ 1.2	SO	Track on left to Gooseberry Guard Station.
5.9 ▲	SO	Track on right to Gooseberry Guard Station.

GPS: N 37°49.36′ W 109°46.36′

▼ 1.3	SO	ATV trail #445 left.
5.8 ▲	SO	ATV trail #445 right.

▼ 1.7	SO	Track on right and left.
5.4 ▲	SO	Track on right and left.

▼ 1.9	SO	Cattle guard, then Duck Lake on left. Campsites at lake.
5.2 ▲	SO	Duck Lake on right, then cattle guard. Campsites at lake.

▼ 2.1	SO	FR 178 on left to Deadman Point.
5.0 ▲	SO	FR 178 on right to Deadman Point.

GPS: N 37°48.69′ W 109°46.48′

▼ 2.4	SO	Track on left into logging area.
4.7 ▲	SO	Track on right into logging area.

▼ 2.7	SO	Track on left.
4.4 ▲	SO	Track on right.

▼ 3.4	SO	FR 154 on right.
3.7 ▲	SO	FR 154 on left.

▼ 3.6	SO	Track on right.
3.5 ▲	SO	Track on left.

▼ 4.3	SO	Track on right.
2.8 ▲	SO	Track on left.

▼ 4.6	SO	ATV trail #210 on right.
2.5 ▲	SO	ATV trail #210 on left.

▼ 4.7	SO	Track on left.
2.4 ▲	SO	Track on right. Sign to Gooseberry Creek ahead.

▼ 5.5	SO	Track on left.
1.6 ▲	SO	Track on right.

▼ 5.7	SO	FR 168 on right to North Notch Spring.
1.4 ▲	SO	FR 168 on left to North Notch Spring.

GPS: N 37°45.84′ W 109°46.20′

▼ 6.4	SO	Trail runs around the rim of Dark Canyon and starts to descend the shelf road switchbacks to the Notch.
0.7 ▲	SO	Trail finishes switchbacks. End of shelf road.

▼ 7.1	SO	Sign, Big Notch. Zero trip meter.
0.0 ▲		Continue north.

GPS: N 37°45.09′ W 109°46.03′

▼ 0.0		Continue southwest.
5.4 ▲	SO	Sign, Big Notch. Zero trip meter.

▼ 0.1	SO	Cattle guard, then Big Notch trailhead.
5.3 ▲	SO	Big Notch trailhead, then cattle guard.

▼ 0.8	SO	End of shelf road, track on left.
4.6 ▲	SO	Track on right, start of shelf road.

▼ 1.3	SO	FR 200 on left.
4.1 ▲	SO	FR 200 on right.

▼ 1.7	SO	FR 208 on left.
3.7 ▲	SO	FR 208 on right.

▼ 2.0	SO	Track on right.
3.4 ▲	SO	Track on left.

▼ 3.0	SO	Cattle guard.
2.4 ▲	SO	Cattle guard.

▼ 3.1	SO	Track on right.
2.3 ▲	SO	Track on left.

▼ 3.3	SO	FR 425 on right to Steamboat Point.
2.1 ▲	SO	FR 425 on left to Steamboat Point.

GPS: N 37°43.36′ W 109°48.15′

▼ 3.4	SO	Track on right and left.
2.0 ▲	SO	Track on right and left.

▼ 3.7	SO	Cattle guard.
1.7 ▲	SO	Cattle guard.

▼ 4.6	SO	Track on left.

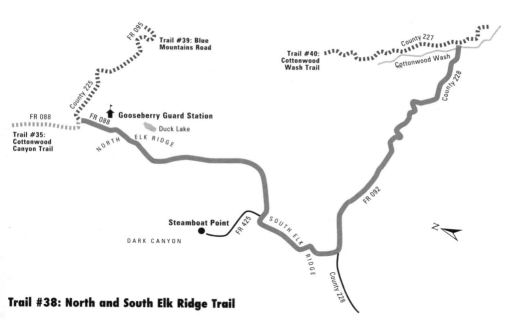

Trail #38: North and South Elk Ridge Trail

0.8 ▲	SO	Track on right.

▼ 5.0	SO	Track on right.
0.4 ▲	SO	Track on left.

▼ 5.4	SO	Little Notch. FR 089 on right (vehicle use) to Kigalia Canyon—wilderness access. Track on left to Hammond Canyon. Zero trip meter.
0.0 ▲		Continue north on FR 088.
		GPS: N 37°41.66' W 109°48.59'

▼ 0.0		Continue south on FR 088.
1.9 ▲	SO	Little Notch. FR 089 on left (vehicle use) to Kigalia Canyon—wilderness access. Track on right to Hammond Canyon. Zero trip meter.

▼ 0.9	SO	FR 337 on right, then corral on left.
1.0 ▲	SO	Corral on right followed by FR 337 on left.

▼ 1.2	SO	Track on right.
0.7 ▲	SO	Track on left.

▼ 1.5	SO	Track on right in logging area. Logged area has been infested by bark beetles.
0.4 ▲	SO	Track on left in logging area. Logged area has been infested by bark beetles.

▼ 1.9	BL	Bear left on FR 092 (CR 228), follow signs for Blanding. Right on FR 088 (CR 228) leads to Natural Bridges National Monument. Zero trip meter.
0.0 ▲		Continue northwest on FR 088.
		GPS: N 37°40.57' W 109°47.82'

▼ 0.0		Continue northeast on FR 092, track on right.
8.4 ▲	BR	Bear right onto FR 088 (CR 225) to Gooseberry Creek. Ahead, FR 088 (CR 228) leads to Natural Bridges National Monument. Zero trip meter.

▼ 0.1	SO	Track on left.
8.3 ▲	SO	Track on right.

▼ 0.4	SO	FR 183 on right to Butts Point.
8.0 ▲	SO	FR 183 on left to Butts Point.

▼ 0.7	SO	Track on right.
7.7 ▲	SO	Track on left.

▼ 1.0	SO	Track on left.
7.4 ▲	SO	Track on right.

▼ 1.6	SO	Cattle guard, then track on left to Hammond Canyon. Corral.

6.8 ▲	SO	Track on right to Hammond Canyon, corral, and cattle guard.
		GPS: N 37°40.83' W 109°46.06'

▼ 2.2	SO	FR 326 on left.
6.2 ▲	SO	FR 326 on right.

▼ 2.3	SO	FR 182 (CR 262A) on right to Milk Ranch Point.
6.1 ▲	SO	FR 182 (CR 262A) on left to Milk Ranch Point.

▼ 5.1	SO	Track on left, Hammond Canyon and Cream Pots Trail. Road is now gravel.
3.3 ▲	SO	Track on right, Hammond Canyon and Cream Pots Trail. Road is now graded dirt.

▼ 5.9	SO	Track on right.
2.5 ▲	SO	Track on left.

▼ 6.4	SO	Cattle guard.
2.0 ▲	SO	Cattle guard.

▼ 8.4	SO	Leaving Manti-La Sal National Forest. Zero trip meter.
0.0 ▲		Continue along gravel road.
		GPS: N 37°39.43' W 109°40.57'

▼ 0.0		Continue along gravel road.
3.2 ▲	SO	Entering Manti-La Sal National Forest. Zero trip meter.

▼ 2.1	SO	CR 229 on right.
1.1 ▲	SO	CR 229 on left.

▼ 3.0	SO	Cross Cottonwood Wash.
0.2 ▲	SO	Cross Cottonwood Wash.

▼ 3.2		End at the midpoint of Trail #40: Cottonwood Wash Trail (CR 227). Continue straight on to Blanding; go left to Round Mountain.
0.0 ▲		Begin at the junction of Trail #40: Cottonwood Wash Trail (CR 227) and CR 228. Zero trip meter and continue west on CR 228.
		GPS: N 37°38.99' W 109°37.57'

Blue Mountains Road

STARTING POINT US 191 in Monticello
FINISHING POINT Junction of Trail #38: North and South Elk Ridge Trail (FR 088) and Trail #35: Cottonwood Canyon Trail (FR 088)
TOTAL MILEAGE 44 miles
UNPAVED MILEAGE 38.9 miles
DRIVING TIME 3 hours
ELEVATION RANGE 7,000–10,200 feet
USUALLY OPEN May to October
DIFFICULTY RATING 2
SCENIC RATING 9
REMOTENESS RATING +0

Special Attractions

- Long trail with many varied views and brilliant scenery along its length.
- Natural features of Chippean Rocks and The Causeway.
- Access to a number of forest trails and backcountry camping areas.
- Aspen viewing in fall.

Description

This long and varied trail travels almost wholly within the Monticello Ranger District of the Manti-La Sal National Forest. It leaves from the center of Monticello, off US 191, two blocks south of the junction with US 666. A sign points to the national forest campgrounds at Dalton Spring, Buckboard, Monticello Lake, and the Blue Mountains ski area.

The pavement road enters the forest after 2 miles. After 4.5 miles, a gravel road heads south to the disused Blue Mountains ski area. The ski lifts remain but were closed in the early 1980s, and the runs are slowly revegetating.

After 5.1 miles, the route bears left onto the dirt FR 079 and starts to climb through some mature stands of aspen and ponderosa pine. At 6.3 miles the route enters the watershed area for the region, and camping is prohibited for the next 11.5 miles. If you plan on backcountry camping, there are a few sites, mainly on side tracks before the watershed area is entered, and numerous sites after exiting from it.

The trail climbs steadily before emerging from the trees at North Creek Pass and the high point of the trail at 10,200 feet. The trail now starts to descend along a shelf road. Although fairly narrow, it has a good surface and grade and ample passing places.

After crossing Indian Creek, the trail starts to climb again over Jackson Ridge before swinging along the top of the plateau. At the halfway mark, the trail leaves FR 079 and turns onto FR 095 toward Elk Ridge. This first part of the descent is not advised in wet or muddy conditions. The vegetation changes in this arid region to predominantly scrub oak and hardier plants. The trail then follows a long shelf road, with extensive views to the southwest over Cliffdwellers Pasture and Chippean Ridge, then north over Trough Canyon and Tuerto Canyon.

The Causeway, at the 31-mile mark, is a natural hogback ridge that separates the drainages of the Colorado River to the north and the San Juan River to the south. The Causeway itself is a narrow saddle with steep drops on either side.

Looking down from the saddle, Blue Mountains Road winds along the hills

The trail winds on, giving glimpses of the Chippean Rocks ahead. Just before the rocks is a grassy valley with some excellent campsites. About 3 miles before the campsites, the Maverick Point overlook gives sweeping views of the national forest, which is managed as a multiple use area: for recreation, grazing, protection of watershed and wildlife habitat, and logging.

Near the end, the trail connects with Trail #40: Cottonwood Wash Trail, and it finishes at the junction of FR 088. From here, you can turn north and follow Trail #35: Cottonwood Canyon Trail (leading to Utah 211), or turn south and follow Trail #38: North and South Elk Ridge Trail (providing access to Blanding). A pleasant day's loop drive back to Monticello can be made by taking either of these trails.

Current Road Information
Manti-La Sal National Forest
Monticello Ranger District
496 East Central; PO Box 820
Monticello, UT 84535
(435) 587-2041

The barren Chippean Rocks rise above the trees along Blue Mountains Road

Map References

BLM   Blanding
USFS   Manti-La Sal National Forest
USGS   1:24,000   Monticello South, Abajo
        Peak, Monticello Lake, Mt. Linnaeus,
        Chippean Rocks, Poison Canyon
        1:100,000 Blanding
Maptech CD-ROM: Moab/Canyonlands
Trails Illustrated, #703
Utah Atlas & Gazetteer, pp. 31, 30, 22
Utah Travel Council #5

Route Directions

▼ 0.0   From US 191 in Monticello (two blocks
           south of junction with US 666), zero
           trip meter and turn west onto FR 105
           (North Creek Road). This intersection
           is marked with a sign for forest
           access.
5.1 ▲   End in Monticello at intersection
           with US 191, two blocks south of
           US 666.
           GPS: N 37°52.19' W 109°20.57'

▼ 2.1   SO Cattle guard, entering Manti-La Sal
           National Forest.
3.0 ▲   SO Cattle guard, leaving Manti-La Sal
           National Forest.
           GPS: N 37°52.16' W 109°23.00'

▼ 3.1   SO Track on left, then track on right.
2.0 ▲   SO Track on left, then track on right.

▼ 3.5   SO Cattle guard, leaving national forest
           into private property.
1.6 ▲   SO Cattle guard, reentering national forest.

▼ 4.2   SO Cattle guard, reentering national forest.
0.9 ▲   SO Cattle guard, leaving national forest
           into private property.

▼ 4.5   SO Gravel road on left to closed Blue
           Mountains ski area.
0.6 ▲   SO Gravel road on right to closed Blue
           Mountains ski area.

▼ 4.7   SO Dalton Spring Campground on left.
0.4 ▲   SO Dalton Spring Campground on right.

▼ 4.9   SO Exit from Dalton Spring Campground
           on left.
0.2 ▲   SO Exit from Dalton Spring Campground
           on right.

▼ 5.1   BL Fork in road. Turn left onto dirt road
           (FR 079) and zero trip meter.
0.0 ▲   Continue east on FR 105.
           GPS: N 37°52.54' W 109°26.34'

▼ 0.0   Continue southwest along FR 079.
8.1 ▲   TR At intersection, turn right onto FR 105.
           Road is now pavement. Zero trip meter.

▼ 0.2   SO Track on left, then track on right. Trail
           is traveling though mature aspens.
7.9 ▲   SO Track on left, then track on right. Trail
           is traveling through mature aspens.

▼ 0.6   SO Track on right.
7.5 ▲   SO Track on left.

▼ 0.9   SO Track on left.
7.2 ▲   SO Track on right.

▼ 1.2   SO Cattle guard, entering culinary watershed
           area; no camping beyond this point.
6.9 ▲   SO Cattle guard, leaving culinary watershed

Trail # 39: Blue Mountains Road

area; camping permitted beyond this
point.
GPS: N 37°52.06′ W 109°26.98′

▼ 2.9　SO　Track on right.
5.2 ▲　SO　Track on left.

▼ 3.2　SO　Track on left.
4.9 ▲　SO　Track on right.

▼ 4.4　BR　Track on left. North Creek Pass, trail
　　　　starts to descend along shelf road.
3.7 ▲　BL　Track on right. North Creek Pass, trail
　　　　starts to descend.
GPS: N 37°50.90′ W 109°28.28′

▼ 4.7　SO　Track on right.
3.4 ▲　SO　Track on left.

▼ 5.0　SO　Hiking trails #020 and #159 on right.
3.1 ▲　SO　Hiking trails #020 and #159 on left.

▼ 7.0　SO　End of shelf road and descent. Cross
　　　　Indian Creek on shallow ford.
1.1 ▲　SO　Cross Indian Creek on shallow ford,
　　　　then ascend on shelf road to North
　　　　Creek Pass.
GPS: N 37°50.53′ W 109°30.19′

▼ 7.6　SO　Track on right, then Aspen Flat hiking
　　　　trail #018 on right.
0.5 ▲　SO　Aspen Flat hiking trail #018 on left, then
　　　　track on left.

▼ 7.7　SO　Track on right.
0.4 ▲　SO　Track on left.

▼ 8.1　SO　Track on right (FR 354) leads to
　　　　Skyline Trail in 1.5 miles. Main trail
　　　　ahead is signed to Blanding and is now
　　　　marked as CR 285. Zero trip meter.
0.0 ▲　　　Continue along FR 079.
GPS: N 37°49.70′ W 109°30.46′

▼ 0.0　　　Start to descend on CR 285 (FR 079).
8.6 ▲　SO　Track on left (FR 354) leads to Skyline
　　　　Trailhead in 1.5 miles. Zero trip meter.

▼ 1.1　SO　Track on left.
7.5 ▲　SO　Track on right.

▼ 1.3　SO　Aqueduct tunnel emerges from hillside
　　　　on right.
7.3 ▲　SO　Aqueduct tunnel emerges from hillside
　　　　on left.

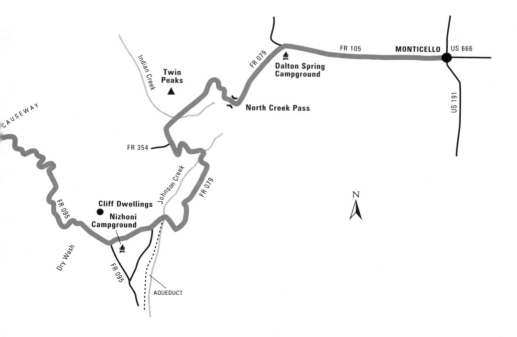

| ▼ 1.5 | SO | Track on right. |
| 7.1 ▲ | SO | Track on left. |

| ▼ 2.3 | SO | Cross Johnson Creek. |
| 6.3 ▲ | SO | Cross Johnson Creek. |

| ▼ 2.8 | SO | Creek crossing. |
| 5.8 ▲ | SO | Creek crossing. |

| ▼ 2.9 | SO | Track on right. |
| 5.7 ▲ | SO | Track on left. |

GPS: N 37°49.01′ W 109°29.24′

| ▼ 3.2 | SO | Track on left. |
| 5.4 ▲ | SO | Track on right. |

| ▼ 4.5 | SO | Cattle guard, exiting culinary watershed area. Camping permitted. |
| 4.1 ▲ | SO | Cattle guard, entering culinary watershed area. No camping beyond this point. |

GPS: N 37°48.04′ W 109°29.98′

| ▼ 4.8 | SO | Track on right. |
| 3.8 ▲ | SO | Track on left. |

| ▼ 5.7 | SO | Two tracks on left. |
| 2.9 ▲ | SO | Two tracks on right. |

| ▼ 6.3 | SO | Track on left. |
| 2.3 ▲ | SO | Track on right. |

| ▼ 6.7 | SO | Campsite, then cross creek. Track on right. |
| 1.9 ▲ | SO | Track on left, then cross creek, followed by campsite. |

| ▼ 6.8 | SO | Track on left. |
| 1.8 ▲ | SO | Track on right. |

| ▼ 7.2 | SO | FR 240 on left. |
| 1.4 ▲ | SO | FR 240 on right. |

| ▼ 7.3 | SO | Track on left. |
| 1.3 ▲ | SO | Track on right. |

| ▼ 8.4 | SO | Track on left into Nizhoni Campground, group and single sites. Track on right. |
| 0.2 ▲ | SO | Track on right into Nizhoni Campground, group and single sites. Track on left. |

| ▼ 8.6 | TR | Turn right onto FR 095 (CR 225) to the Causeway and Elk Ridge. Straight on goes to Blanding. Zero trip meter. |
| 0.0 ▲ | | Continue along FR 079. |

GPS: N 37°46.82′ W 109°32.55′

| ▼ 0.0 | | Descend FR 095; keep off when muddy. |
| 9.2 ▲ | TL | Turn left onto FR 079. The right turn goes to Blanding. Zero trip meter. |

| ▼ 0.2 | SO | Track on right. |
| 9.0 ▲ | SO | Track on left. |

| ▼ 0.9 | SO | Cattle guard. |
| 8.3 ▲ | SO | Cattle guard. |

| ▼ 1.3 | BL | Track on right up Dry Wash to cliff dwellings. |
| 7.9 ▲ | BR | Track on left up Dry Wash to cliff dwellings. |

GPS: N 37°47.39′ W 109°33.36′

| ▼ 3.0 | SO | Track on left. |
| 6.2 ▲ | SO | Track on right. |

| ▼ 3.1 | SO | Track on left, then views over Chippean Ridge. Long wide shelf road gradually climbs through dense oak vegetation. |
| 6.1 ▲ | SO | Track on right, shelf road finishes. |

| ▼ 5.0 | SO | Track on right, Allen Canyon on left. |
| 4.2 ▲ | SO | Allen Canyon on right, track on left. |

| ▼ 5.3 | SO | Hiking Trail #013 on right. |
| 3.9 ▲ | SO | Hiking Trail #013 on left. |

| ▼ 8.0 | SO | Track on left, followed by Skyline hiking trail on right. End of shelf road. |
| 1.2 ▲ | SO | Skyline hiking trail on left, followed by track on right. Shelf road descends with views over Chippean Ridge. |

GPS: N 37°49.82′ W 109°36.23′

| ▼ 8.4 | SO | Tuerto hiking trail on right. |
| 0.8 ▲ | SO | Tuerto hiking trail on left. |

| ▼ 9.2 | SO | Cattle guard, then the Causeway viewpoint. Views left over Deep Canyon, |

right over Trough Canyon and Tuerto Canyon. Zero trip meter.

0.0 ▲ Continue along FR 095.

GPS: N 37°50.55' W 109°36.88'

▼ 0.0 Continue over the Causeway.

5.4 ▲ SO The Causeway viewpoint. Views right over Deep Canyon, left over Trough Canyon and Tuerto Canyon. Zero trip meter at cattle guard.

▼ 0.6 SO FR 349 on right.

4.8 ▲ SO FR 349 on left.

▼ 1.2 SO Maverick Point overlook.

4.2 ▲ SO Maverick Point overlook.

▼ 1.7 SO Track on left.

3.7 ▲ SO Track on right.

▼ 3.9 SO Track on left.

1.5 ▲ SO Track on right.

▼ 4.1 SO Track on right.

1.3 ▲ SO Track on left.

▼ 4.5 SO FR 164 on right and FR 206 on left. Wide grassy, shady area good for camping.

0.9 ▲ SO FR 164 on left and FR 206 on right. Wide grassy, shady area good for camping.

▼ 5.4 BL Fork, bear left to Chippean Ridge and Gooseberry. Right goes to Maverick Point. Zero trip meter.

0.0 ▲ Continue along FR 095.

GPS: N 37°49.70' W 109°41.00'

▼ 0.0 Continue toward Chippean Ridge.

7.6 ▲ SO Track on left to Maverick Point. Zero trip meter.

▼ 1.4 SO Track on left.

6.2 ▲ SO Track on right.

▼ 2.3 SO FR 096 on right.

5.3 ▲ BR FR 096 on left.

GPS: N 37°49.56' W 109°42.20'

▼ 3.4 SO Track on right to Mormon Pasture

Mountain, then cattle guard. Start of shelf road, views over Trail #40: Cottonwood Wash Trail on left.

4.2 ▲ SO Cattle guard, then track on left to Mormon Pasture Mountain. End of shelf road.

GPS: N 37°49.51' W 109°43.20'

▼ 4.1 SO Cattle guard.

3.5 ▲ SO Cattle guard.

▼ 4.5 SO End of shelf road.

3.1 ▲ SO Start of shelf road, views over Trail #40: Cottonwood Wash Trail on right.

▼ 4.8 BL Fork in road. Continue left toward Gooseberry Guard Station. Mormon Pasture is to the right. View of Round Mountain directly ahead.

2.8 ▲ BR Fork in road. Continue right toward The Causeway. Mormon Pasture is on left.

GPS: N 37°50.48' W 109°43.93'

▼ 4.9 SO Left is FR 106, Trail #40: Cottonwood Wash Trail to Blanding. Continue on FR 095 (CR 225).

2.7 ▲ SO Right is FR 106, Trail #40: Cottonwood Wash Trail to Blanding. Follow the sign for Mormon Pasture to the next intersection.

GPS: N 37°50.47' W 109°44.08'

▼ 6.0 SO Cattle guard, then track on right.

1.6 ▲ SO Track on left, then cattle guard.

▼ 7.6 Trail finishes at intersection with FR 088. Right begins Trail #35: Cottonwood Canyon Trail, leading to Utah 211. Left begins Trail #38: North and South Elk Ridge Trail. Gooseberry Guard Station is on left.

0.0 ▲ At the junction of FR 088 (at the endpoints of Trail #35: Cottonwood Canyon Trail and Trail #38: North and South Elk Ridge Trail) and FR 095 (CR 225), zero trip meter and turn northeast onto FR 095.

GPS: N 37°50.42' W 109°46.39'

Cottonwood Wash Trail

STARTING POINT Junction of Trail #39: Blue
    Mountains Road (FR 095) and FR
    106/CR 227
FINISHING POINT Utah 95
TOTAL MILEAGE 24.4 miles
UNPAVED MILEAGE 23.2 miles
DRIVING TIME 2 hours
ELEVATION RANGE 5,200–7,800 feet
USUALLY OPEN May to November
DIFFICULTY RATING 2
SCENIC RATING 7
REMOTENESS RATING +0

Special Attractions

■ Scenic descent from the Manti-La Sal
  National Forest to Cottonwood Wash.
■ Can be combined with a choice of other
  forest roads to make a loop drive.

History

The southern end of Cottonwood Wash and
its many tributaries is the site of one of the
last battlegrounds between Native Americans
and Utah settlers attempting to carve a living
out of the harsh yet beautiful landscape.

Following the arrest of two Ute men near

Crossing at the Cottonwood Creek

Blanding in 1923, Chief Posey helped them
escape and led his people into a series of confrontations with the settlers, which led to
further arrests and deaths. There were skir-
mishes on Murphy Point to the southeast
and on the ridge above Butler Wash, just
southwest of where one of the two Utes had
been arrested. Comb Wash, just west of Cottonwood Canyon, was the site of a siege during which a large posse from Blanding attempted to capture the Utes. Although his
people escaped, Chief Posey was injured and
died two days later in a nearby cave.

With their chief fallen, the Ute people
surrendered and were taken into custody
while the federal government decided their
fate. A reservation was established for the
adult Utes on 8,360 acres of land, where
they received allotments for farming and
grazing. Children were forced to take on Eu-
ro-American haircuts and clothing. In the
1940s and 1950s, the government moved
the Utes again, this time to White Mesa,
about 10 miles south of Blanding.

Though the signs may be old and weath-
ered, you will notice you are passing through
Ute territory as you crisscross Cottonwood
Wash. Time has passed; yet the Ute maintain
a connection with the land.

Description

This trail commences at the junction of FR
106 and FR 095, near the west end of Trail
#39: Blue Mountains Road, and it heads south
through pine forest toward Blanding. It winds
through forest before descending to join Cottonwood Wash. There is a section of shelf road,
but it is wide enough to allow two vehicles to
pass fairly easily. The trail surface is good in dry
weather, but should not be attempted in wet
weather as it would be very hard for even good
mud tires to get an adequate grip.

In the valley there are numerous crossings
of the mainly dry Cottonwood Wash. These
should not pose any problem for a high-
clearance vehicle, since they are predomi-
nately wide and sandy. Cottonwood Wash
runs in a wide red canyon and drops to leave
the pine forest to enter the drier valley floor.
The trail leaves the Manti-La Sal National

Forest after 8.8 miles and then passes
through sections of Ute land and sections of
BLM land until it ends at Utah 95.

Current Road Information

Manti-La Sal National Forest
Monticello Ranger District
496 East Central; PO Box 820
Monticello, UT 84535
(435) 587-2041

Map References

BLM   Blanding
USFS   Manti-La Sal National Forest
USGS   1:24,000   Chippean Rocks, Cream
       Pots, Mancos Jim Butte, Black
       Mesa Butte
       1:100,000 Blanding
Maptech CD-ROM: Moab/Canyonlands
Trails Illustrated, #703
Utah Atlas & Gazetteer, pp. 30, 22
Utah Travel Council #5 (incomplete)

Route Directions

▼ 0.0   At the junction of Trail #39: Blue
         Mountains Road (FR 095) and FR
         106/CR 227, zero trip meter and pro-
         ceed south on FR 106/CR 227.
.8 ▲   Trail finishes at intersection with Trail
         #39: Blue Mountains Road (FR 095)
         and FR 106. Turn right for Monticello
         via Trail #39: Blue Mountains Road;
         turn left to meet Trail #38: North and
         South Elk Ridge Trail and Trail #35:
         Cottonwood Canyon Trail at FR 088.
         GPS: N 37°50.47′ W 109°44.08′

▼ 0.8 SO Track on right.
.0 ▲   SO Track on left.

▼ 0.9 SO Cattle guard.
.9 ▲   SO Cattle guard.

▼ 1.0 SO ATV Trail #445 on right.
.8 ▲   SO ATV Trail #445 on left.

▼ 2.8 SO Cattle guard.
.0 ▲   SO Cattle guard.

▼ 3.2 SO Cottonwood Wash enters on right.
           and runs alongside trail.
5.6 ▲ SO Trail leaves Cottonwood Wash and
           starts to climb out of canyon.

▼ 5.1 SO Track on left and remains of log cabin.
3.7 ▲ SO Track on right and remains of log cabin.

▼ 6.3 SO Track on right to old mine tailings and
           tunnels; mining lease in effect.
2.5 ▲ SO Track on left to old mine tailings and
           tunnels; mining lease in effect.
           GPS: N 37°46.34′ W 109°41.95′

▼ 6.7 SO Cross through creek, then track on
           right.
2.1 ▲ SO Track on left, then cross through creek.

▼ 7.0 SO Track on right.
1.8 ▲ SO Track on left.

▼ 7.3 SO Cross through creek.
1.5 ▲ SO Cross through creek.

▼ 7.6 SO Track on right, then cross through creek.
1.2 ▲ SO Cross through creek, then track on left.

▼ 8.6 SO Cross through creek.
0.2 ▲ SO Cross through creek.

▼ 8.7 SO Cross through creek.
0.1 ▲ SO Cross through creek.

▼ 8.8 SO Cattle guard, leaving Manti-La Sal
           National Forest; entering Ute land. Zero
           trip meter.
0.0 ▲   Continue into Manti-La Sal National
           Forest.
           GPS: N 37°44.52′ W 109°41.29′

▼ 0.0   Continue on along Cottonwood Wash.
7.9 ▲ SO Cattle guard; entering Manti-La Sal
           National Forest. Zero trip meter.

▼ 1.6 SO Two creek crossings.
6.3 ▲ SO Two creek crossings.

▼ 2.1 SO Cross through creek.
5.8 ▲ SO Cross through creek.

Trail #40: Cottonwood Wash Trail

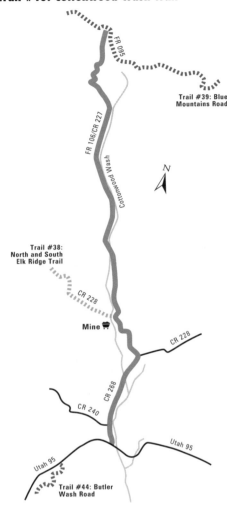

▼ 2.5   SO   Corral on left, cattle guard, cross through creek.
5.4 ▲   SO   Cross through creek, cattle guard, then corral on right.

▼ 3.0   SO   Cross through creek.
4.9 ▲   SO   Cross through creek.

▼ 3.6   SO   Cross through creek.
4.3 ▲   SO   Cross through creek.

▼ 4.2   SO   Wide slickrock creek crossing.
3.7 ▲   SO   Wide slickrock creek crossing.

▼ 4.9   SO   Track on left.
3.0 ▲   SO   Track on right.

▼ 5.0   SO   Cross through creek.
2.9 ▲   SO   Cross through creek.

▼ 5.3   SO   Track on right.
2.6 ▲   SO   Track on left.

▼ 5.4   SO   Cross through creek.
2.5 ▲   SO   Cross through creek.

▼ 5.8   SO   Leaving Ute land.
2.1 ▲   SO   Entering Ute land.
       GPS: N 37°40.52' W 109°38.53'

▼ 6.0   SO   Track on right.
1.9 ▲   SO   Track on left.

▼ 6.1   SO   Track on right.
1.8 ▲   SO   Track on left.

▼ 6.9   SO   Track on right.
1.0 ▲   SO   Track on left.

▼ 7.0   SO   Track on right.
0.9 ▲   SO   Track on left.

▼ 7.4   SO   Entering Ute land.
0.5 ▲   SO   Leaving Ute land.

▼ 7.9   TL   Junction with CR 228. Turn left signed to Blanding. Right is Trail #38: North and South Elk Ridge Trail. Zero trip meter.
0.0 ▲   Continue along South Cottonwood Road.
       GPS: N 37°38.98' W 109°37.55'

▼ 0.0   Continue along CR 228 toward Blanding.
7.7 ▲   TR   Junction with CR 227. Turn right signed South Cottonwood Road. Ahead is CR 228, Trail #38: North and South Elk Ridge Trail. Zero trip meter.

▼ 1.2   SO   Leaving Ute land.
6.5 ▲   SO   Entering Ute land.

▼ 1.5   SO   Cattle guard.
6.2 ▲   SO   Cattle guard.

▼ 2.1   SO Track on right.

5.6 ▲   SO Track on left.

▼ 2.6   BR Two tracks, left to corral and straight on for CR 228. Continue right on CR 268.

5.1 ▲   BL Track on right is second entrance to CR 228, second track goes straight to corral.

▼ 2.9   SO Track on left, second entrance to CR 228.

4.8 ▲   SO CR 228 on right.

▼ 5.2   SO Foundations of old mine works on left, followed by CR 274 on left and track on right.

2.5 ▲   SO CR 274 on right and track on left, followed by foundations of old mine works on right.

▼ 5.4   SO Cross through creek.

2.3 ▲   SO Cross through creek.

▼ 5.7   SO CR 274 on right.

2.0 ▲   SO CR 274 on left.

THE POSEY WAR

The Posey War was not actually a war. Rather, the name refers to a moderately violent series of confrontations between white settlers and Native Americans around 1923 in San Juan County. Tensions began in the 1880s when newly arrived settlers began placing increasing demands on lands traditionally claimed by the Ute and Paiute. By the turn of the century, the new ranchers and settlers had appropriated or destroyed most of the plants and animals that the tribes depended on, which led to much hostility between the whites and Indians.

White settlers would often physically and verbally abuse local Indians. They branded one man, a 60-year-old Paiute named Posey, as an arrogant troublemaker, and he became a symbol for their antagonism. As anti-Indian sentiment increased and the Indian food supplies decreased, the Ute and Paiute began gathering harvests from

Chief Posey

a newly abundant source—the ranches of the settlers. Indians hunted and stole from the flocks and herds of the ranchers.

In 1923, Sheriff William Oliver arrested two young Ute men for robbing a sheep camp, killing a calf, and burning a bridge. During their trial recess in Blanding, the two escaped with assistance from Posey. After Oliver failed to retrieve the pair, he returned to town and deputized a large number of local men to solve the "Indian problem"—that is, to shoot everything and anything that looked like an Indian. Expecting a full-scale war, Oliver and his men vowed to fight to the finish. Frightened by the aggressive whites, the Indians abandoned their homes and sought refuge in the countryside. But short of food and clothing and shivering in the harsh weather, the Ute and Paiute women and children quickly surrendered. The posse took 40 Indians as prisoners. First they were held in a school basement and then in a concentration camp of barbed wire in town. Posey and his men reacted with force. During a skirmish between the parties, Posey was fatally wounded and one young Indian escapee was killed.

In the wake of the "war," the federal government established an 8,360-acre reservation in Allen Canyon. While the adults were confined to this land, most of their children were taken and forced to conform to white culture. Barbers cut their hair while local men restrained them; volunteers bathed and dressed boys in calico shirts and girls in dresses with gingham aprons. They were then sent to attend school in Tawaoc, Colorado.

▼ 6.2	SO	Corral on left.	
1.5 ▲	SO	Corral on right.	

▼ 6.7	SO	CR 240 on right. Road turns to pavement.	
1.0 ▲	SO	CR 240 on left. Road turns to graded dirt.	

▼ 7.7		Cattle guard, then trail ends on Utah 95, 6 miles west of junction with US 191. Turn left for Blanding.
0.0 ▲		Trail commences at intersection of CR 268 and Utah 95. Sign points to South Cottonwood Forest Access. Zero trip meter and proceed northwest on CR 268.

GPS: N 37°33.78' W 109°34.99'

Small cliff dwelling near Johns Canyon Overlook Trail

MOAB REGION TRAIL #41

Johns Canyon Overlook Trail

STARTING POINT 0.1 miles north of mile marker 19 on Utah 261
FINISHING POINT Johns Canyon Overlook
TOTAL MILEAGE 12 miles
UNPAVED MILEAGE 12 miles
DRIVING TIME 1.25 hours (one-way)
ELEVATION RANGE 5,900–6,600 feet
USUALLY OPEN March to December
DIFFICULTY RATING 4
SCENIC RATING 8
REMOTENESS RATING +0

Special Attractions
- Overlook into Johns Canyon.
- Small cliff dwelling.
- Access to Grand Gulch hiking trails.

Description
This fairly short spur trail runs out onto Point Lookout and ends at a dizzying viewpoint over Johns Canyon. The trail starts off as graded dirt road and crosses over Polly Mesa. The grader stopped after 8 miles, however, and the trail becomes rougher and lumpier and crosses several slickrock sections. This section is a narrow winding two-track that threads through the cedars and junipers out to the rim of Johns Canyon. There are several pleasant campsites along the trail.

A small cliff dwelling, 9.7 miles from the start of the trail, sits underneath a rock overhang in the wash. The dwelling is a single room and has incredibly precise stonework forming the door and walls. The Grand Gulch Primitive Area is rich in Anasazi ruins and cliff dwellings, and many other ruins are to be found here and in surrounding canyons. No vehicles are allowed in the primitive areas, so you will need to park and hike in to see them.

Current Road Information
BLM Monticello Field Office
435 North Main; PO Box 7
Monticello, UT 84535
(435) 587-1500

Map References
BLM   Bluff, Navajo Mountain (incomplete)
USGS 1:24,000 Cedar Mesa North, Pollys Pasture, Cedar Mesa South, Slickhorn Canyon East
     1:100,000 Bluff, Navajo Mountain (incomplete)

Maptech CD-ROM: Moab/Canyonlands
Trails Illustrated, #706
Utah Atlas & Gazetteer, p. 22
Utah Travel Council #5

Route Directions

▼ 0.0   0.1 miles north of mile marker 19 on Utah 261, turn west onto graded dirt road. Road is marked as CR 249. Zero trip meter.
GPS: N 37°23.79′ W 109°56.59′

▼ 0.3   SO   Pass through wire gate. Information board and fee station on the left after gate, also track on left.
▼ 0.4   SO   Track on left.
▼ 0.5   SO   Corral on left.
▼ 0.7   SO   Cross through wash.
▼ 0.9   BL   Track on right.
▼ 1.1   SO   Track on left.
▼ 2.4   BL   Track on right goes to Government Trail. Zero trip meter.
GPS: N 37°24.45′ W 109°58.82′

▼ 0.0   Proceed along graded dirt road.
▼ 1.6   SO   Track on right.
GPS: N 37°23.49′ W 110°00.08′

▼ 2.0   SO   Cross through wash.
▼ 2.6   SO   Track on left.
▼ 2.9   SO   Track on right.
▼ 4.2   SO   Track on right.
▼ 4.3   SO   Campsite on left, then drop down and cross through wash.
GPS: N 37°21.17′ W 109°59.59′

▼ 5.0   SO   Cattle guard.
▼ 5.3   SO   Cross through wash.
▼ 5.5   SO   Corral on right and track on right in cleared area. Zero trip meter.
GPS: N 37°20.44′ W 110°00.41′

▼ 0.0   Continue toward Johns Canyon.
▼ 1.0   SO   Cross through wash.
▼ 1.3   SO   Trail becomes rockier.
GPS: N 37°19.18′ W 110°00.84′

▼ 1.6   BL   Track on right.
GPS: N 37°19.06′ W 110°00.81′

▼ 1.8   SO   Cross through wash. Small cliff dwelling is down the wash. To reach it, park and walk west along the wash for 0.1 miles downstream to where the wash feeds over a rocky pour-off into the lower canyon. The dwelling is immediately under this ledge. Walk to the south side of the canyon for the best view and access to the lower wash.
GPS: N 37°18.92′ W 110°00.71′

▼ 2.0   SO   Viewpoint over a tributary of Slickhorn Canyon.
▼ 2.1   BR   Small dam on right, then cross through slickrock wash.
▼ 2.4   SO   Cross through wash.
▼ 2.8   SO   Cross through wash.
GPS: N 37°18.19′ W 110°00.88′

▼ 3.8   BL   Track on right.
▼ 4.1   Trail passes an overlook over Johns Canyon and Trail #42: Johns Canyon Trail below, before finishing at a second overlook.
GPS: N 37°17.17′ W 110°00.66′

Trail #41: Johns Canyon Overlook Trail

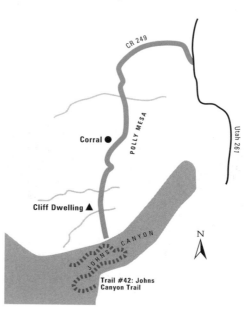

Johns Canyon Trail

STARTING POINT 0.4 miles along the San Juan Goosenecks Road (Utah 316) from Utah 261

FINISHING POINT Johns Canyon

TOTAL MILEAGE 17.3 miles

UNPAVED MILEAGE 17.3 miles

DRIVING TIME 1.5 hours (one-way)

ELEVATION RANGE 4,700–5,400 feet

USUALLY OPEN Year-round

DIFFICULTY RATING 4

SCENIC RATING 9

REMOTENESS RATING +0

Special Attractions
- Scenic Johns Canyon.
- The bluffs of Cedar Point and Muley Point.
- Indian petroglyphs.

History
Johns Canyon was formerly called Douglas Canyon after a prospector in the early 1900s, Jim Douglas, who found gold in the region. However, before he could return to work his find, the San Juan River rose and flooded his claim, and it remained underwater for the next 20 years. Disheartened, Jim jumped to his death into the San Juan River from the old wooden bridge at Mexican Hat. Douglas Mesa, across the river from Johns Canyon, still bears his name.

The name Johns Canyon comes from

Set of petroglyphs found along the trail

Wash crossing at Johns Canyon Creek

John Oliver, who ran cattle in the valley along with his brother, Bill. Their competition for the range was Jimmy Palmer, who was reputed to be a horse rustler and a murderer! Palmer killed John and crossed into Arizona in an attempt to evade the consequences of his crime. He was later captured and died in a Texas jail.

Description
This narrow trail leads into the Glen Canyon National Recreation Area and enters into Johns Canyon, a tributary of the main San Juan River. The trail is graded dirt road for most of its length; only the final part of the trail merits the 3 difficulty rating. The rest of the trail is suitable for high-clearance vehicles in dry weather.

The first part of the trail leaves the San Juan Goosenecks road (Utah 316) and heads west toward the steep face of Cedar Mesa. It enters the Glen Canyon National Recreation Area and passes underneath Cedar Point. The trail narrows as it winds around several deep canyons, containing tributaries of the San Juan River, just to the south. There are some sections of shelf road, but they are short and not especially narrow.

After passing through a gate on a narrow

section of the trail, you can see two sets of petroglyphs. The first set is easier to spot on the return journey, as it is on a large south-west facing boulder. The second set is higher up above the trail. Both sets show several human and animal shapes chipped into the black desert varnish.

The trail passes underneath Muley Point before swinging around to enter Johns Canyon. The canyon is long, with several fingers at the north end. The trail crosses the rocky Johns Canyon creek with a pour-off and several pools below it on the left. Shortly after, the trail forks. The main trail goes left and becomes narrower and ungraded. There is one section, 2 miles after the fork, that can wash out badly. This is also the narrowest section of the entire trail, with a steep drop-off into the canyon! It has been filled with rocks on several occasions but remains a low-traction climb with lots of rubble.

Although shown as continuing on most maps, the latter part of the trail enters an area now managed as wilderness by the Glen Canyon National Recreation Area, and no vehicles, including mountain bikes, are permitted.

The right fork after the Johns Canyon creek leads to a maze of tracks that head up Johns Canyon for another couple of miles. There is a nice campsite immediately after the turn. These sandy tracks often wash out, and there are several alternatives. If you keep to the right, you will pass the remains of a small dugout.

Current Road Information

BLM Monticello Field Office
435 North Main; PO Box 7
Monticello, UT 84535
(435) 587-1500

Map References

BLM   Bluff, Navajo Mountain
     (incomplete)
USGS 1:24,000   The Goosenecks,
     Goulding NE, Slickhorn Canyon
     East, Cedar Mesa South
     1:100,000 Bluff, Navajo Mountain
     (incomplete)
Maptech CD-ROM: Moab/Canyonlands
Trails Illustrated, #706
Utah Atlas & Gazetteer, p. 22
Utah Travel Council #5

Route Directions

▼ 0.0   Along San Juan Goosenecks road (Utah 316), 0.4 miles from Utah 261, turn northwest onto Johns Canyon Trail (CR 244), an unmarked graded dirt road, and zero trip meter.
        GPS: N 37°12.02' W 109°53.23'

▼ 2.5   BR Track on left.
        GPS: N 37°12.18' W 109°55.97'

▼ 4.2   SO Entering Glen Canyon National Recreation Area, followed by small track on right. Zero trip meter.
        GPS: N 37°12.77' W 109°57.79'

Trail #42: Johns Canyon Trail

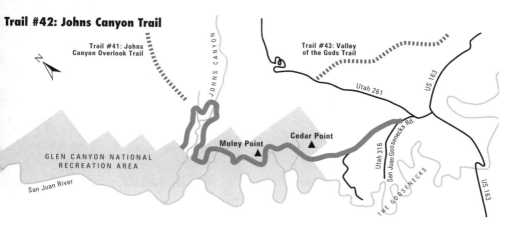

▼ 0.0		Continue into the recreation area. Cedar Point is on the right, Muley Point is ahead.
▼ 0.8	SO	Small track on left.
▼ 1.0	SO	Turnout on left, with views down tributary canyon of the San Juan River.
▼ 2.3	SO	Gate. Please keep closed. Zero trip meter.
		GPS: N 37°14.17' W 109°59.07'

▼ 0.0		Continue underneath the bluff.
▼ 0.3	SO	Petroglyphs to the right. Look back along the trail to see them.
▼ 0.9	SO	Passing underneath Muley Point.
▼ 1.6	SO	Petroglyphs to the right, slightly above the trail.
		GPS: N 37°14.26' W 110°00.08'

▼ 3.2	SO	Cross through wash.
▼ 4.3	SO	Track on left goes 0.2 miles to viewpoint.
▼ 6.9	SO	Cross through wash.
▼ 7.1	SO	Two tracks on right.
		GPS: N 37°16.36' W 110°00.03'

▼ 7.3	SO	Cross through Johns Canyon creek on rocky crossing. Series of small pouroffs below trail on left, followed by track to the right.
		GPS: N 37°16.46' W 109°59.83'

▼ 7.5	BL	Track on right leads up Johns Canyon for approximately 3 miles, passing beside a small dugout. Zero trip meter.
		GPS: N 37°16.60' W 109°59.84'

▼ 0.0		Continue around the rim of Johns Canyon.
▼ 0.9	SO	Cross through wash.
		GPS: N 37°16.78' W 110°00.61'

▼ 2.0	SO	Narrow section of trail, often very washed out.
▼ 3.3		Trail ends for vehicle travel at the boundary of the wilderness area.
		GPS: N 37°15.95' W 110°02.32'

Valley of the Gods Trail

STARTING POINT US 163, 4 miles east of Utah 261
FINISHING POINT Utah 261, at the bottom of the Moki Dugway
TOTAL MILEAGE 15.6 miles
UNPAVED MILEAGE 15.6 miles
DRIVING TIME 1.5 hours
ELEVATION RANGE 4,400–5,200 feet
USUALLY OPEN Year-round
DIFFICULTY RATING 2
SCENIC RATING 9
REMOTENESS RATING +0

Special Attractions
- Eroded rock formations along an easy valley trail.
- The Setting Hen, the Rooster, Balanced Rock, and more rock formations.
- Spectacular backcountry campsites.

Description
This graded dirt road winds through a valley of eroded rock formations not unlike the better-known Monument Valley, just over

The trail approaches Setting Hen Rock on the right and Rooster Butte on the left

Rock spires and Castle Butte

the border in Arizona. The trail passes such imaginatively named formations as the Setting Hen, Rooster Butte, and Rudolph and Santa Claus!

This well-used trail leaves from US 163, 4 miles east of the junction with Utah 261, and in dry weather it is easily traveled by passenger vehicles—though the trail can be washboardy with small sand traps. You immediately cross through Lime Creek, an easy creek crossing, and the trail then winds around the rock formations, with many turnouts to view and photograph the scene.

The floor of the valley is covered with sparse sagebrush, and the buttes and rock formations stand out well in the setting. The valley is rimmed by the white-topped cliffs of Cedar Mesa. There are a number of backcountry campsites, predominantly around Lime Creek near the beginning of the trail, although there are some spectacular ones around the midway point, at the base of the buttes along the ridge. These offer great views down Lime Creek and farther into the valley.

The far end of the trail offers views back over the valley to Rooster Butte and the Setting Hen before the trail finishes at the base of the Moki Dugway, a graded gravel section of Utah 261 that drops abruptly down from Cedar Mesa in a series of switchbacks.

Current Road Information

BLM Monticello Field Office
435 North Main; PO Box 7
Monticello, UT 84535
(435) 587-1500

Map References

BLM   Bluff
USGS 1:24,000   Mexican Hat, Cigarette
          Spring Cave, Cedar Mesa South
          1:100,000 Bluff
Maptech CD-ROM: Moab/Canyonlands
Trails Illustrated, #706
Utah Atlas & Gazetteer, p. 22
Utah Travel Council #5

Route Directions

▼ 0.0   From US 163, 4 miles east of Utah
          261, turn north on the graded dirt road
          at the sign for Valley of the Gods (CR
          242) and zero trip meter.
7.2 ▲   Trail ends at the junction with Utah
          261. Turn right for Mexican Hat, turn
          left for Bluff.
          GPS: N 37°14.10' W 109°48.82'

▼ 0.1 SO Cross through Lime Creek, followed by
          a track to the right along the creek.
7.1 ▲ SO Track on left along Lime Creek, then
          cross through the creek.

▼ 0.2 SO Turnout on right.
7.0 ▲ SO Turnout on left.

▼ 0.3 SO Track on right goes down to Lime
          Creek. Seven Sailors Rock is on the left.
6.9 ▲ SO Seven Sailors Rock is on the right.
          Track on left goes down to Lime Creek.

▼ 0.6 SO Turnout on right gives views along
          Lime Creek.
6.6 ▲ SO Turnout on left gives views along Lime
          Creek.

▼ 0.8 SO Track on left goes to West Fork Lime
          Creek. Setting Hen Rock is ahead, with
          Rooster Butte on the left.
6.4 ▲ SO Track on right goes to West Fork Lime
          Creek.

▼ 2.7 SO Trail passes underneath Setting Hen Rock.

4.5 ▲ SO Trail passes underneath Setting Hen Rock.

▼ 3.5 SO Track on left and track on right.

3.7 ▲ SO Track on left and track on right. Rooster Butte is ahead to the right, and Setting Hen Rock is slightly behind it.
GPS: N 37°16.94' W 109°48.52'

▼ 3.9 SO Turnout on left gives view over Franklin Butte on the left.

3.3 ▲ SO Turnout on right gives view over Franklin Butte on the right.

▼ 4.0 SO Track on right.

3.2 ▲ SO Track on left.

▼ 4.8 SO Track on left alongside wash. Franklin Butte is due left; Battleship Rock is larger butte north of it.

2.4 ▲ SO Track on right alongside wash. Franklin Butte is due right, Battleship Rock is larger butte north of it.
GPS: N 37°17.75' W 109°49.34'

▼ 4.9 SO Track on left.

2.3 ▲ SO Track on right.

▼ 5.5 SO Cross through West Fork Wash.

1.7 ▲ SO Cross through West Fork Wash.
GPS: N 37°18.03' W 109°50.04'

▼ 6.2 SO Track on right.

1.0 ▲ SO Track on left.

▼ 6.4 SO Track on right.

0.8 ▲ SO Track on left.

▼ 6.9 SO Track on right. The rock formation "De

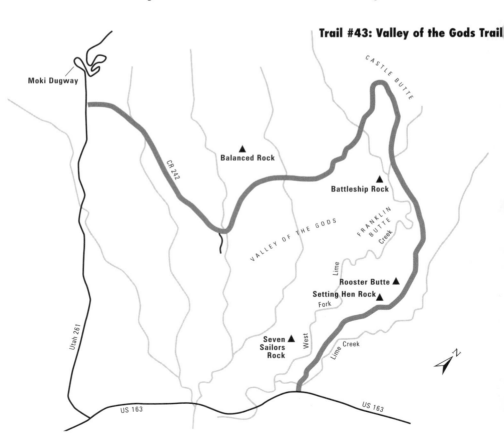

Trail #43: Valley of the Gods Trail

Gaulle and His Troops" on right.

0.3 ▲ SO Track on left. The rock formation "De Gaulle and His Troops" on left.

▼ 7.2 SO Trail passes over a ridge underneath Castle Butte on the left. Track on right at top of the ridge goes to a campsite at the base of the butte. Zero trip meter at the top of the ridge.

0.0 ▲ Continue along the graded trail.

GPS: N 37°18.95' W 109°51.31'

▼ 0.0 Descend along wash.

8.4 ▲ SO Trail passes over a ridge underneath Castle Butte on the right. Track on left at the top of the ridge goes to a campsite at the base of the butte. Zero trip meter at the top of the ridge.

▼ 0.3 SO Cross through wash. "Rudolph and Santa Claus" is ahead to the right of the trail.

8.1 ▲ SO Cross through wash.

▼ 0.9 SO Cross through wash.

7.5 ▲ SO Cross through wash.

▼ 1.1 SO Cross through wash.

7.3 ▲ SO Cross through wash. "Rudolph and Santa Claus" is ahead to the left of the trail.

▼ 1.5 SO Cross through wash.

6.9 ▲ SO Cross through wash.

▼ 1.7 SO Cross through wash.

6.7 ▲ SO Cross through wash.

▼ 2.2 SO Rooster Butte and Setting Hen Rock are visible on the far side of the valley.

6.2 ▲ SO Rooster Butte and Setting Hen Rock are visible on the far side of the valley.

GPS: N 37°17.17' W 109°51.14'

▼ 2.8 SO Turnout on left.

5.6 ▲ SO Turnout on right.

▼ 3.0 SO Track on left.

5.4 ▲ SO Track on right.

▼ 3.1 SO Cross through wash.

5.3 ▲ SO Cross through wash.

▼ 3.6 SO Cross through wash.

4.8 ▲ SO Cross through wash.

▼ 3.7 SO Track on right. Balanced Rock is ahead.

4.7 ▲ SO Track on left.

▼ 4.7 SO Cross through wash.

3.7 ▲ SO Cross through wash.

▼ 4.9 SO Cross through wash.

3.5 ▲ SO Cross through wash.

▼ 5.0 SO Track on left.

3.4 ▲ SO Track on right.

GPS: N 37°15.43' W 109°52.32'

▼ 5.1 SO Oil drilling post and Balanced Rock on right.

3.3 ▲ SO Oil drilling post and Balanced Rock on left.

▼ 5.6 SO Track on left.

2.8 ▲ SO Track on right.

▼ 6.9 SO Cross through wash.

1.5 ▲ SO Cross through wash.

▼ 7.9 SO Cross through wash.

0.5 ▲ SO Cross through wash.

▼ 8.0 SO Valley of the Gods B&B on the right.

0.4 ▲ SO Valley of the Gods B&B on the left.

▼ 8.4 Trail ends on Utah 261, at the bottom of the Moki Dugway. Turn right to ascend the dugway, turn left for Mexican Hat.

0.0 ▲ Trail commences on Utah 261 at the bottom of the Moki Dugway. Turn east on the graded dirt road at the sign for Valley of the Gods (CR 242). Zero trip meter.

GPS: N 37°15.85' W 109°55.90'

Butler Wash Road

STARTING POINT US 163, 18.2 miles east of
Mexican Hat or about 1.4 miles west of
junction of US 163 and Utah 191
FINISHING POINT Utah 95, 9.4 miles west of
US 191
TOTAL MILEAGE 20.2 miles
UNPAVED MILEAGE 20.2 miles
DRIVING TIME 1.5 hours
ELEVATION RANGE 4,400–5,400 feet
USUALLY OPEN Year-round
DIFFICULTY RATING 1
SCENIC RATING 10
REMOTENESS RATING +0

Special Attractions
- Butler Wash Anasazi ruins near the north
  end of the trail.
- Anasazi cliff dwellings in the canyons of
  Comb Ridge.
- Views of the tilted slab of Comb Ridge.

Description
This graded county road follows along the
tilted side of the Comb Ridge monocline
and alongside Butler Wash. From the trail
you can view the canyons cutting deeply into Comb Ridge, many of which contain
very unspoiled Anasazi cliff dwellings. Hikes
to explore these side canyons can reveal

Cliff dwelling at the end of the canyon hike

Red rocks tower above Butler Wash Road

many surprises. However, because of the unspoiled nature of the ruins, the BLM has
asked that exact locations and directions not
be published.

The road starts on US 163, 18.2 miles
east of Mexican Hat; look for the Butler
Wash Road BLM sign. The large bulk of
Tank Mesa is on the right; its red walls provide a contrast to the lighter stone of
Comb Ridge. Many of the numerous side
trails to the right and left lead to good,
small campsites. The northern end of the
trail leaves Butler Wash and winds around
Black Mesa and Black Mesa Butte through
stands of juniper and cedar trees before
joining Utah 95.

The road is graded for its full length and
is suitable for year-round travel. Snow or
heavy rain may temporarily make it impassable for short periods.

Current Road Information
BLM Monticello Field Office
435 North Main; PO Box 7
Monticello, UT 84535
(435) 587-1500

Map References

BLM   Blanding, Bluff
USGS   1:24,000   Bluff SW, Bluff, No
       Mans Island, Bluff NW, Hotel
       Rock, Black Mesa Butte
       1:100,000 Bluff, Blanding
Maptech CD-ROM: Moab/Canyonlands
Trails Illustrated, #706
Utah Atlas & Gazetteer, p. 22
Utah Travel Council #5

Route Directions

▼ 0.0   From US 163, 18.2 miles east of
           Mexican Hat, turn north onto the grad-
           ed dirt road at the BLM sign for Butler
           Wash Road. Pass through gate and
           zero trip meter.
7.9 ▲   Pass through gate, then trail ends at
           the junction with US 163. Turn left for
           Bluff, turn right for Mexican Hat.
           GPS: N 37°15.90' W 109°38.16'

▼ 0.3 BR Track on left.
7.6 ▲ SO Track on right.

▼ 0.9 SO Track on left, then cattle guard and
           information board.
7.0 ▲ SO Cattle guard and information board,
           then track on right.
           GPS: N 37°16.58' W 109°38.44'

▼ 1.7 BL Track on right.
6.2 ▲ SO Track on left.

▼ 2.5 SO Cross through wash.
5.4 ▲ SO Cross through wash.

▼ 3.0 SO Cross through wash.
4.9 ▲ SO Cross through wash.

▼ 3.2 SO Cross through wash.
4.7 ▲ SO Cross through wash.

▼ 3.3 SO Track on left.
4.6 ▲ SO Track on right.

▼ 3.6 SO Track on left.
4.3 ▲ SO Track on right.
           GPS: N 37°18.85' W 109°37.64'

▼ 3.8 SO Track on right, then cross over creek.
4.1 ▲ SO Cross over creek, then track on left.

▼ 4.1 SO Cross through wash.
3.8 ▲ SO Cross through wash.

▼ 4.4 SO Cross through wash.
3.5 ▲ SO Cross through wash.

▼ 4.8 SO Track on right.
3.1 ▲ SO Track on left.

▼ 5.1 SO Track on left, then cross through wash.
2.8 ▲ SO Cross through wash, then track on
           right.

▼ 5.5 SO Cross through wash.
2.4 ▲ SO Cross through wash.

▼ 5.9 SO Track on left.
2.0 ▲ SO Track on right.
           GPS: N 37°20.81' W 109°37.61'

▼ 6.2 SO Track on left.
1.7 ▲ SO Track on right.

▼ 6.5 SO Cross through wash.
1.4 ▲ SO Cross through wash.

▼ 6.7 SO Track on left.
1.2 ▲ SO Track on right.
           GPS: N 37°21.44' W 109°37.74'

▼ 6.8 SO Track on left.
1.1 ▲ SO Track on right.

▼ 7.1 SO Track on left.
0.8 ▲ SO Track on right.

▼ 7.9 BL Cross through fence line, then track to
           the right is Trail #47: Decker Road (CR
           230). Zero trip meter.
0.0 ▲   Continue along Butler Wash Road (CR
           262).
           GPS: N 37°22.33' W 109°37.26'

▼ 0.0   Continue along Butler Wash Road (CR
           262).
1.6 ▲ SO Track to the left is Trail #47: Decker

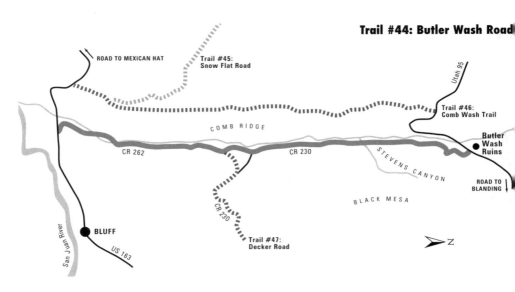

Road (CR 230), then cross through fence line. Zero trip meter.

▼ 0.5   SO   Track on left.
1.1 ▲   SO   Track on right.

▼ 0.6   SO   Track on left.
1.0 ▲   SO   Track on right.
     GPS: N 37°22.82' W 109°37.53'

▼ 1.2   SO   Track on left.
0.4 ▲   SO   Track on right.
     GPS: N 37°23.35' W 109°37.43'

▼ 1.6   TL   T-intersection. Right and left is CR 230. Zero trip meter.
0.0 ▲   Continue along CR 262.
     GPS: N 37°23.54' W 109°37.10'

▼ 0.0   Continue along CR 230 and immediately cross through wash.
10.7 ▲   TR   Cross through wash, then turn right onto CR 262. Zero trip meter.

▼ 0.4   SO   Cattle guard.
10.3 ▲   SO   Cattle guard.

▼ 0.6   SO   Two tracks on left.
10.1 ▲   SO   Two tracks on right.
     GPS: N 37°24.02' W 109°37.39'

▼ 1.0   SO   Oil drilling post on left, then track on left.

9.7 ▲   SO   Track on right, then oil drilling post on right.
     GPS: N 37°24.38' W 109°37.40'

▼ 1.2   SO   Cross through wash.
9.5 ▲   SO   Cross through wash.

▼ 1.3   SO   Track on left, then track on right.
9.4 ▲   SO   Track on left, then track on right.
     GPS: N 37°24.58' W 109°37.49'

▼ 1.7   SO   Cross through wash.
9.0 ▲   SO   Cross through wash.

▼ 2.1   SO   Cross through wash.
8.6 ▲   SO   Cross through wash.

▼ 2.5   SO   Cross through wash, then track on right and track on left. Large cave in Comb Ridge on left.
8.2 ▲   SO   Track on right and track on left, then cross through wash. Large cave in Comb Ridge on right.
     GPS: N 37°25.69' W 109°37.65'

▼ 2.6   SO   Track on left, then cross through fence line.
8.1 ▲   SO   Cross through fence line, then track on right.

▼ 3.0   SO   Cross through wash.
7.7 ▲   SO   Cross through wash.

▼ 3.3 SO Cross through wash.
7.4 ▲ SO Cross through wash.

▼ 3.8 SO Faint track on right, then cross through wash.
6.9 ▲ SO Cross through wash, then faint track on left.

▼ 4.8 SO Cattle guard.
5.9 ▲ SO Cattle guard.
        GPS: N 37°27.71′ W 109°37.81′

▼ 5.1 SO Track on right.
5.6 ▲ SO Track on left.

▼ 6.0 SO Track on right.
4.7 ▲ SO Track on left.
        GPS: N 37°28.66′ W 109°37.73′

▼ 6.5 SO Track on right.
4.2 ▲ SO Track on left.
        GPS: N 37°29.09′ W 109°37.67′

▼ 6.6 SO Track on left.
4.1 ▲ SO Track on right.

▼ 7.4 SO Cross through fence line.
3.3 ▲ SO Cross through fence line.

▼ 7.5 SO Cross through wash.
3.2 ▲ SO Cross through wash.

▼ 8.0 SO Track on left, then cross through fence line.
2.7 ▲ SO Cross through fence line, then track on right.

▼ 9.1 SO Track on right, then cross through wash.
1.6 ▲ SO Cross through wash, then track on left.

▼ 9.3 SO Cross through wash.
1.4 ▲ SO Cross through wash.

▼ 10.4 BL Cross through wash, then track on right.
0.3 ▲ TR Track on left, then cross through wash.
        GPS: N 37°32.04′ W 109°36.90′

▼ 10.5 SO Information board for Cedar Mesa on left.
0.2 ▲ SO Information board for Cedar Mesa on right.

▼ 10.7 Trail ends at the junction with Utah 95. Turn right for Blanding, left for Lake Powell.
0.0 ▲ Trail commences on Utah 95, 0.6 miles west of mile marker 113, 9.4 miles west of US 191. Turn east on unmarked graded dirt road and zero trip meter.
        GPS: N 37°32.09′ W 109°37.19′

MOAB REGION TRAIL #45

Snow Flat Road

STARTING POINT Trail #46: Comb Wash Trail, 2.2 miles north of US 163
FINISHING POINT Utah 261, 0.4 miles south of mile marker 23
TOTAL MILEAGE 21.4 miles
UNPAVED MILEAGE 21.4 miles
DRIVING TIME 1.5 hours
ELEVATION RANGE 4,400–6,600 feet
USUALLY OPEN March to December
DIFFICULTY RATING 3
SCENIC RATING 8
REMOTENESS RATING +0

Special Attractions
■ Old Mormon Pioneer Trail.
■ The Twist—a rocky climb up onto Cedar Mesa.
■ Views of Cedar Mesa and Road Canyon.
■ Snow Flat Spring Cave.

Description
Snow Flat Road follows part of the old Mormon Pioneer Trail that traveled west to the San Juan Mission. The trail leaves Trail #46: Comb Wash Trail and for the first few miles runs along the west side of Comb Wash. This section is very sandy, with several deep, powder-fine sand traps. The trail climbs a slight ridge away from Comb

Looking toward Comb Ridge from Snow Flats Road

Wash, offering spectacular views back to Comb Ridge, north to the Blue Mountains, and south into Road Canyon.

At The Twist, the trail climbs up through the slickrock onto Cedar Mesa. It is not particularly steep, but the surface changes to rock and is lumpy with a few ledges. This is possibly the best scenery of the whole trail, as the dark green of the cedar trees contrasts with the pink sandstone of The Twist. This section has many viewpoints and some of the best camping along the trail, in small sites looking east to Comb Ridge.

Cryptobiotic crust seen along Snow Flats Road

After The Twist, the trail reverts to a narrow, smooth, graded dirt road interspersed with short rocky sections. The turnoff to Snow Flat Spring Cave is not marked but is easy to find. The large shallow cave itself is a short hike down the wash. At the back, under an overhang, two springs drip out of the rock wall into two wooden cowboy tanks. The moisture promotes the growth of ferns and mosses in hanging gardens on the wall above the spring.

After the turnoff to the cave, the trail is smoother graded dirt and not too sandy. There are several small, unmarked tracks to explore, and a hiking trail.

Snow can temporarily close the road in the winter months, as can heavy rain, but it is often passable the entire year. The trail finishes on Utah 261, north of the Moki Dugway.

There are a number of Indian relics in the vicinity of this trail, which are interesting to view, but please respect these sites and don't remove anything.

Current Road Information
BLM Monticello Field Office
435 North Main; PO Box 7
Monticello, UT 84535
(435) 587-1500

Map References
BLM   Bluff
USGS 1:24,000   Bluff SW, Bluff NW,
        Snow Flat Spring Cave, Cedar
        Mesa North
        1:100,000 Bluff
Maptech CD-ROM: Moab/Canyonlands
Trails Illustrated, #706
Utah Atlas & Gazetteer, p. 22
Utah Travel Council #5

Route Directions

▼ 0.0   From Trail #46: Comb Wash Trail,
            2.2 miles north of the junction with
            US 163, turn north onto the graded
            dirt road, marked CR 237, and zero
            trip meter.

2.5 ▲   Trail ends at the junction with Trail
            #46: Comb Wash Trail. Turn right to

exit to US 163, turn left to continue along Comb Wash Road.

GPS: N 37°17.82' W 109°39.61'

▼ 0.2   SO   Cross through wash.
2.3 ▲   SO   Cross through wash.

▼ 2.0   SO   Cross through wash.
0.5 ▲   SO   Cross through wash.

▼ 2.5   SO   Track on right and information board and fee station for Cedar Mesa. Zero trip meter.
0.0 ▲   Continue along graded road.

GPS: N 37°19.85' W 109°39.81'

▼ 0.0   Continue along graded road.
9.4 ▲   SO   Track on left and information board and fee station for Cedar Mesa. Zero trip meter.

▼ 0.2   SO   Cattle guard.
9.2 ▲   SO   Cattle guard.

▼ 0.3   SO   Cross through wash.
9.1 ▲   SO   Cross through wash.

▼ 1.3   SO   Track on left. Trail swings away from wash.
8.1 ▲   SO   Track on right. Trail joins the wash.

▼ 2.2   SO   Track on left to campsite.
7.2 ▲   SO   Track on right to campsite.

GPS: N 37°20.88' W 109°41.34'

▼ 4.3   SO   Track on left, then track on right. You are crossing the Mormon Trail.
5.1 ▲   SO   Track on left, then track on right.

GPS: N 37°22.03' W 109°43.01'

▼ 5.4   SO   Faint track on right, then climb The Twist.
4.0 ▲   SO   Trail reaches bottom of The Twist, then faint track on left.

▼ 5.6   SO   Viewpoint and campsite on right.
3.8 ▲   SO   Viewpoint and campsite on left.

▼ 5.8   SO   Viewpoint and campsite on right.
3.6 ▲   SO   Viewpoint and campsite on left.

Trail #45: Snow Flat Road

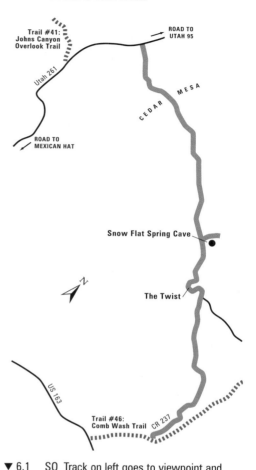

▼ 6.1   SO   Track on left goes to viewpoint and campsite.
3.3 ▲   SO   Track on right goes to viewpoint and campsite.

▼ 6.7   SO   Viewpoint on right at oil drilling post.
2.7 ▲   SO   Viewpoint on left at oil drilling post.

GPS: N 37°22.78' W 109°44.46'

▼ 6.8   SO   Pass through wire gate.
2.6 ▲   SO   Pass through wire gate.

▼ 6.9   SO   Campsite on right.
2.5 ▲   SO   Campsite on left.

▼ 8.7   SO   Track on right goes to viewpoint over the canyon and campsite. Snow Flat Spring Cave is visible from the viewpoint to the north, high on the cliff.

0.7 ▲   SO Track on left goes to viewpoint over the canyon and campsite. Snow Flat Spring Cave is visible from the viewpoint to the north, high on the cliff.
GPS: N 37°23.86' W 109°45.86'

▼ 8.9   SO Track on right.
0.5 ▲   SO Track on left.

▼ 9.4   SO Well-used, ungraded spur track on right goes to Snow Flat Spring and Cave. Zero trip meter.
0.0 ▲   Continue along the graded trail.
GPS: N 37°24.11' W 109°46.57'

Spur to Snow Flat Spring Cave

▼ 0.0   Proceed along small well-used track.
▼ 0.4   TR Cross through small wash, then turn right after wash.
▼ 0.6   UT Trail ends for vehicles at turning circle.
GPS: N 37°24.32' W 109°46.07'

To reach the cave, walk south to join the wash and proceed southeast down the main wash, staying on the north side. After approximately 350 yards the wash goes over a big rocky pour-off. Look for the small trail that stays high on the north side of the wash, and follow this for approximately 175 yards to Snow Flat Spring Cave. There is a small stone ruin just before the cave against the cliff.
GPS at the cave:
N 37°24.19' W 109°45.97'

Continuation of Main Trail

▼ 0.0   Continue along the graded trail.
9.5 ▲   SO Well-used, ungraded spur track on left goes to Snow Flat Spring and Cave. Zero trip meter.

▼ 1.2   SO Cross through wash.
8.3 ▲   SO Cross through wash.

▼ 1.7   SO Track on left and hiking trail to the right.

7.8 ▲   SO Track on right and hiking trail to the left.
GPS: N 37°25.05' W 109°47.94'

▼ 2.9   BR Track on left.
6.6 ▲   BL Track on right.

▼ 3.0   SO Track on left.
6.5 ▲   SO Track on right.

▼ 4.5   SO Pass through fence line.
5.0 ▲   SO Pass through fence line.
GPS: N 37°26.05' W 109°50.48'

▼ 4.6   SO Track on right goes to campsite.
4.9 ▲   SO Track on left goes to campsite.
GPS: N 37°26.09' W 109°50.60'

▼ 4.7   SO Track on right.
4.8 ▲   SO Track on left.
GPS: N 37°26.08' W 109°50.73'

▼ 7.6   SO Faint track on left.
1.9 ▲   BL Faint track on right.

▼ 8.6   SO Information board and fee station for Cedar Mesa on left.
0.9 ▲   SO Information board and fee station for Cedar Mesa on right.
GPS: N 37°26.17' W 109°54.39'

▼ 9.0   SO Track on left.
0.5 ▲   SO Track on right.

▼ 9.1   SO Large track on left, then second faint track on left.
0.4 ▲   BL Faint track on right, then second large track on right.
GPS: N 37°26.34' W 109°54.96'

▼ 9.3   SO Track on left.
0.2 ▲   BL Track on right.

▼ 9.5   Trail finishes at the junction with Utah 261. Turn right to join to Utah 95, turn left for Mexican Hat.
0.0 ▲   Trail starts on Utah 261. Turn east on CR 237 and zero trip meter. BLM sign reads, "Impassable when wet."
GPS: N 37°26.45' W 109°55.32'

Comb Wash Trail

STARTING POINT Utah 95, 13.5 miles west of junction with US 191

FINISHING POINT US 163, 0.7 miles east of mile marker 37

TOTAL MILEAGE 17.4 miles

UNPAVED MILEAGE 17.4 miles

DRIVING TIME 1 hour

ELEVATION RANGE 4,400–5,000 feet

USUALLY OPEN Year-round

DIFFICULTY RATING 2

SCENIC RATING 9

REMOTENESS RATING +0

Special Attractions

- Comb Ridge monocline.
- Anasazi cliff dwellings in the area.
- Significant section of the Mormon Hole-in-the-Rock Expedition.
- Cave Towers near the north end of the trail.

History

Comb Ridge is a long monocline running for almost 80 miles from Elk Ridge in the north down to Kayenta, Arizona. A monocline is the bending of the earth's crust in one direction only, and Comb Ridge has its sheer scarp face on the western side. Formed over 65 million years ago, Comb Wash is a major drainage for the area, with tributaries draining from Cedar Mesa to the west as well as down the face of the monocline. It takes its name from the scalloped appearance of the ridge top, which resembles the comb of a rooster.

The earliest inhabitants of the region were the Anasazi, or Ancient Puebloans, who have left many relics and signs behind them. Various dwellings and structures of stone and mud are found in nearby Mule Canyon and its surroundings (farther west on Utah 95). Some of the best examples are the Butler Wash Ruins (a couple of miles east along Utah 95). Here you can see a large cluster of dwellings high up under an overhang in the cliff, accessed by steep hand and footholds up the cliff wall. Most of the cliff dwellings are oriented toward the south, so that they could take full benefit of the low winter sun for warmth and light. The well-marked site includes a 0.5-mile walk to an overlook over the ruins. Another ruin is Cave Towers (near Mule Canyon Ruins on Utah 95, 0.3 miles west of mile marker 103), a cluster of seven towers in a tributary of Mule Canyon. A short, 0.6-mile, unsigned dirt road leads south from Utah 95; a very short hike at the end of the road leads down the wash to the three remaining towers on either side, above a series of large caves.

To the 1880 Mormon Hole-in-the-Rock Expedition, Comb Ridge appeared an impassable barrier as they descended from Cedar Mesa. They were forced to swing south and eventually succeeded in crossing Comb Ridge at San Juan Hill near where the San Juan River cuts through the ridge.

Looking down over Comb Wash Trail from Utah 95

Description

This trail runs down the west side of Comb Ridge, one of the most prominent features of the region. The trail runs close to both Comb Wash and Comb Ridge for its full length. From this side, Comb Ridge is a series of cliff faces forming an impenetrable barrier to east-west travel.

The trail leaves Utah 95 on a graded dirt road, CR 235. There is no sign at the start other than the county road marker, but a BLM information board can be seen from the highway. The information board gives general information for camping, hiking, and exploring in the region. A large well-used informal camping area is nearby, situated under the cottonwoods alongside Comb Wash. This is a pleasant area, although it's rather close to the highway.

The trail leads south, crossing a few small sandy washes. Other tracks in the first few miles lead to camping areas; the most attractive campsites on the trail are at the northern end.

The trail, traveling almost due north to south, is graded for its full length, but it is loose and sandy with several patches of deep sand traps. It is suitable for high-clearance vehicles, but in dry weather 4WD may be necessary to successfully negotiate the sandy

A small wooden cabin sits at the foot of Comb Ridge

sections. The northern end of the trail is the sandiest; the southern end tends to be firmer, but the trail does cross the wide sandy Comb Wash at the lower end. This trail is impassable during wet weather.

The ever-changing Comb Ridge makes for fascinating scenery. To the west are views over Cedar Mesa. After 8.9 miles, an access track to Cedar Mesa is marked by a BLM information board. The BLM is using the area to try out a day-use fee system. Day hiking and overnight backpacking requires a permit, which can be obtained at the entry points using a self-pay system during winter months. Hikers at other times of the year require advance reservations. Car camping and traveling along the established county roads does not currently require a permit, although camping stays are limited to two nights and you are requested to use existing campsites.

The trail passes the eastern end of Trail #45: Snow Flat Road before finishing at the junction of US 163.

Current Road Information

BLM Monticello Field Office
435 North Main; PO Box 7
Monticello, UT 84535
(435) 587-1500

Map References

BLM   Blanding, Bluff
USGS 1:24,000   Hotel Rock, Bluff NW,
       Bluff SW
       1:100,000 Blanding, Bluff
Maptech CD-ROM: Moab/Canyonlands
Trails Illustrated, #706
Utah Atlas & Gazetteer, p. 22
Utah Travel Council #5

Route Directions

▼ 0.0   From Utah 95, 13.5 miles west of US
             191, turn south on graded gravel road
             CR 235 and zero trip meter. Turn is
             approximately 1 mile west of where
             the highway crosses Comb Ridge.
4.0 ▲   Trail ends on Utah 95 just west of
             Comb Ridge. Turn right for Blanding,

left for Hite Crossing.
GPS: N 37°30.67' W 109°39.18'

Trail #46: Comb Wash Trail

▼ 0.1   SO   Information board and well-used large camping area under cottonwoods alongside Comb Wash. Multiple tracks to the right and left lead to camping areas for the next 0.5 miles.

3.9 ▲   SO   Information board and well-used large camping area under cottonwoods alongside Comb Wash.

▼ 0.6   SO   Cross through wash.
3.4 ▲   SO   Cross through wash. Multiple tracks to the right and left lead to camping areas for the next 0.5 miles.

▼ 1.0   SO   Track on right.
3.0 ▲   SO   Track on left.

▼ 1.4   SO   Cross through sandy wash.
2.6 ▲   SO   Cross through sandy wash.

▼ 2.7   SO   Cross through wash.
1.3 ▲   SO   Cross through wash.

▼ 3.1   SO   Cross through wash.
0.9 ▲   SO   Cross through wash.

▼ 3.7   SO   Track on right.
0.3 ▲   SO   Track on left.

▼ 4.0   SO   Pass through wire gate, then corral on right. Zero trip meter.
0.0 ▲   Continue along Comb Wash.
GPS: N 37°27.29' W 109°39.18'

▼ 0.0   Continue along Comb Wash.
4.9 ▲   SO   Corral on left, then pass through wire gate. Zero trip meter.

▼ 1.1   SO   Track on right.
3.8 ▲   SO   Track on left.

▼ 1.8   SO   Track on right.
3.1 ▲   SO   Track on left.
GPS: N 37°25.79' W 109°39.16'

▼ 2.4   SO   Track on right.
2.5 ▲   SO   Track on left.

▼ 3.8   SO   Track on left.
1.1 ▲   SO   Track on right.
GPS: N 37°24.14' W 109°39.36'

▼ 4.5   SO   Track on right.
0.4 ▲   SO   Track on left.
GPS: N 37°23.47' W 109°39.37'

▼ 4.9   SO   Track on right goes to Cedar Mesa. Information board at intersection. Zero trip meter.
0.0 ▲   Continue along Comb Wash.
GPS: N 37°23.14' W 109°39.38°

▼ 0.0   Continue along Comb Wash.

6.3 ▲ SO Track on left goes to Cedar Mesa.
Information board at intersection. Zero
trip meter.

▼ 0.2 SO Cattle guard.
6.1 ▲ SO Cattle guard.

▼ 0.3 SO Track on left.
6.0 ▲ SO Track on right.
GPS: N 37°22.91′ W 109°39.41′

▼ 1.1 SO Track on right goes to old cabin.
5.2 ▲ SO Track on left goes to old cabin.

▼ 3.5 SO Cattle guard.
2.8 ▲ SO Cattle guard.
GPS: N 37°20.16′ W 109°39.24′

▼ 3.6 BL Track on right.
2.7 ▲ SO Track on left.
GPS: N 37°20.06′ W 109°39.28′

▼ 4.9 SO Track on left.
1.4 ▲ SO Track on right.

▼ 5.9 SO Cross through Comb Wash.
0.4 ▲ SO Cross through Comb Wash.

▼ 6.3 SO Track on right is Trail #45:
Snow Flat Road (CR 237). Zero trip
meter.
0.0 ▲   Continue toward Utah 95.
GPS: N 37°17.85′ W 109°39.69′

▼ 0.0   Continue toward US 163.
2.2 ▲ BR Track on left is Trail #45: Snow Flat
Road (CR 237). Zero trip meter.

▼ 0.9 SO Track on left.
1.3 ▲ SO Track on right.

▼ 1.0 SO Track on left, then cross through wash.
1.2 ▲ SO Cross through wash, then track on
right.

▼ 1.7 SO Cross through wash.
0.5 ▲ SO Cross through wash.

▼ 1.8 SO Cross through wash.
0.4 ▲ SO Cross through wash.

▼ 2.0 SO Faint track on right.
0.2 ▲ SO Faint track on left.

▼ 2.1 SO Information board on left.
0.1 ▲ SO Information board on right.

▼ 2.2   Trail ends at the junction with US
163 just west of Comb Ridge. Turn
left for Bluff, turn right for Mexican
Hat.
0.0 ▲   Trail starts on US 163, 0.7 miles east
of mile marker 37. Turn north on the
graded dirt road and zero trip meter.
Road is marked as CR 235.
GPS: N 37°16.41′ W 109°40.62′

MOAB REGION TRAIL #47

Decker Road

STARTING POINT US 191, at mile marker 33
FINISHING POINT Junction with Trail #44:
Butler Wash Road, 7.9 miles north of
US 163
TOTAL MILEAGE 9.3 miles
UNPAVED MILEAGE 9.3 miles
DRIVING TIME 45 minutes
ELEVATION RANGE 4,600–5,100 feet
USUALLY OPEN Year-round
DIFFICULTY RATING 2
SCENIC RATING 7
REMOTENESS RATING +0

Special Attractions
- Views across to the Comb Ridge
monocline.
- Pretty Black Rock Canyon.
- Many graded county roads for easy
exploration.

Description
There are many graded county roads in the
vicinity of Trail #44: Butler Wash Road, and
these easy trails offer some varied, attractive
scenery for driving and hiking. This trail
covers some of these well-marked roads east
of Butler Wash.

Decker Road leaves US 191, 14.3 miles south of the junction with Utah 95 and travels west across Cottonwood Wash. It passes through some private property around the wash; signs request that you remain on the county roads. The road travels around the south end of No-Mans Island, a large mesa that towers over the sagebrush bench, before dropping to cross through the pretty Black Rock Canyon. This shallow canyon winds north, and a county road runs alongside it for much of its length.

The road ends on the Butler Wash Road; entering from the west there is a good view of Comb Ridge and Butler Wash.

Current Road Information

BLM Monticello Field Office
435 North Main; PO Box 7
Monticello, UT 84535
(435) 587-1500

Map References

BLM   Bluff
USGS   1:24,000   No Mans Island, Bluff
          1:100,000 Bluff
Maptech CD-ROM: Moab/Canyonlands
Utah Atlas & Gazetteer, p. 22
Utah Travel Council #5

Route Directions

▼ 0.0   From US 191, opposite mile marker 33, turn southwest onto graded dirt road and cross over cattle guard. Sign for

          CR 230 is above cattle guard.
2.5 ▲   Cross cattle guard, then the trail ends at junction with US 191. Turn left for Blanding, turn right for Bluff.
          GPS: N 37°22.78′ W 109°30.15′

▼ 0.8 SO Cattle guard.
1.7 ▲ SO Cattle guard.

▼ 1.5 SO Track on left.
1.0 ▲ SO Track on right.
          GPS: N 37°23.38′ W 109°31.26′

▼ 1.8 SO Entering private property. Remain on county road.
0.7 ▲ SO Leaving private property.

▼ 2.1 SO Cabin on right.
0.4 ▲ SO Cabin on left.

▼ 2.2 SO Corral on right, then cattle guard.
0.3 ▲ SO Cattle guard, then corral on left.

▼ 2.5 SO Graded road on right is CR 202A. Zero trip meter.
0.0 ▲   Continue along CR 230.
          GPS: N 37°23.53′ W 109°32.23′

▼ 0.0   Continue along CR 230.
3.8 ▲ SO Graded road on left is CR 202A. Zero trip meter.

▼ 0.1 SO Cross through Cottonwood Wash. Old Buick LeSabre on right before wash.

Looking back at Comb Ridge and Tank Mesa from the start of the trail

Trail #47: Decker Road

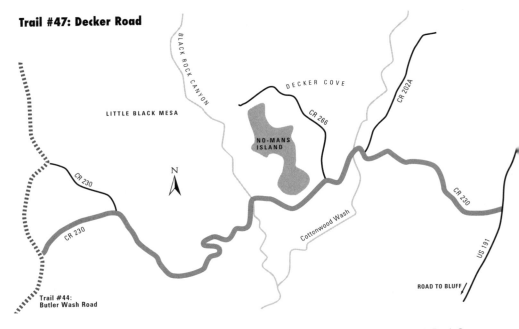

3.7 ▲   SO Cross through Cottonwood Wash. Old Buick LeSabre on left after wash.

▼ 0.7   BR Cattle guard, exiting private property. Faint track on left after cattle guard. No-Mans Island is directly ahead.

3.1 ▲   SO Faint track on right, then cattle guard. Entering private property, remain on county road.
        GPS: N 37°23.15' W 109°32.63'

▼ 0.9   BL Graded road on right is CR 266, which goes to Decker Cove.

2.9 ▲   SO Graded road on left is CR 266, which goes to Decker Cove.
        GPS: N 37°23.21' W 109°32.77'

▼ 1.5   BR Track on left.
2.3 ▲   SO Track on right.

▼ 2.1   SO Graded road on right goes up Black Rock Canyon.
1.7 ▲   SO Graded road on left goes up Black Rock Canyon.
        GPS: N 37°23.00' W 109°33.89'

▼ 2.4   SO Cross through Black Rock Canyon Wash.

1.4 ▲   SO Cross through Black Rock Canyon Wash.

▼ 2.9   SO Cross through wash.
0.9 ▲   SO Cross through wash. No-Mans Island is ahead.

▼ 3.1   SO Cross through small creek, flowing from spring on right.
0.7 ▲   SO Cross through small creek, flowing from spring on left.

▼ 3.3   SO Cross through wash.
0.5 ▲   SO Cross through wash.
        GPS: N 37°22.43' W 109°34.66'

▼ 3.8   BR Graded road to the left is CR 270. Zero trip meter.
0.0 ▲   Continue northeast.
        GPS: N 37°22.15' W 109°34.70'

▼ 0.0   Continue southwest.
1.7 ▲   SO Graded road to the right is CR 270. Zero trip meter.

▼ 0.4   SO Track on left.
1.3 ▲   BL Track on right.

▼ 0.6   SO Cross through wash.

1.1 ▲	SO	Cross through wash.

▼ 0.8	SO	Cross through wash.
0.9 ▲	SO	Cross through wash.

▼ 1.4	SO	Track on left.
0.3 ▲	SO	Track on right.

▼ 1.6	SO	Cross through wash.
0.1 ▲	SO	Cross through wash.

▼ 1.7	TL	Turn onto unsigned graded dirt road and zero trip meter. Comb Ridge is now directly ahead.
0.0 ▲		Continue southeast along graded road.
		GPS: N 37°22.91' W 109°36.08'

▼ 0.0		Continue toward Comb Ridge.
1.3 ▲	TR	T-intersection, turn right onto CR 230 (Decker Road) and zero trip meter.

▼ 1.3		Trail ends at the junction with Trail #44: Butler Wash Road, 7.9 miles north of US 163. Turn left to exit to US 163 for Bluff or Mexican Hat. Turn right to continue along Butler Wash Road.
0.0 ▲		Trail commences on Trail #44: Butler Wash Road, 7.9 miles north of US 163. Turn northeast onto graded dirt road, marked CR 230, and zero trip meter.
		GPS: N 37°22.32' W 109°37.25'

MOAB REGION TRAIL #48

Montezuma Canyon Trail

STARTING POINT Hatch Trading Post, junction of CR 212 and CR 446
FINISHING POINT US 191
TOTAL MILEAGE 41.4 miles
UNPAVED MILEAGE 41.4 miles
DRIVING TIME 2.5 hours
ELEVATION RANGE 4,700–6,900 feet
USUALLY OPEN Year-round
DIFFICULTY RATING 1
SCENIC RATING 9
REMOTENESS RATING +0

Opening of a small cliff dwelling

Special Attractions

■ Many small cliff dwellings and petroglyphs.
■ Ancient Anasazi ruins at Three Kiva Pueblo.
■ 11th-century Bradford Canyon Ruins.

History

The history of this trail stretches as far back as the Anasazi and extends to the uranium boom of the 1940s and 1950s. The most significant feature along the trail is possibly the Three Kiva Pueblo, 13 miles from the start. This 14-room Anasazi site experienced three building phases and three occupations between A.D. 1000 and 1300. It consists of three belowground kivas (ceremonial sites) and the remains of some aboveground stone rooms once used for living and storage areas. One area when excavated revealed a very high concentration of turkey bones, indicating that it was probably used as a turkey run, providing food and feathers for blankets.

The site is managed by the Bureau of Land Management, which has restored one of the three underground kivas. You can descend a ladder to view the kiva as it would have looked when used for the tribal ceremonies of the Anasazi. The floor of the kiva has a fire pit and a sipapu—a hole in the ground representing the opening through which the mythical tribal ancestors first emerged into the world. Benches surround the fire pit, and holes in the side allow fresh air into the chamber.

There are many small Anasazi cliff dwellings along the length of the drive. Those that are next to the trail are mentioned on the directions, but there are others to be found by the keen of sight, notably near the junctions of Montezuma Creek and Monument Canyon as well as at Coal Bed Canyon, slightly off the trail.

At nearly the same time as the Anasazi, around 800 years ago, other inhabitants in the canyon constructed cliff dwellings at what is now called the Bradford Canyon Ruins, found near the junction of Bradford Creek and Montezuma Creek. These dwellings are low down on the cliff face and spread the length of a large crack in the cliff. A fence, erected in the 1960s, protects them from damage.

The Hatch Trading Post, at the southern end of the route, is an example of more recent Native American history. The trading post is one of several that came into existence

Slickrock crossing of the Montezuma Creek ford

between 1900 and 1930. The Shiprock Indian Agency was encouraging the development of arts, crafts, and agriculture, and the trading posts were set up to deal with the corresponding increase in two-way trade. Historically, barter has always been an important part of Native American economy, and the trading posts acted as focal points for the community as well as allowing the Ute and Navajo to trade their goods with the outside world. By the 1980s most trading posts had disappeared, as wages reduced the need for barter. Many traders were unable to compete and went out of business. Hatch, like many of the surviving trading posts, now sells mainly soft drinks and small goods to passing tourists.

The name Montezuma refers to the last Aztec ruler of Mexico, who, the story goes, escaped his captors and fled north. He supposedly eluded them for a while before being recaptured in this corner of Utah and executed. As a result, "Recapture" is a common name in this area, notably Recapture Creek and Reservoir near Blanding. There is no proof of the origin of this tale, but it

A view of the Three Kiva Pueblo

makes for an unusual explanation nevertheless!

The recent history of Montezuma Creek includes some uranium mining—though a painted sign on a rock by the Utomic Corporation is pretty much the only visible remnant. The top end of the road into Montezuma Creek was built by the Civilian Conservation Corps in the late 1930s.

Description

This interest-packed route sees very few visitors. Its entire length is graded county road that poses no difficulties for passenger vehicles in dry weather. It travels mostly along the wide-bottomed floor of Montezuma Canyon; Montezuma Creek flows down the middle of it to join the San Juan River to the south. Montezuma Creek is dry for a large part of the year, but as with all creeks around this region, it has the capacity to be deep and fast flowing, and it's prone to flash floods. Extreme care should be taken if heavy rain is predicted, and if there is any doubt about the crossings, then do not cross. All of the creek crossings have a gentle approach and either a sandy or rocky bottom.

The route starts at the historic Hatch Trading Post and continues north along CR 446. There are a few tricky junctions but for the most part the major county road is correct.

The route passes through a mixture of private property and BLM land. There are some reasonable backcountry camping opportunities, but be sure you are not inadvertently trespassing on private property before making camp.

After 11 miles you come to the first cliff dwelling on the west side of the track. These dwellings can be difficult to spot, as they blend in so well with the surrounding cliffs. If you climb up to investigate the ruins, remember that it is illegal to remove, deface, or destroy any of the structures or artifacts within. Tread Lightly!™ The cliff dwellings along this route are for the most part very small, with only one or two rooms sandwiched into a crack in the cliff face. They are in original condition and unrenovated by the BLM.

At 13 miles, you reach the remains of the Three Kiva Pueblo on a meander in the creek. The BLM has provided a book to track visitor numbers, but there are no interpretive signs for the site.

At the northern end of the canyon there is a thriving community of market gardeners and even a vineyard. Local landowners use the natural caves in the base of the cliffs as sheds and storage areas to house a variety of things. Trailers, hay, farming equipment, and animals are all sheltered here.

The route finishes on US 191, 0.1 miles south of mile marker 67. Turn right for Monticello, left for Blanding.

Current Road Information

BLM Monticello Field Office
435 North Main; PO Box 7
Monticello, UT 84535
(435) 587-1500

Map References

BLM   Bluff, Blanding
USFS   Manti-La Sal National Forest
       (incomplete)
USGS   1:24,000   Hatch Trading Post, Bug
       Canyon, Bradford Canyon, Devil
       Mesa, Monticello South
       1:100,000 Bluff, Blanding
Maptech CD-ROM: Moab/Canyonlands
Utah Atlas & Gazetteer, p. 23
Utah Travel Council #5

Route Directions

▼ 0.0   Immediately northeast of the Hatch
           Trading Post at the fork in the road,
           zero trip meter and bear left on CR
           446. Hovenweep National Monument
           is east along CR 212.

2.3 ▲   Trail ends at the Hatch Trading Post,
           just past the junction to Hovenweep
           National Monument. On CR 212,
           turn east to Hovenweep; straight on
           leads to US 191 and Blanding and
           Bluff.
           GPS: N 37°23.51' W 109°13.55'

▼ 0.4   SO   Cattle guard.
1.9 ▲   SO   Cattle guard.

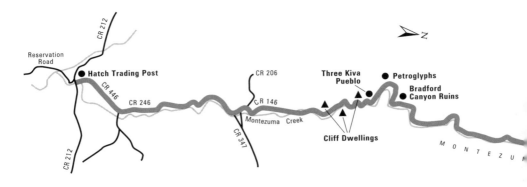

▼ 1.1   SO   Track on right.
1.2 ▲   SO   Track on left.

▼ 2.3   BL   Fork, good gravel road on right. Zero trip meter.
0.0 ▲   Continue on CR 446.
      GPS: N 37°25.25′ W 109°12.62′

▼ 0.0   Continue along CR 446.
6.1 ▲   SO   Good gravel road on left. Zero trip meter.

▼ 0.8   SO   Cattle guard, road becomes CR 246 as the surface deteriorates slightly.
5.3 ▲   SO   Cattle guard, road is now CR 446 as surface improves.

▼ 1.1   SO   Track on right.
5.0 ▲   SO   Track on left.

▼ 1.6   SO   CR 201A on left.
4.5 ▲   SO   CR 201A on right.

▼ 2.7   SO   Track on right.
3.4 ▲   SO   Track on left.

▼ 3.6   SO   Cattle guard.
2.5 ▲   SO   Cattle guard.

▼ 5.6   SO   Track on right.
0.5 ▲   SO   Track on left.

▼ 5.8   SO   CR 347 on right.
0.3 ▲   SO   Second turn onto CR 347 on left.
      GPS: N 37°29.61′ W 109°13.63′

▼ 6.1   SO   Second turn onto CR 347 on right. Zero trip meter.
0.0 ▲   SO   Continue straight.
      GPS: N 37°29.77′ W 109°13.87′

▼ 0.0   Continue straight ahead.
7.2 ▲   SO   CR 347 on left. Zero trip meter.

▼ 0.1   TR   Turn right onto CR 146 at gas pipeline tanks. Straight ahead is CR 206.
7.1 ▲   TL   Turn left at intersection onto CR 246 at gas pipeline tanks. Right is CR 206.

▼ 0.6   SO   Cattle guard. Road is graded dirt.
6.6 ▲   SO   Cattle guard. Road is gravel.

▼ 1.1   SO   Cattle guard.
6.1 ▲   SO   Cattle guard.

▼ 1.4   SO   Ranch sheds on left, small dam on right.
5.8 ▲   SO   Small dam on left, ranch sheds on right.

▼ 2.0   SO   Cattle guard.
5.2 ▲   SO   Cattle guard.

▼ 2.3   SO   Track on right, then cattle guard, then second track on right.
4.9 ▲   SO   Track on left, then cattle guard, then second track on left.

▼ 3.0   BL   Bear left at pipeline sheds.
4.2 ▲   SO   Track on left to pipeline sheds.

Trail #48: Montezuma Canyon Trail

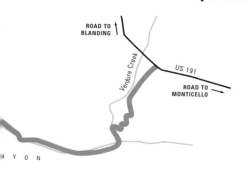

▼ 3.6 SO Track on right, followed by track on left.
3.6 ▲ SO Track on right, followed by track on left.

▼ 4.2 SO Old corral on left.
3.0 ▲ SO Old corral on right.

▼ 4.4 SO Cross Montezuma Creek.
2.8 ▲ SO Cross Montezuma Creek.
     GPS: N 37°32.86′ W 109°14.06′

▼ 4.8 SO Immediately on left, a third of the way up the cliff is a small cliff dwelling.
2.4 ▲ SO Immediately on right, a third of the way up the cliff is a small cliff dwelling.
     GPS: N 37°33.01′ W 109°14.36′

▼ 5.0 SO Small cliff dwelling on right, halfway up cliff under overhang. On private land.
2.2 ▲ SO Small cliff dwelling on left, halfway up cliff under overhang. On private land.
     GPS: N 37°33.14′ W 109°14.42′

▼ 5.1 SO Track on right, then cattle guard.
2.1 ▲ SO Cattle guard, then track on left.

▼ 5.6 SO Old painted sign on rock on right— Buckhorn Mine.
1.6 ▲ SO Old painted sign on rock on left (look back slightly)—Buckhorn Mine.

▼ 6.0 SO Faint track on right up Tank Canyon.
1.2 ▲ SO Faint track on left up Tank Canyon.

▼ 6.5 BR Private track on left to pipeline works.
0.7 ▲ SO Private track on right to pipeline works.

▼ 7.2 SO Three Kiva Pueblo on left with small parking area. Zero trip meter.
0.0 ▲   Continue south on CR 146.
     GPS: N 37°33.91′ W 109°15.09′

▼ 0.0   Continue north on CR 146.
21.0 ▲ SO Three Kiva Pueblo on right with small parking area. Zero trip meter.

▼ 0.5 SO Track on right to campsite, then cross Montezuma Creek on rocky ford. Low-clearance vehicles beware of rock holes slightly on left of midline, bear slightly right.
20.5 ▲ SO Cross Montezuma Creek on rocky ford. Low-clearance vehicles beware of rock holes slightly on right of midline, bear slightly left. Track on left to campsite after ford.

▼ 0.6 TL Immediately after creek, turn left on small sandy track.
20.4 ▲ TR Rejoin main track.

▼ 0.7 TR Turn right before corral onto small sandy track. Small cliff dwelling immediately on left.
20.3 ▲ TL Small cliff dwelling immediately on right before turn. Corral on right at turn.
     GPS: N 37°34.23′ W 109°15.31′

▼ 0.8 SO Track on left.
20.2 ▲ SO Track on right.

▼ 0.9 TL Rejoin main track.
20.1 ▲ TR Turn right onto small sandy track.

▼ 1.1 SO Petroglyphs immediately beside track on left; look hard!
19.9 ▲ SO Petroglyphs immediately beside track on right; look hard!
     GPS: N 37°34.49′ W 109°15.37′

▼ 1.3 SO Track on right.
19.7 ▲ SO Track on left.

▼ 2.4 SO Track on right.
18.6 ▲ SO Track on left.

▼ 2.5 SO CR 238A on left. Proceed straight ahead on CR 146 and cross Bradford Creek.
18.5 ▲ SO Cross Bradford Creek, then CR 238A on right. Proceed straight ahead on CR 146.
GPS: 37°35.00' W 109°16.22'

▼ 2.6 SO Bradford Canyon Ruins on left, protected by fence.
18.4 ▲ SO Bradford Canyon Ruins on right, protected by fence.

▼ 3.4 SO Remains of old mine hopper halfway up cliff on far side of creek on right.
17.6 ▲ SO Remains of old mine hopper halfway up cliff on far side of creek on left.
GPS: N 37°35.10' W 109°15.61'

▼ 4.3 SO Corral on left, then cattle guard.
16.7 ▲ SO Cattle guard, then corral on right.

▼ 4.4 SO Track on left.
16.6 ▲ SO Track on right.

▼ 4.9 SO Cross creek.
16.1 ▲ SO Cross creek.

▼ 7.6 SO Entering private land over cattle guard.
13.4 ▲ SO Entering BLM land over cattle guard.

▼ 8.9 SO Cattle guard.
12.1 ▲ SO Cattle guard.

▼ 9.3 SO Log cabin on left, then cattle guard.
11.7 ▲ SO Cattle guard, then log cabin on right.

▼ 10.4 SO Track on left and right. Road is now gravel.
10.6 ▲ SO Track on left and right. Road is now graded dirt.

▼ 10.8 SO Track on left to private property.
10.2 ▲ SO Track on right to private property.

▼ 10.9 SO Cattle guard.
10.1 ▲ SO Cattle guard.

▼ 11.1 SO Track on left. Canyon becomes narrower and steeper.
9.9 ▲ SO Track on right. Canyon opens out.
GPS: N 37°39.80' W 109°14.91'

▼ 12.4 SO Cattle guard.
8.6 ▲ SO Cattle guard.

▼ 14.2 SO Cattle guard, then grapevines on right.
6.8 ▲ SO Cattle guard.

▼ 14.4 SO Track on right.
6.6 ▲ SO Track on left.

▼ 14.9 SO Bridge.
6.1 ▲ SO Bridge.

▼ 15.9 SO Cattle guard.
5.1 ▲ SO Cattle guard.

▼ 16.7 SO Cattle guard.
4.3 ▲ SO Cattle guard.

▼ 21.0 SO Bridge. Leaving Montezuma Creek. Zero trip meter.
0.0 ▲ Continue along valley floor with Montezuma Creek on left.
GPS: N 37°46.92' W 109°16.52'

▼ 0.0 Climb out of valley with Verdure Creek on left.
4.8 ▲ SO Bridge. Leaving Verdure Creek to run south along Montezuma Creek. Zero trip meter.

▼ 4.4 SO Cattle guard, then road on right.
0.4 ▲ BR Fork, then cross cattle guard on right-hand road.
GPS: N 37°47.59' W 109°20.19'

▼ 4.8 Trail ends at intersection with US 191. Turn right for Monticello, left for Blanding.
0.0 ▲ Begin trail at junction of US 191 and Montezuma Creek Road (CR 146), 0.1 miles south of mile marker 67. Turn southeast on Montezuma Creek Road and zero trip meter.
GPS: N 37°47.99' W 109°20.26'

Hurrah Pass Trail

STARTING POINT Junction of Main Street and Kane Creek Boulevard, Moab

FINISHING POINT Hurrah Pass

TOTAL MILEAGE 13.9 miles

UNPAVED MILEAGE 9.3 miles

DRIVING TIME 1 hour (one-way)

ELEVATION 3,900–4,780 feet

USUALLY OPEN Year-round

DIFFICULTY RATING 1 to Kane Creek Ford, 2 to Hurrah Pass

SCENIC RATING 9

REMOTENESS RATING +0

Special Attractions

- Ancient petroglyphs in Moonflower Canyon.
- Colorado River access and views of the vista from Hurrah Pass.
- Camping in Kane Springs Canyon.

History

Kane Springs Canyon has several rock art sites along its length. The easiest to find is the roadside cliff gallery at Moonflower Canyon, 2.9 miles from the start of the trail. The site is a panel of rock carvings of animals (plus a Barrier Canyon style figure) etched by ancient tribes into the sandstone cliffs. An interpretive sign at the site outlines the meaning of the most prominent figures. To the left of the panel are logs jammed in an apparently haphazard fashion into a large crack; these served as a ladder so the artists could access the higher portions of the cliff face. Unfortunately, this site has been vandalized in the past by graffiti and illegal moldings of the carvings.

Approximately 1.7 miles after the trail leaves the Colorado River, and some 80 feet below the trail, is Birthing Rock. This large boulder is covered with depictions of animals, stylized human figures, and a birth scene.

More recent history can be seen along this trail in the form of mining remains. The Climax and Climota uranium mines are set in the sheer-walled Kane Springs Canyon.

Kane Springs, to the southwest at the headwaters of Kane Creek, was a valuable watering place along the Old Spanish Trail, a trade route between New Mexico and present-day Los Angeles. This annual caravan of 200 horsemen crossed the Colorado River approximately 1.5 miles upstream from Moonflower Canyon. The timing of their trip was crucial—they had to leave Santa Fe in October before heavy rains made travel impossible, and the return trip had to depart California in April before the river fords were impassable following the spring snowmelt.

Since the 1940s, the Moab region has been featured in many movies and TV specials. In 1950, *Rio Grande,* starring John Wayne, was set in this region. Columbia Picture's 1983 movie *Spacehunter—Adventures in the Forbidden Zone* was partially filmed at Kane Creek. The 1997 film *The Perfect Getaway* included scenes at Hurrah Pass, and a 1998 SUV commercial depicts a vehicle riding along a sub-

Kane Creek Road winds through the high walls of Kane Creek Canyon

way, past "Moab Station" and emerging on the eastern side of Hurrah Pass.

Description

This trail, beginning in the center of Moab, is an excellent introduction to canyon country. It has a little bit of everything—stunning views in the canyon and from the plateau and the pass, ancient petroglyphs, the Colorado River, and access to hiking and 4WD trails.

The pavement road enters Kane Springs Canyon through The Portal, a gap in the Moab Rim, and it winds alongside the Colorado River through the canyon. The high Wingate sandstone walls are very popular with rock climbers. Camping in the Colorado Riverway area is restricted to designated sites, but there are plenty to choose from (a fee is charged).

This trail is passable to passenger vehicles as far as Kane Creek ford in dry conditions. The ford is impassable at high water. Under normal conditions it is only a couple of inches deep, but it can change after a thunderstorm very quickly. Do not enter the ford if the water is deep or fast flowing. From the ford, the trail becomes rougher and a high-clearance vehicle is preferred. It winds underneath the Anticline Overlook to finish at Hurrah Pass (4,780 feet). From Hurrah Pass, there are views over the Colorado River to the potash evaporation ponds on the far side, Chimney Rock, and back down Kane Springs Canyon. Trail #50: Chicken Corners Trail continues from this point.

Looking toward Hurrah Pass from an upper section of the track

Current Road Information

BLM Moab Field Office
82 East Dogwood, Suite M
Moab, UT 84532
(435) 259-2100

Map References

BLM   Moab, La Sal
USFS   Manti-La Sal National Forest
USGS   1:24,000   Moab, Trough Springs
       Canyon
       1:100,000 Moab, La Sal
Maptech CD-ROM: Moab/Canyonlands
Trails Illustrated, #501
Utah Atlas & Gazetteer, p. 30
Utah Travel Council #5 (incomplete)
Other: Latitude 40—Moab West
       Canyon Country Off-Road Vehicle
       Trail Map—Canyon Rims &
       Needles Areas

Route Directions

▼ 0.0   From Main Street in Moab, turn north-west onto Kane Creek Boulevard.
          GPS: N 38°33.83' W 109°32.94'

▼ 0.7   BL Follow Kane Creek Boulevard, 500W road on right.

▼ 1.6   SO Road follows Colorado River through

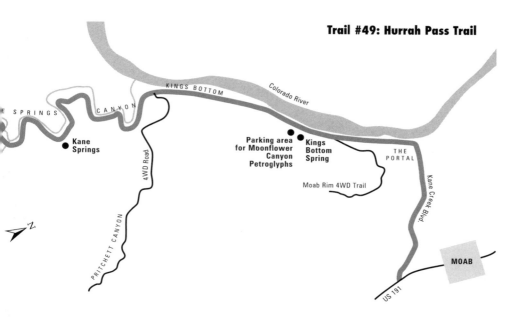

The Portal into Kane Springs Canyon. Enter Colorado Riverway Recreation Area. Camping in designated sites only (fee area).

▼ 2.5   SO   Moab Rim, an extreme Jeep trail on left.
GPS: N 38°33.54' W 109°34.94'

▼ 2.7   SO   Kings Bottom Recreation Site on right.

▼ 2.9   SO   Moonflower Canyon Petroglyphs, parking area on left.
GPS: N 38°33.24' W 109°35.20'

▼ 3.3   SO   Road on left.

▼ 3.6   SO   Dugouts used as work sheds in base of cliff on left.

▼ 4.3   SO   Pritchett Canyon, an extreme Jeep trail, leads off through campground on left. Pavement turns to graded dirt road.
GPS: N 38°33.24' W 109°35.20'

▼ 4.4   SO   Cattle guard. Road climbs away from Colorado River.

▼ 4.8   SO   Popular rock climbing area on left.

▼ 5.5   SO   Track on right is Amasa Back 4WD and mountain bike trail.
GPS: N 38°31.46' W 109°36.06'

▼ 6.5   SO   Spring Site Recreation Area on right. Kane Springs in rock face on left.

▼ 7.4   SO   Hunters Canyon on left, walk-in camping.

▼ 7.6   SO   Echo Recreation Site on right.

▼ 8.1   SO   Leaving Colorado Riverway Recreation Area. Leave narrow part of canyon.

▼ 9.7   SO   As road passes through a rocky outcrop, look left to see remains of a mine high on canyon walls.

▼ 10.2   SO   Numerous tracks right and left, mainly to campsites.

▼ 10.5   SO   Kane Creek ford. Impassable in high water. Zero trip meter. After ford, this becomes a 2-rated track.
GPS: N 38°28.25' W 109°36.09'

▼ 0.0   Leave Kane Creek ford.

▼ 0.1   SO   Track on left to campsite.

▼ 0.4   SO   Track on left to campsite.

▼ 0.5   SO   Track on left, Kane Springs Canyon, difficult Jeep trail.

▼ 0.7   SO   Track on left.

▼ 1.8   SO   Road is smoother and wider.

▼ 2.6   SO   Track on right to overlook over Kane Springs Canyon.

▼ 3.2   SO   Track on right to overlook.

▼ 3.3   SO   Cattle guard.

▼ 3.4   Trail ends at Hurrah Pass, elevation 4,780 feet. Continue to Trail #50: Chicken Corners Trail, or retrace your steps back to Moab.
GPS: N 38°28.92' W 109°37.46'

Chicken Corners Trail

STARTING POINT Hurrah Pass
FINISHING POINT Chicken Corners
TOTAL MILEAGE 11.2 miles
UNPAVED MILEAGE 11.2 miles
DRIVING TIME 2 hours (one-way)
ELEVATION RANGE 3,700–4,780 feet
USUALLY OPEN Year-round
DIFFICULTY RATING 4
SCENIC RATING 10
REMOTENESS RATING +0

Special Attractions

- Far-reaching views of Canyonlands area.
- Views of the Colorado River and potash evaporation ponds.

Description

The very popular spur trail to Chicken Corners continues from the top of Hurrah Pass, at the end of Trail #49: Hurrah Pass Trail. It gradually descends along a rough shelf road, wrapping around gullies etched in the bluff to level off above the Colorado River. It winds along the river, at times coming very close to the edge. It continues on sandy tracks to the start of the Lockhart Basin Trail after 6.7 miles. Lockhart Basin trail takes two days to complete and has a very difficult, potentially vehicle-damaging section at its northernmost end. Route finding on the plateau above the Colorado River can be difficult in places as trails go off in all directions, but most of them either dead-end or rejoin the main trail later.

The trail wraps around the Chicken Rocks, at a point overlooking the Colorado River, and comes to a dead end a mile later. The trail used to continue on as a horse trail, but it would be a brave horse or foolhardy person who would continue around the outcrop on the old trail. Dead Horse Point State Park is almost directly opposite.

The name "Chicken Corners" comes from the local guides who used to let the nervous passengers walk rather than ride the narrow trail around these rocks.

Driving past the Chicken Rocks as the Colorado River flows through the valley below

Trail #50: Chicken Corners Trail

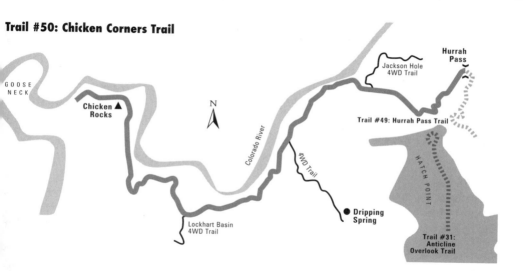

Current Road Information

BLM Moab Field Office
82 East Dogwood, Suite M
Moab, UT 84532
(435) 259-2100

Map References

BLM   La Sal
USGS 1:24,000   Trough Springs Canyon,
          Shafer Basin
          1:100,000 La Sal
Maptech CD-ROM: Moab/Canyonlands
Trails Illustrated, #501
Utah Atlas & Gazetteer, p. 30
Utah Travel Council #5 (incomplete)
Other: Latitude 40—Moab West
          Canyon Country Off-Road Vehicle
          Trail Map—Canyon Rims &
          Needles Areas

Route Directions

0.0   Trail commences at the top of Hurrah
          Pass (4,780 feet) marked by a BLM
          sign, at the end of Trail #49: Hurrah
          Pass Trail. Zero trip meter, bear left,
          proceed southwest over the pass, and
          continue down the shelf road.
          GPS: N 38°28.94' W 109°37.48'

▼ 1.5   SO Trail leaves the cliff edge and descends
          across plateau to Colorado River.
          Chimney Rock is directly ahead on the
          far side of the river.

▼ 2.4   SO Track on right is Jackson Hole trail.
          GPS: N 38°28.29' W 109°38.95'

▼ 2.5   BR Leave creek wash and bear right up
          hill.
          GPS: N 38°28.22' W 109°39.08'

▼ 2.7   SO Colorado River overlook on right. Trail
          runs along edge of rim over river.

▼ 3.8   TR Trail runs along wash. Track on left up
          wash.

▼ 4.1   SO Track on left.

▼ 4.3   SO Track on left to Dripping Spring. Sign to
          Lockhart Basin straight on.
          GPS: N 38°27.21' W 109°40.08'

▼ 4.9   SO Cross wash.

▼ 5.4   SO Cross wash.

▼ 6.7   SO Track on left down wash, sign to
          Lockhart Basin.
          GPS: N 38°25.76' W 109°41.34'

▼ 9.7   BL Trail passes around Chicken Rocks
          above the Colorado River.
          GPS: N 38°27.02' W 109°42.91'

▼ 11.2 Trail ends, old horse trail continues, but
          unsafe for foot travel. Views north
          toward Dead Horse Point and the
          Goose Neck in the Colorado River.
          GPS: N 38°26.47' W 109°44.14'

Gemini Bridges Trail

STARTING POINT US 191 and Gemini Bridges turnoff, north of Moab

FINISHING POINT Utah 313 and Gemini Bridges turnoff, north of Island in the Sky Visitor Center

TOTAL MILEAGE 12.7 miles

UNPAVED MILEAGE 12.7 miles

DRIVING TIME 2.5 hours

ELEVATION RANGE 4,600–5,900 feet

USUALLY OPEN Year-round

DIFFICULTY RATING 5

SCENIC RATING 9

REMOTENESS RATING +0

Special Attractions

- Gemini Bridges double arch.
- Moderately challenging 4WD trail in stunning desert scenery.
- Connects with Trail #52: Bull Canyon Trail.

The Gooney Bird Rock overlooks the Gemini Bridges Trail

Description

Gemini Bridges is a wonderful trail for a novice four-wheeler wanting a bit more of a challenge, yet not wanting to risk vehicle damage. The entire length of the trail is incredibly scenic, with red rock formations sandstone cliffs, far-ranging views over to the La Sal Mountains, and the highlight of the trail, the twin arch of Gemini Bridges.

The trail leaves US 191 and winds along the northern end of the Moab Rim. Looking east you can see Arches National Park on a clear day Balanced Rock is visible. The graded shelf road winds around through the gap into Little Canyon, crossing and recrossing a small creek as the canyon narrows. At the 4-mile mark, you pass by the aptly named Gooney Bird Rock immediately on your left.

After passing the turnoffs for the difficult Gold Bar Rim Trail (not covered in this guide) and Trail #52: Bull Canyon Trail, the trail becomes more challenging and earns it 5 rating. It travels over slickrock pavement and rocky ledges interspersed with sandy sections. A couple of sections call for careful wheel placement, but all high-clearance 4WDs should handle this with ease. It may be impassable following light snow or heavy rain.

After 7.3 miles, you come to the small parking area for Gemini Bridges. A short walk takes you out to the bridges; look down to see the 4WD trail in Bull Canyon far below.

From the bridges, the trail winds across the southernmost end of Arths Pasture. To the north is a flat sagebrush plain; to the south, the depression of Crips Hole. There are many short tracks leading to some good backcountry camping and viewpoints of Bull Canyon to the south and Monitor and Merrimac Buttes to the north.

The trail ends on Utah 313, a few miles north of the Island in the Sky Visitor Center

Current Road Information

BLM Moab Field Office
82 East Dogwood, Suite M
Moab, UT 84532
(435) 259-2100

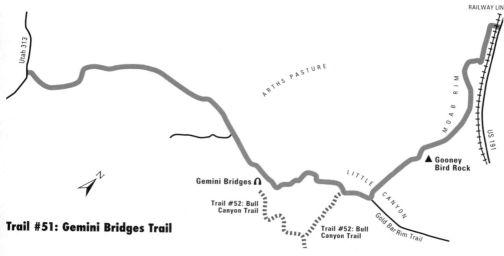

Trail #51: Gemini Bridges Trail

Map References

BLM Moab
USGS 1:24,000 Merrimac Butte, Gold
      Bar Canyon, The Knoll
      1:100,000 Moab
Maptech CD-ROM: Moab/Canyonlands
Trails Illustrated, #211; #501
Utah Atlas & Gazetteer, pp. 30, 40
Utah Travel Council #5
Other: Latitude 40—Moab West
      Canyon Country Off-Road Vehicle
      Trail Map—Island Area

Route Directions

▼ 0.0   Turn west off US 191 onto Gemini
            Bridges Trail, 9.8 miles north of Moab.
            Cross cattle guard, then railroad tracks.
5.1 ▲   Cross railroad tracks, then a cattle
            guard; the trail ends at US 191. Moab
            is 9.8 miles south.
            GPS: N 38°39.36' W 109°40.58'

▼ 1.2 SO Trail climbs the face of Moab Rim.
3.9 ▲ SO Bottom of descent.

▼ 2.1 SO Trail descends through gap into Little
             Canyon.
3.0 ▲ SO Trail ascends through the gap to run
             across face of Moab Rim.

▼ 2.5 BR Track on left.
2.6 ▲ BL Track on right.

GPS: N 38°37.69' W 109°39.91

▼ 2.7 SO Track on left.
2.4 ▲ SO Track on right.

▼ 2.8 SO Track on left.
2.3 ▲ SO Track on right.

▼ 3.8 SO Track on left.
1.3 ▲ SO Track on right.

▼ 4.0 SO Gooney Bird Rock on left at wash.
1.1 ▲ SO Gooney Bird Rock on right at wash.

▼ 4.6 TR Track on right, followed by T-intersec-
            tion. Sign, Gemini Bridges on right,
            Gold Bar Rim on left.
0.5 ▲ TL Sign, US 191 left, Gold Bar Rim
            straight on. Followed by second track
            on left.
            GPS: N 38°36.02' W 109°40.37'

▼ 4.7 SO Cattle guard.
0.4 ▲ SO Cattle guard.

▼ 5.0 SO Track on left at crest.
0.1 ▲ SO Track on right at crest.

▼ 5.1 BR Sign, Gemini Bridges on right, Trail
            #52: Bull Canyon Trail on left.
0.0 ▲   Continue west.
            GPS: N 38°35.80' W 109°40.83'

▼ 0.0   Continue northeast.
2.2 ▲   SO   Sign, US 191 straight ahead, Trail #52: Bull Canyon Trail on right.

▼ 0.2   SO   Faint track on right.
2.0 ▲   SO   Faint track on left.

▼ 0.8   BL   Fork. Sign, Gemini Bridges on left. Trail travels over slickrock.
1.4 ▲   SO   Track on left.
       GPS: N 38°35.78′ W 109°41.59′

▼ 1.6   SO   Track on left.
0.6 ▲   SO   Track on right.

▼ 2.0   TL   Sign, Gemini Bridges on left, followed by campsite.
0.2 ▲   TR   Campsite, then turn right.

▼ 2.2   SO   Gemini Bridges parking area. Short walk to bridges. Zero trip meter.
0.0 ▲   Turn east out of parking area; follow signs for US 191.
       GPS: N 38°35.33′ W 109°42.57′

▼ 0.0   Turn north out of parking area; follow sign for Utah 313.
5.4 ▲   SO   Gemini Bridges parking area. Short walk to bridges. Zero trip meter.

▼ 0.1   TL   T-intersection, immediately followed by track on right.
5.3 ▲   TR   Track on left, then turn right.

▼ 0.9   TR   Four Arch Trail on left. Follow route marker and bear left; tracks on right

MOAB

Named for the biblical "land beyond Jordan," Moab sits on the banks of the Colorado River in southeastern Utah. Ute Indians lived here long before Mormons arrived to settle the area. In 1855, 41 Mormon men tried to establish the Elk Mountain Mission at the site of present-day Moab, but Indian attacks made life far too difficult and the project was abandoned.

It was not until the late 1870s that the Mormons were able to create a permanent settlement. By 1881, a railroad spur connected the town with the Denver to Salt Lake City line. Soon after, a ferry system was set up across the Colorado River. By 1912, it was replaced with a bridge.

In its early years, Moab's economy depended on farming, ranching, and fruit orchards. Still, as early as 1906, local newspapers were promoting the area as a tourist spot; the first settlers were not blind to the natural beauty surrounding them.

In the 1950s, Moab experienced its largest economic boom—large quantities of uranium were discovered and a small oil bonanza hit the area, lasting into the 1960s. The population of Moab quadrupled. After uranium mining slowed down, potash mining (used in the manufacture of fertilizer) became an important industry.

As more people came to the area and saw the striking landscape, the tourism industry began to take off. After the establishment of Arches National Park to the north and Canyonlands National Park to southwest, Moab became a prime location for the exploration of southeastern Utah. For the past 20 years, with the marking of the Slickrock trails, it has become a worldwide center for mountain biking.

Tourists were not the only ones flocking to this stunning countryside. Hollywood has arrived on a number of occasions. *Wagon Master* (1949), about the Hole-in-the-Rock journey, was filmed here, and such recent movies as *Indiana Jones and the Last Crusade* (1989), *Thelma and Louise* (1991), and *City Slickers II* (1994) have been filmed in and around Moab.

Moab and the surrounding area continue to grow in popularity as a tourist spot for amateur geologists, outdoor athletes, and people who just want to experience its primal landscape.

are detour around rocky section.

4.5 ▲	TL	Tracks on left are detour around rocky section, then turn left, Four Arch Trail is on right.

GPS: N 38°35.51′ W 109°43.43′

▼ 1.3	SO	Track on left.
4.1 ▲	SO	Track on right.

▼ 1.6	TL	Intersection.
3.8 ▲	TR	Intersection, follow sign for Gemini Bridges.

GPS: N 38°35.75′ W 109°44.11′

▼ 1.8	SO	Track on right. Graded road starts. Numerous side tracks between here and the highway lead to viewpoints and camping areas.
3.6 ▲	SO	Track on left, trail becomes packed dirt.

▼ 5.4		Trail ends at intersection with Utah 313. Turn left for Island in the Sky Visitor Center, right for Moab.
0.0 ▲		Trail starts on Utah 313, north of the Island in the Sky Visitor Center. Zero trip meter and turn east on graded dirt road at the sign for Gemini Bridges. For the first 3.6 miles, numerous side tracks lead to viewpoints and camping areas.

GPS: N 38°34.39′ W 109°47.52′

Bull Canyon Trail

STARTING POINT 5.1 miles along Trail #51: Gemini Bridges Trail

FINISHING POINT Bull Canyon

TOTAL MILEAGE 5.4 miles

UNPAVED MILEAGE 5.4 miles

ELEVATION RANGE 4,600–5,000 feet

DRIVING TIME 2.5 hours (both canyons)

USUALLY OPEN Year-round

DIFFICULTY RATING 4 (Bull Canyon), 3 (Dry Fork Bull Canyon)

SCENIC RATING 8

REMOTENESS RATING +0

Looking through a dead tree at Gemini Bridges

Special Attractions

- Different perspective of the canyon country.
- Unusual view of Gemini Bridges.
- Towering red canyon walls and scenery.

Description

These two interesting side trips make a wonderful addition to Trail #51: Gemini Bridges Trail. They add an enjoyable perspective of the canyons that few people see. They are generally much quieter than the popular Gemini Bridges Trail along the canyon rim.

Bull Canyon dips down into a tight wash and twists between large boulders. It is wide enough for a full-size SUV, but this can be more difficult following heavy rain. The scenic route along the canyon floor, between towering red cliffs of Wingate sandstone, finishes directly below the twin arches of Gemini Bridges. In ranching days, Bull Canyon had a series of steps cut into the rock from the canyon rim to the floor,

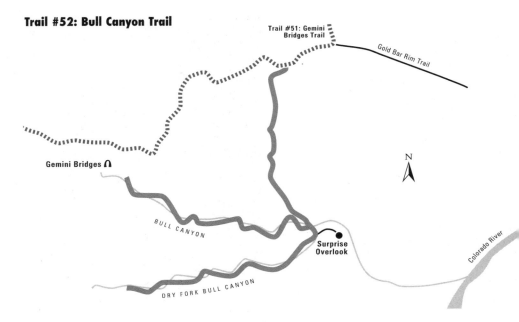

which allowed stock to descend precariously into the canyon to drink from a spring. Both trails follow a creek wash, dipping down to ride in the creek bed on occasion.

Dry Fork Bull Canyon twists through a narrow wash before opening out into a wider canyon with equally stunning scenery. An observant eye will spot the overgrown tailings piles left over from old mine workings—the reason for the existence of the trail. Though Dry Fork Bull Canyon continues for another 1.5 miles, it becomes very difficult to drive—beyond the difficulty rating of this guide—and is not suitable for large unmodified vehicles; it is extremely tight with large boulders and deep washouts making underbody damage likely.

An additional bonus is a short 0.2-mile spur trail in Dry Fork Bull Canyon that travels to Surprise Overlook. A short scramble up a sand dune reveals a panoramic vista: you can see into Day Canyon and over the rims to the La Sal Mountains.

Current Road Information

BLM Moab Field Office
82 East Dogwood, Suite M
Moab, UT 84532
(435) 259-2100

Map References

BLM   Moab
USGS 1:24,000   Gold Bar Canyon
         1:100,000 Moab
Maptech CD-ROM: Moab/
         Canyonlands
Trails Illustrated, #211; #501
Utah Atlas & Gazetteer, p. 30
Other: Latitude 40—Moab West Canyon
         Country Off-Road Vehicle Trail
         Map—Island Area

Route Directions

▼ 0.0   5.1 miles from the east end of Trail #51:
           Gemini Bridges Trail, zero trip meter and
           turn southwest onto
           graded dirt road, following sign to
           Bull Canyon.
           GPS: N 38°35.80' W 109°40.82'

▼ 1.0   SO Track on left. Small campsite on first bend.
▼ 1.3   SO Cattle guard.
▼ 1.5   SO Junction of Bull Canyon and Dry Fork
           Bull Canyon trails. Zero trip meter. Bear
           right to Bull Canyon, left to Dry Fork
           Bull Canyon.
           GPS: N 38°34.69' W 109°40.62'

▼ 0.0		Bear right at intersection and descend down to sandy/stony wash.
		GPS: N 38°34.69' W 109°40.62'

▼ 1.0	BR	Fork, continue along in wash.
▼ 1.5	SO	Track on left.
▼ 1.9	UT	Track on left. End of recommended vehicle trail. Park here and walk 300 yards to the base of Gemini Bridges on the left. To the right is an arch in the making—high on the cliff face. Vehicle tracks ahead and left are difficult to follow; there is risk of vehicle and environmental damage.
		GPS: N 38°35.01' W 109°42.21'

Return to the junction of trails to Bull Canyon and Dry Fork Bull Canyon and zero your trip meter.

ry Fork Bull Canyon

▼ 0.0		From junction of Bull Canyon and Dry Fork Bull Canyon trails, continue to the southeast.
		GPS: N 38°34.69' W 109°40.62'

▼ 0.1	TR	Climb up rise out of creekbed. Left-hand trail goes 0.2 miles to Surprise Overlook.
▼ 0.6	SO	Small arch on right just after right-hand bend. Enter wash.
▼ 1.2	SO	Canyon opens out.
▼ 1.3	SO	Old stock tank on right.
▼ 1.5	SO	Dip down to cross creek, then look for small fragile arch high on sandstone column on right.
▼ 1.9	SO	Track on left.
▼ 2.0	UT	Old mining track on right, dried up dam on left. End of recommended vehicle trail. Ahead it is more difficult than our trail rating indicates and is not suitable for large unmodified vehicles. It is extremely tight with large boulders and deep washouts making underbody damage likely. You can hike another 1.5 miles to the trail end.
		GPS: N 38°34.25' W 109°42.08'

Castleton-Gateway Road

STARTING POINT Colorado 141, south of Gateway, Colorado
FINISHING POINT La Sal Mountain Road (FR 062), Utah
TOTAL MILEAGE 27.1 miles
UNPAVED MILEAGE 21.1 miles
DRIVING TIME 2 hours
ELEVATION RANGE 5,000–8,500 feet
USUALLY OPEN Early June to Late October
DIFFICULTY RATING 2
SCENIC RATING 8
REMOTENESS RATING +0

Special Attractions

- Spectacular canyon scenery around Gateway.
- Interstate trail providing alternative access to slickrock country.
- Far-ranging views across Beaver Creek and Fisher Valley in Utah.

History

The tiny settlement of Gateway, Colorado, lies along a route used by the Ute to reach the Uncompahgre Plateau, named after one of their chiefs. Gateway, set on the Dolores River, is a natural amphitheater. Overshadowed to the north by the Palisade, a gigantic sandstone monolith over 2,000 feet high, Gateway is surrounded by towering red sandstone buttes.

During the 1870s, gold was discovered in the beds of the Dolores and San Miguel Rivers. The gold boom didn't last long, and cattle ranching took over the valley's economy. The Washington Treaty signed in 1880 removed the Ute from the region by the following year, which was then settled by pioneers eager to claim their new ranches. Inevitably, with cattle ranching there were cattle rustlers. Sewemup Mesa to the south of John Brown Canyon is named after a band of rustlers that would cut the brands off the hide of the stolen cattle, sew 'em up again, and rebrand them with its own insignia.

Mining once again became the focus of the economy with the uranium boom in the 1950s. Carnotite, vanadium, and uranium ore were all mined around the Gateway and John Brown Canyon area.

At the western end of the route, in Utah, the trail wraps around the southern end of Castle Valley. The settlement of Castleton, named after the massive castlelike rock formation nearby, has today all but vanished. A supply town, built in the early 1890s, it had a hotel, saloons, a sheriff, a school, and stores. In its heyday, it competed with Moab to supply the mining camps and ranches in the area.

Looking back at the Gateway from the trail

Today the Castleton-Gateway region is heavily used by recreationalists. A hut-to-hut mountain bike route from Telluride to Moab passes through here, rock climbers scale the sandstone towers in Castle Valley, and 4WD vehicles explore the many trails in the region.

Description

If you're driving from Colorado to Moab, this road provides an excellent scenic alternative to I-70. The route starts at Gateway, a small settlement set in a valley on the Dolores River, and follows the well-marked John Brown Canyon just south of town on Colorado 141. The road is subject to frequent washouts after heavy rain and can be rough. The surface is roughly graded packed dirt, with a high rock content. It switchbacks alongside the creek for the first few miles and then levels out on top of the mesa. Just before the Colorado-Utah state line, a sign warns of the dangers of abandoned uranium mines. The state line is marked by an unofficial sign on a gatepost.

Once in Utah, the track quality drops as the trail undulates across open pasture into the La Sal Mountain State Forest. After heavy rain, this section becomes very difficult, turning into sloppy mud. The La Sal Mountain State Forest is used for cattle grazing in summer. There are some nice backcountry camping areas along this section, but there are sites with more spectacular views farther along near Castle Valley.

The vegetation ranges from sagebrush, prickly pear, small oaks, and pinyon pine in John Brown Canyon to stands of pine, rolling sagebrush, and the occasional stand of aspen on the plateau.

As the track continues, the views become more spectacular. First there are North and South Beaver Mesas and then, in the lower trail sections, the wide, red Fisher Valley, surrounded by towering sandstone cliffs, buttes, and outcrops. A couple of forest camping areas are along this stretch, plus many spur trails leading to quiet camping areas with great views. The route ends at the junction with La Sal Mountain Road (FR 062), 30 miles from Moab.

Current Road Information
BLM Moab Field Office
82 East Dogwood, Suite M
Moab, UT 84532
(435) 259-2100

Manti-La Sal National Forest
Moab Ranger District
62 East 100 North
Moab, UT 84532
(435) 259-7155

Map References
BLM   Delta, CO; Moab, UT
USFS Manti-La Sal National Forest
USGS 1:24,000 Gateway, CO;
       Dolores Point North, CO;
       Dolores Point South, CO &
       UT; Mt. Waas, UT; Warner
       Lake, UT
       1:100,000 Delta, CO; Moab, UT
Maptech CD-ROM: Grand Junction/
       Western Slope, CO; Moab/
       Canyonlands, UT
Utah Atlas & Gazetteer, pp. 31, 41
Utah Travel Council #5 (incomplete)
Other: Latitude 40—Moab East

Route Directions

▼ 0.0   At the intersection of Colorado 141 and CR 4.40 (John Brown Canyon), south of Gateway and the Dolores River crossing, zero trip meter and turn west up CR 4.40.

8.1 ▲   Route finishes at the intersection of Highway 141 and CR 4.40. Turn left for Gateway.
       GPS: N 38°40.61' W 108°58.62'

▼ 0.5 SO Cattle guard, road turns to graded dirt. No winter maintenance from December to June from this point.
7.6 ▲ SO Cattle guard, road turns to pavement.

▼ 5.1 SO Mine on right, on far side of canyon.
3.0 ▲ SO Mine on left, on far side of canyon.

▼ 5.7 SO Track on left, CR Z2.40, unmarked.
2.4 ▲ SO Track on right, CR Z2.40, unmarked.

GPS: N 38°36.84' W 109°01.24'

▼ 5.9 SO Track on left.
2.2 ▲ SO Track on right.

▼ 6.6 SO Willow Spring on right.
1.5 ▲ SO Willow Spring on left.

▼ 7.1 BL Track on right.
1.0 ▲ BR Track on left.

▼ 8.1 SO Colorado-Utah state line at cattle guard. Zero trip meter.
0.0 ▲   Continue into Colorado.
       GPS: N 38°36.57' W 109°03.60'

▼ 0.0   Continue into Utah.
9.2 ▲ SO Colorado-Utah state line at cattle guard. Zero trip meter.

▼ 0.8 SO Track on left into private property.
8.4 ▲ SO Track on right into private property.

▼ 1.4 BL Track on right.
7.8 ▲ BR Track on left.

▼ 4.1 SO Faint track on left.
5.1 ▲ SO Faint track on right.

▼ 4.3 SO Track on right at small clearing.
4.9 ▲ SO Track on left at small clearing.

▼ 4.7 SO Cattle guard.
4.5 ▲ SO Cattle guard.

▼ 5.4 SO Entering La Sal Mountain State Forest. Road on left is Taylor Flat Road. View ahead to Mount Waas.
3.8 ▲ SO Leaving La Sal Mountain State Forest. Road on right is Taylor Flat Road.
       GPS: N 38°35.00' W 109°07.96'

▼ 5.7 SO Cattle guard, old corral on left.
3.5 ▲ SO Cattle guard, old corral on right.

▼ 6.5 SO Track on left.
2.7 ▲ SO Track on right.

▼ 7.0 SO Track on left to 5 Bar A Ranch.
2.2 ▲ SO Track on right to 5 Bar A Ranch, Gateway

Trail #53: Castleton-Gateway Road

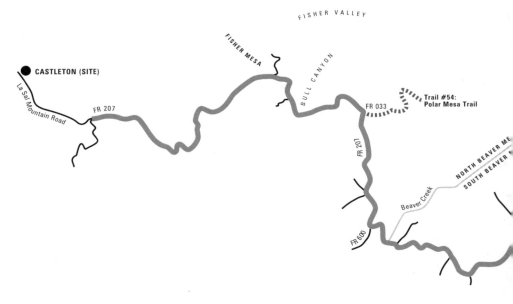

and Kirks Basin are signed straight on.
GPS: N 38°34.64' W 109°09.20'

▼ 8.5   SO   Track on right.
0.7 ▲   SO   Track on left.

▼ 8.8   SO   Enter private property over cattle guard.
0.4 ▲   SO   Leave private property over cattle guard.

▼ 9.2   BR   Track on left, Beaver Basin trail, FR 600. Zero trip meter.
0.0 ▲   Continue along forest road.
      GPS: N 38°34.83' W 109°10.99'

▼ 0.0   Continue along forest road.
2.4 ▲   BL   Track on right, Beaver Basin trail, FR 600. Zero trip meter.

▼ 0.7   SO   Track on left, small stock pond on right.
1.7 ▲   SO   Track on right, small stock pond on left.

▼ 2.1   SO   Entering Manti-La Sal National Forest over cattle guard. Road is now FR 207.
0.3 ▲   SO   Leaving Manti-La Sal National Forest over cattle guard.

▼ 2.4   BL   Trail #54: Polar Mesa Trail on right, FR

033. Zero trip meter.
0.0 ▲   Continue along FR 207.
      GPS: N 38°36.70' W 109°11.70'

▼ 0.0   Continue along FR 207.
7.4 ▲   BR   Trail #54: Polar Mesa Trail on left, FR 033. Zero trip meter.

▼ 0.6   SO   Track on right to a small campsite.
6.8 ▲   SO   Track on left to a small campsite.

▼ 2.1   SO   Track on left at small dam, FR 622. Road wraps around Bull Canyon and Fisher Valley. Road turns to pavement.
5.3 ▲   SO   Track on right at small dam, FR 622. Road wraps around Bull Canyon and Fisher Valley. Road turns to graded dirt.

▼ 2.6   SO   Track on right.
4.8 ▲   SO   Track on left.

▼ 5.2   SO   Gravel road, FR 622, on right.
2.2 ▲   SO   Gravel road, FR 622, on left.

▼ 6.9   SO   Leaving Manti-La Sal National Forest.
0.5 ▲   SO   Entering Manti-La Sal National Forest.

▼ 7.4   Trail finishes at the junction with La Sal

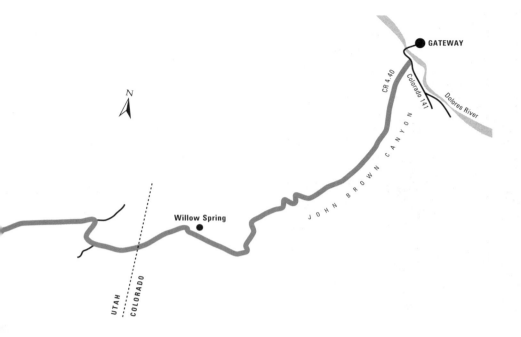

Mountain Road. Both directions lead to Moab, approximately 30 miles away.

0.0 ▲ Trail starts at the junction of La Sal Mountain Road (FR 062) and the Castleton-Gateway Road, approximately 30 miles from Moab. Zero trip meter and turn east on the Castleton-Gateway Road.
GPS: N 38°35.74′ W 109°17.38′

Polar Mesa Trail

STARTING POINT Junction FR 207 (Trail #53: Castleton-Gateway Road) and FR 033
FINISHING POINT Polar Mesa, uranium mining ruins
TOTAL MILEAGE 9.7 miles
UNPAVED MILEAGE 9.7 miles
DRIVING TIME 1 hour (one-way)
ELEVATION RANGE 7,000–8,200 feet
USUALLY OPEN May to November
DIFFICULTY RATING 3
SCENIC RATING 8
REMOTENESS RATING +0

Special Attractions

- Old uranium mining camp ruins on Polar Mesa.
- Spectacular views over Fisher Valley and Dolores River valley.

Description

Polar Mesa is a spur trail off Trail #53: Castleton-Gateway Road. The majority of the road surface is roughly graded dirt; the final part traversing Polar Mesa is rockier and less maintained. It is suitable for a high-clearance vehicle in dry weather, but it should not be attempted in wet weather or immediately following a rainstorm, as the earliest sections turn treacherous and greasy.

The first part of the track winds around on a wide spur, with the upper reaches of Fisher Valley to the north and Beaver Creek canyon to the south. It climbs gradually to North Beaver Mesa and winds through scattered pine and open grassy areas. A couple of fairly well used tracks lead off toward Beaver Creek canyon.

The trail intersects with Trail #55: Onion Creek and Thompson Canyon Trail, which is part of the Kokopelli Trail for mountain bikes, hikers, and in parts, 4WD vehicles.

An old mine shed on Polar Mesa

As you approach the mining area, numerous trails appear to the right and left; most are little used and of a higher difficulty rating than the main trail. There are several old mining buildings to be found down these tracks, as well as tailings piles and mine tunnels and shafts. Polar Mesa in its heyday supplied extremely high quality uranium oxide—as much as 1.57 percent uranium. As with all ex-uranium mining areas, extreme care must be taken around the mine workings—tailings piles should be considered radioactive, and there is a danger of radon gas around the tunnels. Care with tire placement is needed, too—there are many old timbers, nails, tin, glass, and other hazards that may puncture a tire.

The track dead-ends at a small loop with a spectacular viewpoint.

Current Road Information
BLM Moab Field Office
82 East Dogwood, Suite M
Moab, UT 84532
(435) 259-2100

Manti-La Sal National Forest
Moab Ranger District
62 East 100 North
Moab, Utah 84532
(435) 259-7155

Map References
BLM   Moab
USFS   Manti-La Sal National Forest
USGS   1:24,000   Mt. Waas, Fisher Valley
       1:100,000 Moab

A wide landscape view spreads out behind an old signpost

Trail #54: Polar Mesa Trail

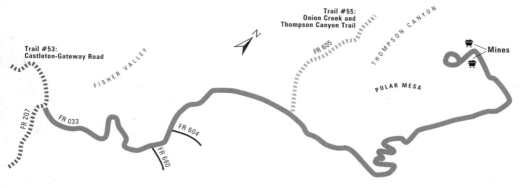

Maptech CD-ROM: Moab/Canyonlands
Trails Illustrated, #501
Utah Atlas & Gazetteer, p. 41
Utah Travel Council #5 (incomplete)
Other: Latitude 40—Moab East
       Canyon Country Off-Road Vehicle
       Map—La Sal Area

Route Directions

▼ 0.0   From FR 207 along Trail #53:
            Castleton-Gateway Road, turn east
            on FR 033 (Polar Mesa Road), and
            zero trip meter. Follow sign to North
            Beaver Creek, Polar Mesa, and
            Fisher Valley.
            GPS: N 38°36.73' W 109°11.67'

▼ 0.3 SO Cross a small bridge over an irrigation
            ditch and continue past a corral on
            right. Views left over Fisher Valley and
            right over Beaver Creek. Road surface
            changes to red dirt.

▼ 1.8 SO Sign reads "North Beaver Mesa."

▼ 1.9 SO Track on right is FR 680.
            GPS: N 38°37.29' W 109°10.32'

▼ 2.0 SO Track on left.

▼ 2.4 SO Track on right is FR 604.
            GPS: N 38°37.70' W 109°10.36'

▼ 3.0 SO Cattle guard.

▼ 4.0 SO Track on left is Trail #55: Onion Creek
            and Thompson Canyon Trail (FR 605).
            Sign points left to Fisher Valley,

straight on to Polar Mesa. A second
BLM sign points left to the Kokopelli
Trail. Continue over cattle guard.
GPS: N 38°38.68' W 109°09.44'

▼ 5.3 BL Track on right. Continue over cattle
            guard and start to climb up mesa.
            GPS: N 38°38.97' W 109°07.99'

▼ 6.2 SO Cattle guard. Trail switchbacks up
            mesa.

▼ 6.8 SO Track on right.
            GPS: N 38°39.45' W 109°08.09'

▼ 7.4 SO Leaving Manti-La Sal National Forest
            and entering private land.

▼ 7.9 SO Track starts to descend, with views
            over the Dolores River valley.

▼ 8.3 SO Track on right. There are now many
            faint tracks on left and right;
            proceed straight ahead on main track.

▼ 9.1 SO More-used track on left goes to mining
            remains.
            GPS: N 38°40.51' W 109°08.50'

▼ 9.3 SO Old mine shed on right.

▼ 9.5 BR Start of final loop.

▼ 9.6 TL Track on right, straight ahead track is
            blocked. A short walk straight ahead
            takes you to a tunnel and loading hop-
            per. Wonderful view over Thompson
            Canyon.

▼ 9.7 TR End of loop. Return the way you came.
            GPS: N 38°40.47' W 109°08.50'

Onion Creek and Thompson Canyon Trail

STARTING POINT Junction of Utah 128 and Onion Creek Road
FINISHING POINT Junction of FR 605 and FR 033, at Trail #54: Polar Mesa Trail
TOTAL MILEAGE 20.7 miles
UNPAVED MILEAGE 20.7 miles
DRIVING TIME 4.5 hours
ELEVATION RANGE 4,200–7,600 feet
USUALLY OPEN April to November
DIFFICULTY RATING 3
SCENIC RATING 8
REMOTENESS RATING +0

Special Attractions

- Spectacular variety of scenery.
- Numerous crossings of Onion Creek.
- Backcountry camping opportunities.
- Great one-day route from Moab when combined with Trail #54: Polar Mesa Trail.

Description

This entire trail winds through a spectacular variety of scenery. The route commences 19.3 miles east along Utah 128 from the junction of US 191. Onion Creek Road is

Rocky section of the trail near Cowhead Hill

A pointy rock formation rises above Onion Creek Canyon

clearly marked. The first half of the trail is graded dirt until the start of the Thompson Canyon Trail. However, the numerous creek crossings mean it is best suited for a high-clearance 4WD vehicle. Do not attempt this route after heavy rain or if thunderstorms are threatening. Onion Creek often washes out, and flash flooding is possible. The second half of the trail is rougher, rocky, and sandy in places.

The first 7.2 miles of the trail are in the Colorado Riverway Recreation Area, and camping is restricted to designated sites. A portable toilet is required; these can be hired in Moab. There are many marked sites in the first 2.3 miles; they become less frequent as the trail winds tighter into the canyon.

The trail follows the canyon, either criss-crossing Onion Creek or on a shelf road above it. The red canyon walls and weird rock formations make for an incredibly scenic drive. After 6 miles, the trail passes Stinking Spring, easily recognizable by the strong sulphur smell.

Leaving the Colorado Riverway Recreation Area, the trail winds up a ridge before descending into Fisher Valley. Onion Creek

Road joins the Kokopelli Trail and turns north, winding up toward Thompson Canyon. It skirts right around Hideout Canyon before snaking onto a rocky ledge. A quiet BLM campsite here has picnic tables, a pit toilet, fire rings, plenty of shade, and good views. This is the most difficult part of the trail, with some rock ledges and large boulders, but all high-clearance 4WDs should have no problem. The top of this ridge provides expansive views over the Dolores River valley and later over Hideout Canyon and Polar Mesa.

The trail ends 4 miles from the start of Trail #54: Polar Mesa Trail on FR 033. Turn right for Moab along Trail #53: Castleton-Gateway Road, turn left to explore Polar Mesa.

Current Road Information

BLM Moab Field Office
82 East Dogwood, Suite M
Moab, UT 84532
(435) 259-2100

Map References

BLM   Moab
USFS Manti-La Sal National Forest (incomplete)
USGS 1:24,000 Fisher Towers, Fisher Valley
       1:100,000 Moab
Maptech CD-ROM: Moab/Canyonlands
Utah Atlas & Gazetteer, p. 41
Utah Travel Council #5
Other: Latitude 40—Moab East Canyon Country Off-Road Vehicle Map—La Sal Area

Route Directions

▼ 0.0   From Utah 128, turn south at sign for Onion Creek Road, and zero trip meter. Camp only in marked areas.

9.3 ▲   Trail finishes at the junction with Utah 128. Turn right for Dewey Bridge, left for Moab.

       GPS: N 38°43.44′ W 109°21.29′

▼ 0.6 SO Track on left to campsite. Numerous

tracks right and left to campsites.

8.7 ▲ SO Track on right to final campsite before Utah 128.

▼ 0.7 SO Parking area.
8.6 ▲ SO Parking area.

▼ 0.9 SO Cross Onion Creek. There are numerous creek crossings for the next 6 miles.
8.4 ▲ SO Final creek crossing.

▼ 1.8 SO Trail enters canyon.
7.5 ▲ SO Trail exits canyon.

▼ 3.7 SO Bridge over Onion Creek.
5.6 ▲ SO Bridge over Onion Creek. Numerous tracks on right and left to campsites.

▼ 5.0 SO Track on right.
4.3 ▲ SO Track on left.
       GPS: N 38°42.04′ W 109°17.37′

▼ 5.9 SO Stinking Spring on left.
3.4 ▲ SO Stinking Spring on right.

▼ 7.2 SO Leaving Colorado Riverway Recreation Area, end of designated site camping. Trail climbs away from Onion Creek toward the Fisher Valley.
2.1 ▲ SO Entering Colorado Riverway Recreation Area, camping in designated sites only. Trail descends to run along Onion Creek. Numerous creek crossings for the next 6 miles.

▼ 8.6 SO Gate followed by track on left.
0.7 ▲ SO Track on right followed by gate. Trail leaves the Fisher Valley.

▼ 9.3 SO Track on left is Kokopelli Trail. This leads up a very difficult 4WD trail to Entrada Bluffs Road. Zero trip meter.
0.0 ▲ SO Continue on up sandy track.
       GPS: N 38°41.32′ W 109°13.19′

▼ 0.0 SO Continue on down sandy track.
11.4 ▲ SO Track on right is Kokopelli Trail. This leads up a very difficult 4WD trail to Entrada Bluffs Road. Zero trip meter.

Trail #55: Onion Creek and Thompson Canyon Trail

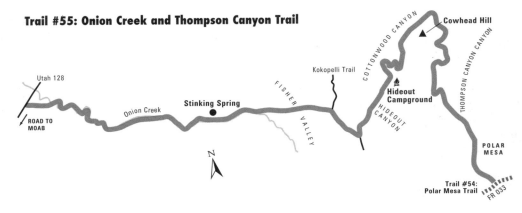

▼ 0.4 SO Gate, entering Fisher Valley Ranch (private property).
11.0 ▲ SO Gate, leaving Fisher Valley Ranch, entering BLM land.

▼ 0.6 SO Track on right to farm shed.
10.8 ▲ SO Track on left to farm shed.

▼ 0.9 TL Turn northeast; follow sign to North Beaver Mesa, La Sal Mountains, Thompson Canyon, and Kokopelli Trail.
10.5 ▲ TR Turn northwest; follow sign to Utah 128, Moab, and Kokopelli Trail.
GPS: N 38°40.63' W 109°12.69'

▼ 1.6 SO Gate at top of rise, entering BLM land. Descend to Hideout Canyon.
9.8 ▲ SO Gate at top of rise, entering Fisher Valley Ranch (private property). Descend to Fisher Valley.

▼ 2.6 SO Track on right to Hideout Campground. Remains of log cabin down track to campsite on left.
8.8 ▲ SO Track on left to Hideout Campground. Remains of log cabin down track to campsite on left.
GPS: N 38°41.57' W 109°11.41'

▼ 2.9 SO Small creek crossing.
8.5 ▲ SO Small creek crossing.

▼ 3.2 SO Views left over Cottonwood Canyon from ridge, and right to Cowhead Hill and Hideout Canyon.
8.2 ▲ SO Views right to Cottonwood Canyon

from ridge, and left over Cowhead Hill and Hideout Canyon.

▼ 3.8 SO Rocky section of track.
7.6 ▲ SO Rocky section of track.

▼ 4.5 SO Track on right.
7.1 ▲ SO Track on left.

▼ 4.9 SO Track on left, expansive views over Dolores River valley.
6.7 ▲ SO Track on right, expansive views over Dolores River valley.

▼ 7.6 BR Old road on left. Bear right for views of Hideout Canyon and Onion Creek to the right, Thompson Canyon and Polar Mesa to the left.
3.8 ▲ BL Old road reenters on right.
GPS: N 38°41.56' W 109°10.17'

▼ 8.4 BR Old road reenters on left.
3.0 ▲ BL Old road on right. Bear left for views of Hideout Canyon and Onion Creek to the left, Thompson Canyon and Polar Mesa to the right.

▼ 8.9 SO Track on left.
2.5 ▲ SO Track on right.

▼ 9.7 SO Leaving BLM land, entering Manti-La Sal National Forest. Road becomes FR 605.
1.7 ▲ SO Leaving Manti-La Sal National Forest, entering BLM land.
GPS: N 38°40.00' W 109°09.75'

▼ 9.9   SO   Track on left.
1.5 ▲   SO   Track on right.

▼ 11.4   Trail ends at the intersection with FR
              033, Trail #54: Polar Mesa Trail. Turn
              right for Moab along Trail #53:
              Castleton-Gateway Road, left to
              explore Polar Mesa.
0.0 ▲   Trail begins at the junction of FR 605
              and FR 033, 4 miles from start of Trail
              #54: Polar Mesa Trail. Zero trip meter
              and turn north onto FR 605; follow sign
              to Fisher Valley.
              GPS: N 38°38.69' W 109°09.41'

Rock formations just off Sand Flats Road

Sand Flats Road

STARTING POINT Junction of La Sal Mountain
Road (FR 062) and Sand Flats Road
(FR 067)
FINISHING POINT Mill Creek Drive, Moab
TOTAL MILEAGE 18.7 miles
UNPAVED MILEAGE 16 miles
DRIVING TIME 1 hour
ELEVATION RANGE 4,200–7,800 feet
USUALLY OPEN March to December
DIFFICULTY RATING 2
SCENIC RATING 9
REMOTENESS RATING +0

Special Attractions

■ Access to mountain bike and 4WD trails.
■ Arid desert scenery and rock formations.
■ Sand Flats Recreation Area.

Description

Sand Flats Road is popular with mountain
bikers and 4WD vehicles, as it provides access to a network of trails plus excellent
camping in the Sand Flats Recreation Area.
It is an alternative route into Moab to
the more-used Castle Valley and La Sal
Mountain Roads.
    The start of the trail is at the junction of
the La Sal Mountain Road (FR 062) and
Sand Flats Road (FR 067); a sign directs

travelers to the two major routes to Moab.
The trail gradually descends with views over
Spanish Valley to the Canyons Rims Recreation Area. The surface is rough and sandy in
places, but should be passable to high-clearance vehicles in dry weather. Heavy rains or
light snow may make this trail impassable.
The scenery is varied and rewarding, with

Looking along the trail from the top end of Rill Creek

Trail #56: Sand Flats Road

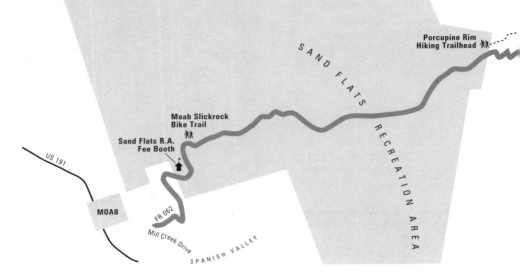

red sandstone cliffs and rugged desert vistas.

After 12 miles, the trail enters the Sand Flats Recreation Area at the mountain bike trailhead to Porcupine Rim. A camping and day-use fee is required for all hikers, 4WDs, and mountain bikes, and camping is permitted in designated areas only. Further information on this area can be obtained at the entrance station or in Moab.

Sand Flats Road improves at this point to

THE SLICKROCK BIKE TRAIL

Editor and newspaper correspondent Dick Wilson had a place where he loved to ride his dirt bike: Moab's garbage dump. Just four miles east of Moab lay the cliff faces of the Sand Flats. Where the townspeople saw a garbage dump, Wilson saw a splendid beauty that could rival a national park. When his dirt bike's tires enabled him to race up the slippery slickrock, Wilson also envisioned a bike trail. He asked the BLM if he could create a motorcycle trail and surprisingly very little resistance surfaced. No one cared what happened to this piece of rocky, overgrazed land. The dump was moved to another location and in 1969 Dick Wilson replaced his previous trail markings, scuffs made by his tires, with easily seen paint. Twenty motorcyclists were there for the trail's dedication. No one was prepared for the popularity the trail would receive when the mountain bike arrived in the mid-1980s. Today, at least 10,000 mountain-bikers ride the trail per year and the number of visitors keeps getting higher. The trail proves to be exciting, gravity defying, and is used as a proving ground for mountain bike design. Mountain bike magazines shoot many of their photographs in this eye-catching area.

Now the temptation has been for bikers to discover their own routes and often these routes hurt the environment. For those who want to stray from his painted trail, Wilson has these words: "If the crowds are causing a terrible impact on the juniper trees, cacti, and pinyon pines in the area, they have missed the whole point of the trail. This is the most indestructible trail in the world. The game the bikers should play is to try and stay on the rock and see how far they can go without riding on the sand and fragile environment." With this trail, Dick Wilson had unknowingly vaulted Moab into the status of mountain bike Mecca.

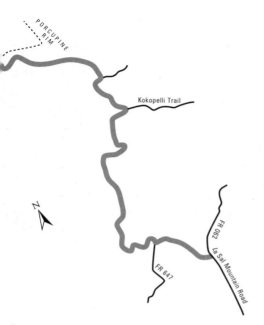

Kokopelli Trail

PORCUPINE RIM

FR 062

La Sal Mountain Road

FR 647

N

become a graded dirt road, although it is still subject to washouts and can be washboardy. It winds across the sandstone plateau between Negro Bill Canyon and the Mill Creek Wilderness Study Area, passing spectacular rock formations on the way. The final part of the trail passes by the Slickrock Bike Trail and the Alcove Recreation Site, before finishing in Moab at Mill Creek Drive.

Current Road Information
BLM Moab Field Office
82 East Dogwood, Suite M
Moab, UT 84532
(435) 259-2100

Map References
BLM   Moab
USFS Manti-La Sal National Forest
USGS 1:24,000 Warner Lake, Rill Creek, Moab
      1:100,000 Moab
Maptech CD-ROM: Moab/Canyonlands
Trails Illustrated, #501 (incomplete)
Utah Atlas & Gazetteer, pp. 30, 31
Utah Travel Council #5
Other: Latitude 40—Moab East
       Canyon Country Off-Road Vehicle
       Map—La Sal Area

Route Directions

▼ 0.0   From La Sal Mountain Road (FR 062), turn northwest onto Sand Flats Roads (FR 067), and zero trip meter.
18.7 ▲   End at La Sal Mountain Road (FR 062). A signpost directs you back to Moab.
      GPS: N 38°31.34' W 109°20.26'

▼ 1.1 SO Track on left, FR 647, followed by cattle guard.
17.6 ▲ SO Cross cattle guard, then track on right, FR 647.

▼ 2.0 SO Views left over Spanish Valley and out to the Canyon Rims Recreation Area.
16.7 ▲ SO Views right over Spanish Valley and out to the Canyon Rims Recreation Area.

▼ 2.9 SO Track on left.
15.8 ▲ SO Track on right.
      GPS: N 38°32.51' W 109°21.65'

▼ 3.1 SO Track on right.
15.6 ▲ SO Track on left.

▼ 3.4 SO Cattle guard.
15.3 ▲ SO Cattle guard.

▼ 4.0 SO Track on right. Track becomes sandier with areas of slickrock pavement.
14.7 ▲ SO Track on left.

▼ 4.4 SO Cattle guard.
14.3 ▲ SO Cattle guard.

▼ 4.6 SO Track on left.
14.1 ▲ SO Track on right.

▼ 4.9 SO Track on left.
13.8 ▲ SO Track on right.

▼ 5.2 SO Kokopelli Trail enters on right over ledge.
13.5 ▲ SO Kokopelli Trail enters on left over ledge.
      GPS: N 38°33.84' W 109°21.07'

▼ 5.8 BL Two tracks on right. Crossing slickrock and sandy section.
12.9 ▲ BR Crossing slickrock and sandy section. Two tracks on left.

View of the landscape as the Sand Flats Road meanders away

▼ 6.2   BL   Track on right to Porcupine Rim camping area.
12.5 ▲   BR   Track on left to Porcupine Rim camping area.

▼ 6.5   SO   Leaving Manti-La Sal National Forest over cattle guard.
12.2 ▲   SO   Entering Manti-La Sal National Forest over cattle guard; road is now FR 067.
         GPS: N 38°34.71' W 109°21.48'

▼ 7.1   SO   Track on left.
11.6 ▲   SO   Track on right.

▼ 8.3   SO   Tracks on left and right.
10.4 ▲   SO   Tracks on left and right.

▼ 8.4   BR   Track on left.
10.3 ▲   BL   Track on right.

▼ 10.3   SO   Porcupine Rim Trailhead. Entering Sand Flats Recreation Area (fee area). Past this point, the trail improves to graded dirt road. There are numerous tracks on right and left to camping areas and 4WD trails.
8.4 ▲   SO   Leaving Sand Flats Recreation Area. Porcupine Rim Trailhead and parking area. Trail is now smaller with sandy areas interspersed with slickrock pavement.

GPS: N 38°34.90' W 109°24.94'

▼ 15.2   SO   Gravel road left to Campsite Cluster E.
3.5 ▲   BL   Gravel road right to Campsite Cluster E.
         GPS: N 38°34.88' W 109°29.97'

▼ 16.0   SO   Pavement starts.
2.7 ▲   SO   Pavement turns to graded gravel road. Numerous tracks right and left to camping areas and 4WD trails (not listed here).

▼ 16.3   SO   Moab Slickrock Bike Trail on right, followed by parking area and toilets.
2.4 ▲   SO   Parking area and toilets followed by Moab Slickrock Bike Trail on left.

▼ 16.7   SO   Alcove Recreation Site on right.
2.0 ▲   SO   Alcove Recreation Site on left.

▼ 17.1   SO   Leaving Sand Flats Recreation Area, pass entrance booth.
1.6 ▲   SO   Entering Sand Flats Recreation Area (fee area).
         GPS: N 38°34.51' W 109°31.37'

▼ 17.7   SO   "America's Most Scenic Dump" on left.
1.0 ▲   SO   "America's Most Scenic Dump" on right.

▼ 18.7   End at intersection with Mill Creek Drive in Moab.
0.0 ▲   Trail starts on Mill Creek Drive in

Moab. Turn east onto paved Sand Flats Road and zero trip meter. The Grand Valley Cemetery is on the corner.

GPS: N 38°33.91' W 109°32.08'

Miners Basin Trail

STARTING POINT Junction of La Sal Mountain Road (FR 062) and FR 065 (Miners Basin Trail)
FINISHING POINT Hiking trailhead for Miners Basin
TOTAL MILEAGE 2.7 miles
UNPAVED MILEAGE 2.7 miles
DRIVING TIME 30 minutes (one-way)
ELEVATION RANGE 7,800–9,750 feet
USUALLY OPEN June to October
DIFFICULTY RATING 2
SCENIC RATING 8
REMOTENESS RATING +0

Special Attractions

■ Access to Miners Basin hiking trails and cabins.
■ Mountain vegetation and scenery, including aspen viewing in fall.
■ Views over the Castle Valley.

History

Ten years after the discovery of gold-bearing gravel in 1888 on the upper reaches of Mount Waas, the town of Miners Basin was developed. Nestled at an elevation of 10,000 feet just above two scree faces, the town grew to a population approaching a hundred, serving several nearby gold, silver, and copper mines. "The Basin," as it became known, supported a hotel, a post office, and two saloons. In the northeastern part of the La Sal Mountains, Mount Waas, which is snow-capped throughout winter, is named after a Ute chief; another prominent peak farther south, Tukuhnikavats, is also named after a Ute and means "dirt seer." The La Sal Mountains, which mean Salt Mountains in Spanish, gained their name from the Domínguez-Escalante expedition, which passed this way in 1776. The mountains have unusual salty springs at their base.

Only 10 years after its establishment, The Basin began to fade as the surrounding mines ran out. Some mines only reached a depth of 150 feet. Today, little remains of the promising settlement except for a few log cabins constructed from the surrounding forests. Still intact, they are occasionally occupied and best treated as private property. Hauling the necessary mining and construction equipment to this elevation was quite a feat for the haulage contractors of the 19th century. Sturdy wagons and strong mules were a definite necessity. The present-day traveler can still appreciate the rocky ascent to Miners Basin; today's trail runs close to the original wagon and mule road.

View of the lake from the end of the Miners Basin Trail

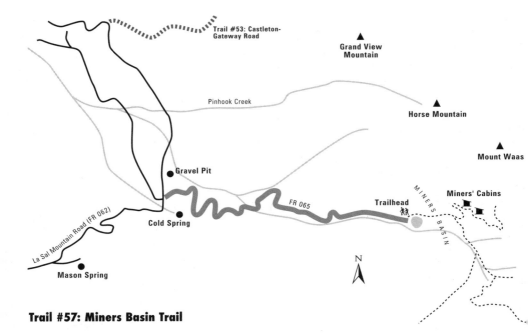

Trail #57: Miners Basin Trail

Description
This short trail leaves La Sal Mountain Road (FR 062) and steadily switchbacks through pines and stands of aspen up to the hiking trailhead for Bachelors Basin and Miners Basin. The lower portions of the trail have spectacular views over Castle Valley. The second half of the trail crosses a couple of small talus slopes before finishing at a small reservoir at the hiking trailhead. From here, it is a gradual 0.75-mile hike to the cabins at Miners Basin.

The trail surface is mainly packed dirt and rock. It is graded, but there are a couple of loose rock sections at the lower end. Under normal conditions, it is suitable for high-clearance vehicles.

Current Road Information
Manti-La Sal National Forest
Moab Ranger District
62 East 100 North
Moab, UT 84532
(435) 259-7155

Map References
BLM   Moab
USFS   Manti-La Sal National Forest

USGS 1:24,000   Warner Lake
       1:100,000 Moab
Maptech CD-ROM: Moab/Canyonlands
Trails Illustrated, #501
Utah Atlas & Gazetteer, p. 31
Utah Travel Council #5
Other: Latitude 40—Moab East
       Canyon Country Off-Road Vehicle
       Map—La Sal Area

Route Directions

▼ 0.0   From La Sal Mountain Road (FR 062), turn east onto FR 065. Coming from the north, the trail is just past, not immediately at, the signpost.
       GPS: N 38°32.82′ W 109°17.44′

▼ 1.1   SO Gate.
▼ 2.6   SO Cattle guard.
▼ 2.7   Trail ends at the hiking trailhead at a small lake. There is a pit toilet and trail information. Hiking trail 034 takes you to Bachelor Basins, trail 143 to Warner Lake Campground. It is approximately 0.75 miles to the cabins at Miners Basin.
       GPS: N 38°32.34′ W 109°15.65′

Selected Further Reading

Akens, Jean. *High Desert Treasures: The State Parks of Southeastern Utah.* Moab, Utah: Four Corners Publications, Inc., 1990.

Akens, John. "Utah Rails." *Canyon Legacy: Planes, Trains and Automobiles: A Regional History 8.* Moab, Utah: The Southeastern Utah Society of Arts and Sciences, Winter 1990.

Alexander, Thomas G. *Utah, the Right Place.* Salt Lake City: Gibbs M. Smith, Inc., 1996.

Allen, Diane, and Larry Frederick. *In Pictures: Arches and Canyonlands the Continuing Story.* Las Vegas: KC Publications, 1993.

American Park Network, Utah's National Parks. San Francisco: American Park Network, 1998.

Athearn, Robert. *The Denver and Rio Grande Western Railroad.* Lincoln, Nebr.: University of Nebraska Press, 1962.

Arizona. Salt Lake City: Gibbs M. Smith, Inc., 1983.

Baars, Donald L. *The Colorado Plateau, A Geologic History.* Albequerque, N.Mex.: University of New Mexico Press, 1972.

Baker, Pearl. *The Wild Bunch at Robbers Roost.* Lincoln, Nebr.: University of Nebraska Press. 1989.

Barnes, F. A. *Canyonlands National Park: Early History and First Descriptions,* vol. 16. Moab, Utah: Canyon Country Publications, 1988.

—. *Canyon Country Explorer 2.* N.p: Canyon Country Publications, 1996.

—. *Canyon County: Off-Road Vehicle Trails—Arches and La Sals Areas.* Moab, Utah: Canyon Country Publications, 1989.

—. *Canyon County: Off-Road Vehicle Trails—Canyon Rims & Needles Areas.* Moab, Utah: Canyon Country Publications, 1990.

—. *Canyon Country: Off-Road Vehicle Trails—Canyon Rims Recreation Area.* Moab, Utah: Canyon Country Publications, 1991.

—. *Canyon Country: Off-Road Vehicle Trails—Island Area.* Moab, Utah: Canyon Country Publications, 1988.

—. *Canyon Country Camping.* Salt Lake City: Wasatch Publishers, 1991.

Barnes, Fran, and Terby Barnes. *Canyon Country Historic Remnants: Bits and Pieces of the Past.* Moab, Utah: Canyon Country Publications, 1996.

Bennett, Cynthia Larsen. *Roadside History of Utah.* Missoula, Mont.: Mountain Press Publishing Company, 1999.

Benson, Joe. *Scenic Driving Utah.* Helena, Mont.: Falcon Publishing, Inc., 1996.

Best Western: Utah Fun Tours. N.p, n.d.

Bickers, Jack. *Canyon Country: Off-Road Vehicle Trails—Maze Area.* Edited by F. A. Barnes. Moab, Utah: Canyon Country Publications, 1988.

Boren, Kerry Ross, and Lisa Lee Boren. *The Gold of Carre-Shinob.* Salt Lake City: Bonneville Books, 1998.

Campbell, Todd. *Above and Beyond Slickrock,* rev. ed. Salt Lake City: Wasatch Publishers, 1995.

Canyon Legacy: A Journal of the Dan O'Laurie Museum—Moab, Utah. No. 8, 9, 10, 18, 22.

Carr, Stephen L. *The Historical Guide to Utah Ghost Towns.* Salt Lake City: Western Epics, 1972.

Carr, Stephen L., and Robert W. Edwards. *Utah Ghost Rails.* Salt Lake City: Western Epics, 1989.

Chronic, Halka. *Roadside Geology of Utah.* Missoula, Mont.: Mountain Press Publishing Co., 1990.

Clark, Carol. *Explorers of the West.* Salt Lake City: Great Mountain West Supply, 1997.

Crampton, C. Gregory. *Standing Up Country: The Canyon Lands of Utah and Arizona.* Salt Lake City: Peregrine Smith

Books, 1983.

DeCourten, Frank. *Dinosaurs of Utah.* Salt Lake City: University of Utah Press, 1998.

Egan, Ferol. *Frémont: Explorer for a Restless Nation.* Reno, Neva.: University of Nevada Press, 1985.

Fife, Carolyn Perry, and Wallace Dean Fife, eds. *Travelers' Choice: A Guide to the Best of Utah's National Parks, Monuments, and Recreation Areas.* Salt Lake City: D and C Publishing, 1998.

Harris, Edward D. *John Charles Frémont and the Great Western Reconnaissance.* New York: Chelsea House Publishers, 1990.

Heck, Larry E. *The Adventures of Pass Patrol. Vol. 1, In Search of the Outlaw Trail.* Aurora, Colo.: Outback Publications, Inc., 1996.

—. *The Adventures of Pass Patrol. Vol. 2, 4-Wheel Drive Trails and Outlaw Hideouts of Utah.* Aurora, Colo.: Outback Publications, Inc., 1999.

—. *The Adventures of Pass Patrol. Vol. 6, 4-Wheel Drive Roads to Hole in the Rock.* Aurora, Colo.: Outback Publications, Inc., 1998.

Hemingway, Donald W. *Utah and the Mormons.* Salt Lake City: Great Mountain West Supply, 1994.

Hinton, Wayne K. *Utah: Unusual Beginning to Unique Present.* New York: Windsor Publications, Inc., 1988.

Huegel, Tony. *Utah Byways: Backcountry Drives for the Whole Family.* Idaho Falls, Idaho: Post Company, 1996.

Johnson, David W. *Canyonlands: The Story Behind the Scenery.* N.p.: KC Publication, 1990.

Kelly, Charles. *The Outlaw Trail: A History of Butch Cassidy and His Wild Bunch.* Lincoln, Nebr.: University of Nebraska Press, 1996.

Kelsey, Michael R. *Hiking, Biking and Exploring in Canyonlands National Park and Vicinity.* Provo, Utah: Kelsey Publishing, 1992.

—. *Canyon Hiking Guide to the Colorado Plateau,* 4th ed. Provo, Utah: Kelsey Publishing, 1999.

—. *Hiking and Exploring Utah's Henry Mountains and Robbers Roost,* rev. ed. Provo, Utah: Kelsey Publishing, 1990.

Korns, J. Roderic, and Dale L. Morgan, eds. *West from Fort Bridger: The Pioneering of Immigrant Trails across Utah, 1846-1850.* Logan, Utah: Utah State University Press, 1994.

May, Dean L. *Utah: A People's History.* Salt Lake City: University of Utah Press, 1987.

McGrath, Roger D. *Gunfighters, Highwaymen and Vigilantes.* Los Angeles: University of California Press, 1984.

Nabhan, Gary Paul, and Caroline Wilson. *Canyons of Color: Utah's Slickrock Wildlands.* Del Mar, Calif.: Tehabi Books, 1995.

The Outlaw Trail Journal, 1992-1999.

Patterson, Richard. *Historical Atlas of the Outlaw West.* Boulder, Colo.: Johnson Publishing Co., 1997

Peterson, Charles S. *Utah: A Bicentennial History.* New York: W. W. Norton and Co., Inc., 1977.

Poll, Richard D., ed. *Utah's History.* Logan, Utah: Utah State University Press, 1989.

Powell, Allan Kent. *The Utah Guide.* Golden, Colo.: Fulcrum Publishing, 1995.

—. *The Utah History Encyclopedia.* Salt Lake City: University of Utah Press, 1994.

Rutter, Michael. *Utah: Off the Beaten Path.* Guilford, Conn.: The Globe Pequot Press, 1999.

Schneider, Bill. *Exploring Canyonlands and Arches National Parks.* Helena, Mont.: Falcon Publishing, 1997.

Thompson, George A. *Some Dreams Die: Utah's Ghost Towns and Lost Treasures.* Salt Lake City: Dream Garden Press, 1999.

Thrapp, Dan L. *Encyclopedia of Frontier Biography.* 3 vols. London: University of Nebraska Press, 1988.

Utah Historical Quarterly. Spring 2000, vol. 68, no. 2.

Utah State Historical Society. Utah History Suite CD-ROM. Provo, Utah: Historical

Views, 1998-99.

Van Cott, John W. *Utah Place Names.* Salt Lake City: University of Utah Press, 1990.

Weibel, Michael R. *Utah Travel Smart.* Santa Fe, N.Mex.: John Muir Publications, 1999.

——. *Utah: Travel Smart.* Santa Fe, N.Mex.: John Muir Publications, 1999.

Wells, Charles A. *Guide to Moab, UT Backroads and 4-Wheel Drive Trails.* Colorado Springs, Colo.: FunTreks, Inc., 2000.

Wharton, Gayen, and Tom Wharton. *It Happened in Utah.* Helena, Mont.: Falcon Publishing, 1998.

——. *Utah.* Oakland, Cali.: Fodor's Travel Publications, 1995.

——. *Utah.* Oakland, Cali.: Compass American Guides, 1950.

About the Authors

Peter Massey grew up in the outback of Australia, where he acquired a life-long love of the backcountry. After retiring from a career in investment banking in 1986 at the age of thirty-five, he served as a director of a number of companies in the United States, the United Kingdom, and Australia. He moved to Colorado in 1993.

Jeanne Wilson was born and grew up in Maryland. After moving to New York City in 1980, she worked in advertising and public relations before moving to Colorado in 1993.

After traveling extensively in Australia, Europe, Asia, and Africa, the authors covered more than 80,000 miles touring the United States and the Australian outback between 1993 and 1997. Since then they have traveled more than 25,000 miles doing research for their guidebook series: *Backcountry Adventures* and *Trails*.

more
utah trails
backroad guides

Utah Trails—Northern

This field guide includes meticulous trail details for 35 off-road routes near the towns of Vernal, Logan, Salt Lake City, Price, Wendover, Beaver, and Milford. **ISBN-10, 1-930139-30-0; ISBN-13, 978-1-930193-30-7; Price $16.95**

Utah Trails—Central

This volume is composed of comprehensive trail statistics for 34 trails near the towns of Green River, Richfield, Hanksville, Crescent Junction, and Castle Dale. **ISBN-10, 1-930193-31-9; ISBN-13, 978-1-930193-31-4; Price $16.95**

Utah Trails—Southwest

This travel guide outlines detailed trail information for 49 off-road routes in the Four Corners region and around the towns of Escalante, St. George, Kanab, Boulder, Bryce Canyon, Hurricane, and Ticaboo. **ISBN-10, 1-930193-10-6; ISBN-13, 978-1-930193-10-9; Price $19.95**

to order
call 800-660-5107 or
visit 4WDbooks.com

4WDBOOKS.COM

california trails
backroad guides

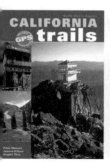
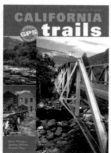

California Trails—Northern Sierra This book outlines detailed trail information for 55 off-road routes located near the towns of Sacramento (east), Red Bluff (east), Truckee, South Lake Tahoe, Sonora, Susanville, Chico, Oroville, Yuba City, Placerville, Stockton (east), Jackson, and Sonora. **ISBN-10, 1-930193-23-8; ISBN-13, 978-1-930193-23-9; Price $19.95**

California Trails—High Sierra This guidebook navigates and describes 50 trails located near the towns of Fresno (north), Oakhurst, Lone Pine, Bishop, Bridgeport, Coulterville, Mariposa, and Mammoth Lakes. **ISBN-10, 1-930193-21-1; ISBN-13, 978-1-930193-21-5; Price $19.95**

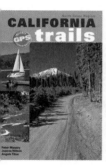
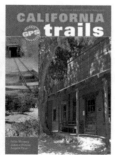

California Trails—North Coast This guide meticulously describes and rates 47 off-road routes located near the towns of Sacramento, Redding (west), Red Bluff, Clear Lake, McCloud, Mount Shasta, Yreka, Crescent City, and Fort Bidwell. **ISBN-10, 1-930193-22-X; ISBN-13, 978-1-930193-22-2; Price $19.95**

California Trails—Central Mountains This guide is comprised of painstaking detail and descriptions for 52 trails located near the towns of Big Sur, Fresno, San Luis Obispo, Santa Barbara, Bakersfield, Mojave, and Maricopa. **ISBN-10, 1-930193-19-X; ISBN-13, 978-1-930193-19-2; Price $19.95**

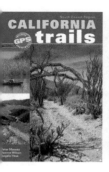

California Trails—South Coast This field guide includes meticulous trail details for 50 trails located near the towns of Los Angeles, San Bernardino, San Diego, Salton Sea, Indio, Borrego Springs, Ocotillo and Palo Verde. **ISBN-10, 1-930193-24-6; ISBN-13, 978-1-930193-24-6; Price $19.95**

California Trails—Desert This edition of our Trails series contains detailed trail information for 51 off-road routes located near the towns of Lone Pine (east), Panamint Springs, Death Valley area, Ridgecrest, Barstow, Baker and Blythe. **ISBN-10, 1-930193-20-3; ISBN-13, 978-1-930193-20-8; Price $19.95**

to order
call 800-660-5107 or
visit 4WDbooks.com

arizona trails
backroad guides

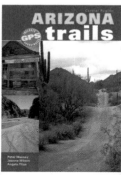

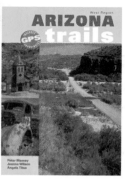

Arizona Trails—Northeast

This guidebook consists of meticulous details and directions for 47 trails located near the towns of Flagstaff, Williams, Prescott (northeast), Winslow, Fort Defiance and Window Rock. **ISBN-10, 1-930193-02-5; ISBN-13, 978-1-930193-02-4; Price $19.95**

Arizona Trails—West

This volume consists of comprehensive statistics and descriptions for 33 trails located near the towns of Bullhead City, Lake Havasu City, Parker, Kingman, Prescott (west), and Quartzsite (north). **ISBN-10, 1-930193-00-9; ISBN-13, 978-1-930193-00-0; Price $19.95**

Arizona Trails—Central

This field guide includes meticulous trail details for 44 off-road routes located near the towns of Phoenix, Wickenburg, Quartzsite (south), Payson, Superior, Globe and Yuma (north). **ISBN-10, 1-930193-01-7; ISBN-13, 978-1-930193-01-7; Price $19.95**

Arizona Trails—South

This handbook is composed of comprehensive statistics and descriptions for 33 trails located near the towns of Tucson, Douglas, Mammoth, Reddington, Stafford, Yuma (southeast), Ajo and Nogales. **ISBN-10, 1-930193-03-3; ISBN-13, 978-1-930193-03-1; Price $19.95**

colorado trails
backroad guides

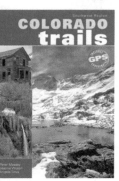

Colorado Trails—North-Central
This guidebook is composed of comprehensive statistics and descriptions of 28 trails, including 8 trails additional to those profiled in the Adventures Colorado book, around Breckenridge, Central City, Fraser, Dillon, Vail, Leadville, Georgetown, and Aspen. **ISBN-10, 1-930193-11-4; ISBN-13, 978-1-930193-11-6; Price $16.95**

Colorado Trails—South-Central
This edition of our Trails series includes meticulous trail details for 30 off-road routes located near the towns of Gunnison, Salida, Crested Butte, Buena Vista, Aspen, and the Sand Dunes National Monument. **ISBN-10, 1-930193-29-7; ISBN-13, 978-1-930193-29-1; Price $16.95**

Colorado Trails—Southwest
This field guide is comprised of painstaking details and descriptions for 31 trails, including 15 trails additional to those described in the Adventures Colorado book. Routes are located around Silverton, Ouray, Telluride, Durango, Lake City, and Montrose. **ISBN-10, 1-930193-32-7; ISBN-13, 978-1-930193-32-1; Price $19.95**

to order
call 800-660-5107 or
visit 4WDbooks.com

4WDBOOKS.COM

backcountry adventures
guides

Each book in the award-winning *Adventures* series listed below is a beautifully crafted, high-qual ity, sewn, 4-color guidebook. In addition to meticulously detailed backcountry trail directions an maps of every trail and region, extensive information on the history of towns, ghost towns, an regional history is included. The guides provide wildlife information and photographs to help reac ers identify the great variety of native birds, plants, and animals they are likely to see. This serie appeals to everyone who enjoys the backcountry: campers, anglers, four-wheelers, hikers, mour tain bikers, snowmobilers, amateur prospectors, sightseers, and more...

Backcountry Adventures Northern California

Backcountry Adventures Northern California takes readers along 2,65 miles of back roads from the rugged peaks of the Sierra Nevada, throug volcanic regions of the Modoc Plateau, to majestic coastal redwoo forests. Trail history comes to life through accounts of outlaws like Blac Bart; explorers like Ewing Young and James Beckwourth; and the bigge mass migration in America's history—the Gold Rush. Contains 152 trail 640 pages, and 679 photos.
ISBN-10, 1-930193-25-4; ISBN-13, 978-1-930193-25-3; Price, $39.95.

Backcountry Adventures Southern California

Backcountry Adventures Southern California provides 2,970 miles routes that travel through the beautiful mountain regions of Big St across the arid Mojave Desert, and straight into the heart of the apt named Death Valley. Trail history comes alive through the accounts Spanish missionaries; eager prospectors looking to cash in durir California's gold rush; and legends of lost mines. Contains 153 trails, 64 pages, and 645 photos.
ISBN-10, 1-930193-26-2; ISBN-13, 978-1-930193-26-0; Price, $39.95.

to order
call 800-660-5107 or
visit 4WDbooks.com

backcountry adventures
guides

Backcountry Adventures Utah

Backcountry Adventures Utah navigates 3,721 miles through the spectacular Canyonlands region, to the top of the Uinta Range, across vast salt flats, and along trails unchanged since the riders of the Pony Express sped from station to station and daring young outlaws wreaked havoc on newly established stage lines, railroads, and frontier towns. Trail history comes to life through the accounts of outlaws like Butch Cassidy; explorers and mountain men; and early Mormon settlers. Contains 175 trails, 544 pages, and 532 photos.

ISBN-10, 1-930193-27-0; ISBN-13, 978-1-930193-27-7; Price, $39.95.

Backcountry Adventures Arizona

Backcountry Adventures Arizona guides readers along 2,671 miles of the state's most remote and scenic back roads, from the lowlands of the Yuma Desert to the high plains of the Kaibab Plateau. Trail history is colorized through the accounts of Indian warriors like Cochise and Geronimo; trailblazers; and the famous lawman Wyatt Earp. Contains 157 trails, 576 pages, and 524 photos.

ISBN-10, 1-930193-28-9; ISBN-13, 978-1-930193-28-4; Price, $39.95.

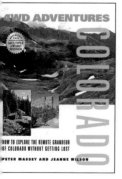

4WD Adventures Colorado

4WD Adventures Colorado takes readers to the Crystal River or over America's highest pass road, Mosquito Pass. This book identifies numerous lost ghost towns that speckle Colorado's mountains. Trail history is brought to life through the accounts of sheriffs and gunslingers like Bat Masterson and Doc Holliday; millionaires like Horace Tabor; and American Indian warriors like Chief Ouray. ains 71 trails, 232 pages, and 209 photos.

ISBN 0-9665675-5-2; Price, $29.95.

to order
call 800-660-5107 or
visit 4WDbooks.com